Understanding Higher Education Internationalization

GLOBAL PERSPECTIVES ON HIGHER EDUCATION

VOLUME 39

Series Editors:

Philip G. Altbach, *Center for International Higher Education,*
   Boston College, USA
Hans de Wit, *Center for International Higher Education,*
   Boston College, USA
Laura E. Rumbley, *Center for International Higher Education,*
   Boston College, USA

Scope:

Higher education worldwide is in a period of transition, affected by globalization, the advent of mass access, changing relationships between the university and the state, and the new technologies, among others. *Global Perspectives on Higher Education* provides cogent analysis and comparative perspectives on these and other central issues affecting postsecondary education worldwide.

This series is co-published with the Center for International Higher Education at Boston College.

Understanding Higher Education Internationalization

Insights from Key Global Publications

Edited by

Georgiana Mihut, Philip G. Altbach and Hans de Wit
Center for International Higher Education, Boston College, USA

SENSE PUBLISHERS
ROTTERDAM/BOSTON/TAIPEI

A C.I.P. record for this book is available from the Library of Congress.

ISBN: 978-94-6351-159-9 (paperback)
ISBN: 978-94-6351-160-5 (hardback)
ISBN: 978-94-6351-161-2 (e-book)

Published by: Sense Publishers,
P.O. Box 21858,
3001 AW Rotterdam,
The Netherlands
https://www.sensepublishers.com/

All chapters in this book have undergone peer review.

Printed on acid-free paper

TABLE OF CONTENTS

ACKNOWLEDGEMENTS

This book emerged from the collaboration between *International Higher Education* (IHE), the quarterly publication of the Boston College Center for International Higher Education and *University World News* (UWN), the weekly on-line publication. Both publications provide news and analysis to the higher education community worldwide. We have selected for this book some of the most relevant articles over the past five years on aspects of lasting interest on the topic of internationalization. This book follows a first book focused on aspects relevant to the field of higher education broadly.

We are indebted to our colleagues at *UWN* for their continuing collaboration. Brendan O'Malley, Mandy Garner, and Karen MacGregor have been especially helpful. At the CIHE, we thank Salina Kopellas for her continuing staff support and Lisa Unangst for editorial assistance. We thank Peter de Liefde of Sense Publishers for his ongoing support to the Book Series on Global Perspectives in Higher Education, in which this book is published as number 39.

Georgiana Mihut has taken the main responsibility for selecting and organizing the articles included here and for drafting the introductions to the sections.

GEORGIANA MIHUT, PHILIP G. ALTBACH AND HANS DE WIT

INTRODUCTION

This volume brings together selected articles published in *University World News* (UWN) and *International Higher Education* (IHE) focused on aspects of internationalization. The articles are logically organized by key themes that reflect the most central issues within the broad phenomena of internationalization. While both publications are freely available online, this book provides a thematically coherent selection of articles, offering an accessible and analytic perspective on the pressing concerns of contemporary higher education and internationalization.

Researchers, policy makers and practitioners alike further the development of higher education as a field of study through public, dynamic conversations. It is news, analysis, and commentary publications like UWN and IHE that facilitate this dialogue and keep pace with the most up-to-date developments in the field. *Understanding Higher Education Internationalization: Insights from Key Global Publications* draws on the contributions of both IHE and UWN to highlight major trends in higher education internationalization in the last five years, and may be best understood as an exercise in curation. With few exceptions, articles published between the 1st of January 2011 and 31st of May 2016 were considered for inclusion. Our philosophy in selecting articles was to prioritize breadth of content and perspective. As editors, we tried to select works that are insightful, clear, and representative—we have not necessarily attempted to select the "best" articles of the respective publications. Lastly, we have grouped selected works by themes of internationalization that are recurrent in both publications—and that we feel have a continued relevance and importance to higher education worldwide.

This book is the second publication resulting from a qualitative analysis of 1,897 published pieces in UWN and IHE. The first book—*Understanding Global Higher Education: Insights from Key Global Publications*—is centered on general aspects of global higher education. This volume is built around internationalization, as the most frequently addressed higher education topic within both IHE and UWN. Altogether, 454 articles among those analyzed focus on aspects connected to higher education internationalization. The 86 articles included in this publication were chosen from among this subset. Most themes included in this book will be familiar to higher education readers, but some will seem less obvious. In order to help the reader make sense of our selected articles, each section of the book will start with a brief introduction that aims to tie together the articles included.

WHAT PROMPTED THIS BOOK?

An established tradition in the field of higher education seeks to map activity and important developments within the field as a whole, often reflected in published surveys of higher education publications and websites. It is likely the disparate nature of higher education as a field that draws researchers to review and analyze the products of their own discipline.

Indeed, higher education, by most standards, is a new field of inquiry (Sadlak & Altbach, 1997). The field itself is very diverse, prompting Macfarlane and Grant (2012) to describe it as "multiple series of intersecting cognate fields" (p. 1). Philip Altbach considered the emergence of the field and provided a sense of its history and current status (Altbach, 2014). Tight (2012) defines the field of higher education in relation to the topics it approaches, the methods it uses, the theories it employs, and the levels of analysis at which research is conducted. To support his definition, which resulted from a similar mapping exercise as the one on which this book is based, Tight (2012) engaged in an analysis of the academic articles and books published in the field of higher education with the purpose of defining its contemporary features. Similarly, Horta and Jung (2014) pursued an indexing exercise of internationally published higher education articles for the purpose of mapping the research approaches employed as well as common themes. At the end of the process, the authors were able to illustrate that publications by Asian higher education researchers cluster around one of two motifs: policy or teaching and learning. Later, Jung (2015) replicated this methodology to analyze the research output of South Korean higher education researchers, identifying a national-centric approach as predominant. Using a similar thematic and longitudinal approach, Kehm (2015) mapped scholarly activity among members of the Consortium of Higher Education Researchers, one of the largest communities of higher education researchers. The results of this inquiry illustrate an increased focus on governance, management, and organizational issues in the field of higher education. Other attempts at defining the field have focused on mapping the curriculum taught to PhD students in higher education, specifically in the United States. This analysis reveals that while a focus on administration, leadership, and organization seems common across all reviewed programs, topics such as community colleges and multiculturalism receive less representation (Card, Chambers, & Freeman, 2016).

However, similar exercises have not been conducted on news and editorial publications relevant to the field of higher education. Importantly, these publications offer broad scope and up to date analysis, which is atypical of more formal academic literature. The Boston College Center for International Higher Education has a strong tradition of mapping the field of higher education and is well positioned to fill this gap. Its most prominent mapping exercise to date is the *Worldwide Higher Education Inventory of research centers, academic programs, and journals and publications*. The most up to date edition of the inventory was published in 2014 (Rumbley et al., 2014), and an interactive online version is available on the center's website.

WHY HIGHER EDUCATION INTERNATIONALIZATION

While the first book, *Understanding Global Higher Education*, was focused on international developments in higher education, this volume addresses the international dimensions of higher education. Internationalization has its own dynamics, but more important, it is transversal to all aspects of higher education. Internationalization is defined as the "the intentional process of integrating an international, intercultural or global dimension into the purpose, functions, and delivery of post-secondary education, in order to enhance the quality of education and research for all students and staff and to make a meaningful contribution to society" (de Wit, Hunter, Howard, & Egron-Polak, 2015, p. 283). Internationalization has become one of the key drivers in higher education worldwide and has impacted all its aspects, as the structure of this volume shows.

ABOUT INTERNATIONAL HIGHER EDUCATION
AND UNIVERSITY WORLD NEWS

International Higher Education (IHE) is a quarterly publication published by the Boston College Center for International Higher Education which offers contributions from authors worldwide who address local, regional, and global issues in the field of higher education. It is currently translated into 6 languages (French, Spanish, Portuguese, Russian, Chinese, and Vietnamese). In addition, IHE is also published in English as a supplement to the *Deutsche Universitätszeitung*, the main magazine focusing on higher education in German-speaking countries.

University World News (UWN) is the oldest and most comprehensive global news outlet for the field of higher education. The publication provides reporting and commentary on developments in higher education and related issues of concern. It also reports on international conferences of higher education and holds webinars with a view to provoking debate and sharing opinion and expertise globally. UWN distributes its e-newspaper weekly to higher education professionals worldwide, most of them senior academics, university leaders, higher education managers, and policy-makers. UWN is read in 150 countries and enjoys a strong readership base in all regions, particularly in Europe, North America, and Africa. The e-newspaper has gained a reputation as a high-quality publication, was the sole media partner of the UNESCO World Conference on Higher Education (2009), and has had media partnerships with OECD, the Talloires Network, British Council, CHEA and the MasterCard Foundation, among others. Launched in 2007, *University World News* has nearly 50,000 readers who receive its weekly global edition newsletter, and nearly 27,000 subscribers to its Africa edition weekly newsletter; its website has 1.5 million hits a month and the publication has 14,000 twitter followers as well as 16,000 Facebook "likes."

While IHE includes standardized articles in terms of length and structure, UWN is more flexible in the type of pieces published. However, both publications encourage a diversity of authors, topics and perspectives and frequently include short pieces about relevant research published in the field, as well as book reviews, analysis of policy initiatives, and debates on different topics. The two publications also closely collaborate: UWN publishes IHE articles on a regular basis. In addition, as of 2017 the two publications are working together as partners. Thus, through an analysis of these publications we may derive insights about higher education research and practice.

STRUCTURE OF THE BOOK

Before introducing the sections of this book, we offer a few observations about the reproduction of the articles from IHE and UWN in book format. First, we note that the UWN articles included were retrieved from the UWN website. Online articles traditionally have different layout standards than printed materials, particularly with respect to paragraph structure, which tends to be shorter, sometimes comprised of one sentence alone. Being cognizant of the reader's experience, articles included here have been re-formatted with the print publication in mind. Another distinct feature of online news articles is the use of hyperlinks as opposed to traditional referencing systems; in this book, hyperlinks representing relevant content references were transformed into in-text citations following the American Psychological Association referencing system. Hyperlinks that linked the name of an organization to the corresponding website were excluded during this process. Lastly, while UWN is published in British English, IHE uses American English, and reproductions in this volume match the original language versions of each publication.

This book is structured in thirteen distinct sections, each of them addressing a major internationalization-related theme resulting from a coding process which included all articles reviewed for this publication. These themes are by no means exhaustive, but do capture the main areas of focus in both IHE and UWN. Each section includes a different number of articles, generally beginning with a global focus, followed by articles addressing regions, and then country-specific pieces. Each section of the book is accompanied by a brief introduction that aims to draw a connective thread among selected articles. The titles of the articles include a note about the respective geographical unit of focus: if an article has a global perspective, "Global" appears at the beginning of the title. The country or region of focus is similarly labeled.

The first section of this book attempts to offer an accessible introduction to the topic of internationalization. The articles included in this section offer different takes on what internationalization is and what it is not, how it has evolved over time, and some of the imperatives it responds to. The second section includes articles focused on transnational education, branch campuses, and higher education hubs, as specific means through which internationalization occurs. Section three draws awareness to the commercialization of internationalization. The articles included in this section include important debates on fees, the use of agents, neoliberalism, and the privilege associated with access to internationalization. Quality assurance, featured in section four, represents another concern associated with internationalization. Section five includes articles focused on internationalization policies and strategies. This section reveals that internationalization policies are increasingly developed at a supranational level, but that different countries, too, attempt to both take advantage of and steer the direction of internationalization. Partnerships are essential in promoting internationalization at regional, national, and institutional levels; section six of this book discusses some of the complexities associated with partnerships and networks. The following two sections of the book address internationalization with a focus on students: section seven highlights relevant factors and perspectives on access, recruitment, and student choice for international students, including standardized examinations, parental involvement, and push and pull factors. Part eight reflects on and highlights the mixed experience of mobile students.

In recent years, faculty and staff have been more involved with and affected by internationalization, and section nine includes articles that speak to the ways in which the academic profession has changed as an effect of internationalization, offering discussion on the importance of training university staff for internationalization processes. In addition to affecting students, academics, and staff, internationalization has shifted governance practices and priorities of the higher education sector. Aspects of the internationalization of governance are captured in section ten. As sections seven, eight, nine, and ten illustrate, key actors within the higher education arena are entrenched in internationalization, and indeed this also applies to the key missions of universities. Section eleven discusses the impacts of internationalization on research; section twelve addresses the intersections of teaching and internationalization. The concluding section of the book discusses the importance of internationalization for the service mission of universities, while highlighting the relation between internationalization and peace, diplomacy, and social service.

This book brings together not only articles written by authors located in different geographic regions, but also from diverse professional backgrounds. Contributions from journalists, doctoral students, higher education researchers, and higher education practitioners are included. Together, the articles included in this volume—alongside the section introductions—offer a rich and relevant picture of the dynamic state of internationalization of higher education globally.

REFERENCES

Altbach, P. G. (2014). The emergence of a field: Research and training in higher education. *Studies in Higher Education, 39*(8), 1306–1320.

Card, K., Chambers, C. R., & Freeman, Jr. S., (2016). Is there a core curriculum across higher education doctoral programs? *International Journal Of Doctoral Studies, 11*, 127-146.

Clark, B. R. (1983). *The higher education system: Academic organization in cross-national perspective.* Berkeley, CA: University of California Press.

de Wit, H., Hunter, F., Howard, L., & Egron-Polak, E. (2015). *Internationalisation of higher education.* Brussels: European Parliament.

Horta, H., & Jung, J. (2014). Higher education research in Asia: an archipelago, two continents or merely atomization? *Higher Education, 68*(1), 117–134.

Jung, J. (2015). Higher education research as a field of study in Korea: Inward but starting to look outward. *Higher Education Policy, 28*(4), 495–515.

Kehm, B. M. (2015). Higher education as a field of study and research in Europe. *European Journal of Education, 50*(1), 60–74.

Macfarlane, B., & Grant, B. (2012). The growth of higher education studies: From forerunners to pathtakers. *Higher Education Research & Development, 31*(5), 621–624. doi:10.1080/07294360.2012.719283

Rumbley, L. E., Altbach, P. G., Stanfield, D. A., Shimmi, Y., de Gayardon, A., & Chan, R. Y. (2014). *Higher education: A worldwide inventory of research centers, academic programs, and journals and publications* (3rd ed.). New York, NY: Lemmens.

Sadlak, J., & Altbach, P. G. (1997). *Higher education research at the turn of the new century: Structures, issues, and trends* (Vol. 10). New York, NY & London: Garland Studies in Higher Education.

Tight, M. (2008). Higher education research as tribe, territory and/or community: A co-citation analysis. *Higher Education, 55*(5), 593–605.

PART 1

UNDERSTANDING INTERNATIONALIZATION

INTRODUCTION

In a time when societies around the world grow further apart, some within the sphere of higher education have put their hopes for global understanding, solidarity, and acceptance in internationalization—the guided encounter between those far away. This first section of this book discusses broader themes and concepts related to internationalization, what it is, and what it is not, and how it can be better understood.

In the first article of the section, Nico Jooste and Savo Heleta draw attention to the need to understand and research internationalization in the broader societal context in which it takes place. This requires awareness of power relations between the global south and the global north, as well as critical engagement with multifaceted challenges such as armed conflict, climate change, inequality, migration, xenophobia, and oppression. The article written by Hans de Wit highlights some of the misconceptions associated with mainstreaming internationalization, thus paving the way for a more comprehensive and productive understanding of the phenomenon. Complementing the article written by de Wit, Jane Knight offers her take on the cannons that should guide internationalization endeavors, including the importance of respecting local context, acknowledging unintended consequences, and the difference between globalization and internationalization. In the next article, Peta Lee provides a comprehensive summary of the report *Internationalization of Higher Education* requested by the European Parliament's Committee on Culture and Education. The report serves as an important update on the state of internationalization in multiple countries around the world.

Philip Altbach and Hans de Wit offer here an overview of the historical development of internationalization and its relation with global political and military tensions, including the two World Wars and the Cold War. In an article focused on Europe, Hans de Wit, and Fiona Hunter provide an optimistic yet cautious take on the future of internationalization of higher education on the continent. The final article in the section, written by Guillaume Tronchet, tries to understand the present-day features of internationalization trends in France by employing a historical lens.

Together, the articles in this section offer a broad yet comprehensive take on the internationalization of higher education, ranging from key guiding principles, historical analyses, and socio-political imperatives, to national-level descriptions and institutional-level rationales.

G. Mihut et al. (Eds.), Understanding Higher Education Internationalization, 3.
© *2017 Sense Publishers. All rights reserved.*

NICO JOOSTE AND SAVO HELETA

1. GLOBAL: CHANGING THE MINDSET IN INTERNATIONALISATION RESEARCH

University World News, 23 October 2015, Issue 387

Higher education internationalisation research and debates have, for decades, been dominated by organisations and individuals from the developed world, lacking inclusivity and genuine collaboration. This has mainly been due to the power imbalances and dominance of the global North in all spheres of life, including higher education. In addition, the passivity from many parts of the global South has added to its lack of representation and voices in this space. In order to develop an inclusive and truly international engagement in the higher education internationalisation arena, the existing paradigms, research approaches, and practices need to be reconsidered.

Instead of the powerful and "mainstream" organisations and experts co-opting the voices from the global South to make their research and agendas look more "inclusive," real collaboration between equals is needed. Such collaboration will not happen if the higher education internationalisation researchers and practitioners from the global South remain passive and do not engage more actively in research, analysis, and knowledge production in the field. In addition, the active voices from the South, many of whom were for far too long ignored and excluded from the mainstream debates on internationalisation should no longer be called the "new" or "emerging" voices but "previously unheard" voices—as many of them have been there all along, but have been ignored or sidelined in the mainstream debates and publications.

The existing theories and approaches, developed in the global North, are in most cases the primary references for all. Higher education institutions in the global South often tend to copy the approaches, strategies and frameworks developed and used in the global North. The problem with this is that what works for one setting will not necessarily work in another setting. In anything we do—in any field of study or work—context is important. There is no "one-size-fits-all" solution to anything. The "copy and paste" approach needs to be replaced by practices and approaches developed for specific settings and informed by sound research.

G. Mihut et al. (Eds.), Understanding Higher Education Internationalization, 5–7.

RETHINKING THE RESEARCH FOCUS

The research focus in internationalisation needs urgent rethinking. For years, the focus of research and debates has been student and staff mobility, student recruitment, study abroad, internationalisation at home, internationalisation of the curriculum, joint degrees, partnerships, and other topics. While these topics are important, Leonard Engel, executive director of the European Association for International Education, points out that they are often addressed "as if they are entities in their own right" and not "in the context of the world in which we live."

Where is higher education internationalisation research in relation to global challenges such as conflict, poverty, environment, climate change, inequality, migration, xenophobia, political, and other kinds of oppression, and post-conflict reconstruction? What is the role and responsibility of academia and internationalisation in peace-building, development, and social justice around the world? Why are these issues not an integral part of our work, debates, research, and practices? The complex and constantly changing world requires from higher education institutions the development of graduates who possess critical thinking skills and global competencies. The world needs graduates who can understand and engage with the environmental, social, economic, political, and other challenges of today and tomorrow.

We propose that future research in the higher education internationalisation field follows the critical social research approach, which questions how institutions, policies, and frameworks are formulated and implemented in practice. This approach does not accept existing frameworks, paradigms, power structures, world orders and ways of thinking as given; instead, it challenges them in order to highlight and transform inequalities and injustices and thereby improve future paradigms and practices. Engaging in critical social research could lead to the creation of a new body of knowledge that would help us in the development of the above-described globally competent graduates.

In terms of research collaboration, higher education internationalisation researchers and practitioners need to think critically about a number of issues related to research paradigms, approaches, and practices. Some of the key questions to consider are: What kind of collaboration and engagement in research do we need in order to develop an inclusive and representative international dialogue where all are given space, heard, and represented? How do we engage in collaboration that is grounded in respect?

GLOBAL RESEARCH COMMONS

An inclusive and truly international dialogue in the higher education internationalisation arena can be developed through the establishment of interlinked global research commons to act as vehicles for the enhancement of research capacity and collaboration around the world. The higher education internationalisation field needs high-quality critical research and analysis from all parts of the globe in order to develop a better understanding among diverse peoples and bring about positive change in the world. There will be many challenges along the way—such as funding and attitude change—but these can be overcome if the interest and will to engage and collaborate are there. We also need to be careful that the proposed research commons do not become—or be perceived as—an elitist project for the chosen few. Research commons need to be inclusive and open to all those with the capacity to engage as well as those who require support to build capacity to be on par with others. Research commons can be places where required capacity building takes place.

Grounding research commons in the global commons concept would provide the necessary spaces for collaboration in higher education internationalisation research and debates. Dr. Nico Jooste wrote about the global commons concept in relation to higher education partnerships, but the same concept can be applied to research collaboration. Participants in the global research commons would need to accept rules that guide the behaviour within the commons. Everyone would need to recognise complex interdependent relations and resist a paternalistic mindset.

Finally, to prevent a new form of the "tragedy of the commons" within the higher education internationalisation space, global research commons would need to be spaces where the collaborators see themselves as equals who are willing to share, innovate and work towards the common good of those "in the commons" as well as their broader communities. Power dynamics would need to be neutralised in order to lift all through consensus-seeking engagement. This will require a shift in attitudes from many. However, if we are to move forward and engage in an inclusive and truly international research and dialogue where all are represented, we do not have an alternative.

HANS DE WIT

2. GLOBAL: INTERNATIONALIZATION OF HIGHER EDUCATION: NINE MISCONCEPTIONS

International Higher Education, Summer 2011, Number 64

Internationalization in European higher education has developed over the last 20 years, from a marginal point of interest to a central factor—also called mainstreaming of internationalization. Indisputably, globalization of our societies and economies has expanded the influence of competition and market processes on the manner in which internationalization is implemented. Internationalization distinguishes many motives and approaches. The mainstreaming of internationalization assumes a more integral process-based approach, aimed at a better quality of higher education and competencies of staff and students. Reality is less promising, however, although the international dimension takes an increasingly central role in higher education. Still, there is a predominantly activity-oriented or even instrumental approach toward internationalization, which leads to major misconceptions about the nature of this development.

Nine misconceptions will be described (two of them coinciding with a myth as described in IHE by Jane Knight in "Five Myths About Internationalization", no. 62, winter 2011), whereby internationalization is regarded as synonymous with a specific programmatic or organizational strategy to promote internationalization— in other words, where the means appear to have become the goal.

EDUCATION ON THE ENGLISH LANGUAGE

The influence of the English language as a medium of communication in research has been dominant for a long period of time. Also, over the past 20 years the tendency in higher education has been to teach in English, as an alternative for teaching in one's mother tongue. There are several unintended negative effects. Increasingly, education offered in the English language is regarded as the equivalent of internationalization, which results in a decreasing focus on other foreign languages; in an insufficient focus on the quality of the English spoken by students and teachers for whom English is not their native language; and thus, leading to a decline in the quality of education.

G. Mihut et al. (Eds.), Understanding Higher Education Internationalization, 9–12.

STUDYING OR STAYING ABROAD

A study or internship abroad as part of your home studies is often regarded as the equivalent of internationalization. In particular, the European Commission's policy to stimulate this manner of mobility has contributed to that instrumental approach over the last 25 years. It is questionable, however, whether the imbalanced and oversimplified approach to mobility matches internationalization. As well, it can be said that mobility is merely an instrument for promoting internationalization and not a goal in itself. Mobility needs to be finely embedded in the internationalization of education. It should be determined whether these added values are developed among students; and more innovative reflection is required on alternative ways of achieving these added values, for instance by the use of distance education and virtual mobility.

AN INTERNATIONAL SUBJECT

A third misconception that continues to surface persistently is that internationalization is synonymous with providing training based on international content or connotation: European studies, international business, or universal music. Within the institutions and schools offering these programs, the prevailing opinion seems to imply that, in this way, internationalization has been properly implemented. Without meaning to ignore the valuable contribution of such programs, again, it is too simplistic and instrumental an argument to declare regional studies as synonymous with internationalization.

HAVING MANY INTERNATIONAL STUDENTS

A fourth misconception of internationalization is the assumption that having many international students equals that trend. Without denying that the combination of local and international students in the lecture room can make a significant contribution to internationalization, simply having international students is not sufficient. Unfortunately, countless examples can be given of programs that are oriented exclusively toward international students or where international students are being added as an isolated group.

FEW INTERNATIONAL STUDENTS GUARANTEE SUCCESS

The other side of the preceding misconception occurs as well. In particular, many international programs have developed a distorted proportion between the number of local and international students. Partly as a result of the increasing national and international competition for international students, the proportion between local and international students becomes more and more unequal. Thus, one can hardly speak of an international classroom setting. Conversely, this development has a negative effect on the internationalization of mainstream, non-English-language programs. Local students with a certain, whether or not motivated, international interest preferably enroll in the international programs—which means the interest of mainstream education in the local language dwindles. Also, in these programs, the presence of a small number of international students creates tensions. Should the courses be taught in English if there are only one or two international students in the lecture room? How can the integration of international students be realized in such distorted proportions?

NO NEED TO TEST INTERCULTURAL AND INTERNATIONAL COMPETENCIES

A sixth misconception assumes that students normally acquire intercultural and international competencies if they study or serve their internship abroad or take part in an international class. This misconception is closely related to the previous ones about mobility, education in English, and the presence of international students. If these kinds of activities and instruments are considered synonymous with internationalization, then it is obvious to assume that intercultural and international competences will therefore also be acquired. Once again, reality is more complicated. It is not guaranteed from the outset that these activities will actually lead to that result. After all, students can completely seclude themselves from sharing experiences with other students and other sections of the population in the countries they visit.

THE MORE PARTNERSHIPS, THE MORE INTERNATIONAL

A seventh misconception on internationalization is the focus on partnerships: the more partnerships, the more success of internationalization. Globalization, competition, and market processes have reinforced the development toward strategic partnerships. This tendency toward strategic partnerships often implicates intentions, however. The majority of partnerships remain bilateral, and in several institutions and schools the number far exceeds the number of students and teachers being exchanged.

HIGHER EDUCATION—INTERNATIONAL BY NATURE

At universities and among their researchers, the general opinion identified a truly international characteristic, and thus there is no need to stimulate and guide internationalization. Thereby, references are made to the Renaissance, the time of the philosopher Erasmus (ca. 1467–1536), whom the European exchange program is named after. This historic reference ignores the fact that universities, mostly originated in the 18th and 19th century, had a clear national orientation and function. Internationalization does not arrive naturally in general universities and universities of applied sciences, but needs to be introduced. That is why the rather widely accepted definition of internationalization by Jane Knight refers to an integration process.

11

INTERNATIONALIZATION AS A PRECISE GOAL

Most of the mentioned misconceptions conceive an activity or instrument as synonymous with internationalization. The last, also fairly prevailing, misconception regards internationalization as a main goal, and therefore it is in line with the misconceptions mentioned earlier. Internationalization is a process to introduce intercultural, international, and global dimensions in higher education; to improve the goals, functions, and delivery of higher education; and thus, to upgrade the quality of education and research. If internationalization is regarded as a specific goal, then it remains ad hoc and marginal.

To comprehend the challenges and opportunities for the internationalization of higher education it is compelling to recognize that these misconceptions are still fairly common.

JANE KNIGHT

3. GLOBAL: FIVE TRUTHS ABOUT INTERNATIONALIZATION

International Higher Education, Fall 2012, Number 69

After several decades of intense development, internationalization has grown in scope, scale, and value. University strategic plans, national policy statements, international declarations, and academic articles all indicate the centrality of internationalization in the current world of higher education. My recent article on the "Five Myths of Internationalization" (IHE no. 62, 2011) brought to light some misconceptions about internationalization. The myths challenged internationalization as a proxy for quality, foreign students as agents of internationalization, institutional agreements and international accreditations as indicators of the level of internationalization, and internationalization as a strategy for high rankings in league tables.

BUILDING ON AND RESPECTING THE LOCAL CONTEXT

Internationalization acknowledges and builds on national and regional priorities, policies, and practices. The attention now given to the international dimension of higher education should not overshadow or erode the importance of local context. Thus, internationalization is intended to complement, harmonize, and extend the local dimension—not to dominate it. If this fundamental truth is not respected, a strong possibility exists of a backlash and for internationalization to be seen as a homogenizing or hegemonic agent. Internationalization will lose its true north and its worth, if it ignores the local context.

A CUSTOMIZED PROCESS

Internationalization is a process of integrating an international, intercultural, and global dimension into the goals, functions, and delivery of higher education. As such it is a process of change—tailored to meet the individual needs and interests of each higher education entity. Consequently, there is no "one size fits all" model of internationalization. Adopting a set of objectives and strategies that are "in vogue" and for "branding" purposes only negates the principle that each program, institution, or country needs to determine its individual approach to internationalization—based on its own clearly articulated rationales, goals, and expected outcomes.

G. Mihut et al. (Eds.), Understanding Higher Education Internationalization, 13–15.

BENEFITS, RISKS, AND UNINTENDED CONSEQUENCES

While there are multiple and varied benefits of internationalization, to focus only on benefits is to be unaware of the risks and unintended negative consequences. Brain drain from international academic mobility is one example of an adverse effect. The current concept of brain circulation does not acknowledge the threat of academic mobility and the great brain race for those countries at the bottom of the brain chain. Second, the desirability of an international qualification is leading to bogus certificates from degree mills, multiple credentials from double-degree programs, and the rise of accreditation mills certifying rogue operations. Third, in some countries, the overreliance on income from international student fees is leading to lower academic standards and the rise of "visa factory programs." Fourth, increased commodification and commercialization of cross-border franchising and twinning programs are threatening the quality and relevance of higher education, in some regions of the world. Moreover, recent surveys show that higher education leaders still believe that the benefits of internationalization still outweigh the risks. However, it is imperative to be vigilant to the different impacts, both positive and negative of internationalization.

NOT AN END UNTO ITSELF

Internationalization is a means to an end, not an end unto itself. This is a common misunderstood truism, which can lead to a skewed understanding of what internationalization is or can do. The suffix of "-ization" signifies that internationalization is a process or means of enhancing or achieving goals. For example, internationalization can help develop international and intercultural knowledge, skills, and values in students—through improved teaching and learning, international mobility, and a curriculum that includes comparative, international, and intercultural elements. The goal is not a more internationalized curriculum or increased academic mobility per se. Rather the aim is to ensure that students are better prepared to live and work in a more interconnected world. Understanding internationalization, as a means to an end and not an end unto itself, ensures that the international dimension is integrated in a sustainable manner into the major functions of higher education teaching and learning, research and knowledge production, and service to the community and society.

GLOBALIZATION AND INTERNATIONALIZATION ARE DIFFERENT BUT LINKED

Globalization focuses on the worldwide flow of ideas, resources, people, economy, values, culture, knowledge, goods, services, and technology. Internationalization emphasizes the relationship between and among nations, people, cultures, institutions, and systems. The difference between the concept of worldwide flow and the notion of relationships among nations is both striking and profound. Internationalization of higher education has been positively and negatively influenced by globalization, and that the two processes, while fundamentally different, are closely connected. For instance, the competitiveness and commercialism agenda, often linked to globalization, has had a major impact on cross-border education development. In turn, the growth of cross-border education and its inclusion in bilateral and regional trade agreements have strengthened globalization.

The fundamental principles guiding internationalization always means different objects to various people, institutions, and countries. Yet, forecasting that internationalization would have evolved from what has been traditionally considered a process, based on values of cooperation, partnership, exchange, mutual benefits, and capacity building. Now, internationalization is increasingly characterized by competition, commercialization, self-interest, and status building. More attention is called for discovering truths and values underpinning the internationalization of higher education.

PETA LEE

4. GLOBAL: INTERNATIONALISATION: VARIATIONS AND VAGARIES

University World News, 21 August 2015, Issue 378

Over the past three decades, there's been growing awareness of the importance of internationalisation at all levels—and its myriad accompanying factors such as, for instance, programmes and policies, funding and stakeholder involvement, cross-border linkages and collaboration. European programmes for research and education, specifically the Erasmus programme but also others like the Marie Curie Fellowships, have driven a broader approach to internationalisation in higher education right across Europe, viewed as an example for institutions, nations, and regions in other parts of the world.

An eye-opening study released recently entitled Internationalisation of Higher Education requested by the European Parliament's Committee on Culture and Education, is one of the most significant to emerge on internationalisation (de Wit, Hunter, Howard, & Egron-Polak, 2015). Compiled by the International Association of Universities and written by Hans de Wit and Fiona Hunter of the Centre for Higher Education Internationalisation, Laura Howard of the European Association for International Education, and Eva Egron-Polak of the International Association of Universities, it unpacks trends and strategies at European, national, and institutional level, and also examines internationalisation strategies in higher education elsewhere.

The authors said that while Europe is seen worldwide as the best-practice case for internationalisation, "there is increased competition from emerging economies and developing countries, but also opportunities for more collaboration as they become stronger actors in the higher education field." For that reason, the study focuses not just on European countries (Finland, France, Germany, Italy, the Netherlands, Norway, Poland, Romania, Spain, and the UK), but also on seven outside Europe—Australia, Canada, Colombia, Japan, Malaysia, South Africa, and the USA.

In a separate, but linked feature article in this issue, University World News highlighted the European countries' progress, approaches and strategies regarding internationalisation. In this feature, we focus on the seven countries outside Europe that were part of the study.

AUSTRALIA

In Australia, higher education institutions have been actively engaged in internationalisation for 50 years. The focus has been on recruiting international students, teaching and support but there's also been major engagement by researchers. "Australian universities are among the most internationalised in the world," said the study's authors. However, complex policy changes and systemic failures saw international student applications drop between 2010 and 2012 with international enrolments declining by almost one-fifth. International education's value as an export dropped from $19.1 billion in 2009–2010 to $14.1 billion in 2012–2013.

These trends are reversing, with the government setting up units like Australian Education International to coordinate international education matters. The Australia Awards, an international scholarship programme, promotes knowledge, education links and ties between Australia and other countries, especially those within the region, while the New Colombo Plan promotes knowledge of the Asia-Pacific region by supporting Australian undergraduate study, internships, mentorships, work placements and research: A$100 million over five years has been committed to this. In 2013, international students represented 25% of students in Australian HE institutions and 30% of all postgraduate research students. With more than half a million international students in 2013, Australia ranked third among English-speaking study destinations, after the US and Britain. It attracts more than 6% of the world's globally mobile students.

USA

In the USA, funding for international education is generous, and key programmes also provide back-up (such as the Fulbright and Fulbright-Hayes programmes). In 2013, general support for international education was a hefty US$375 million from the state department and US$75 million from the education department. The US$250 billion federal student financial aid programme funds can be used for study abroad and the US Agency for International Development's budget of US$1.58 billion (2012) provided international research opportunities.

CANADA

In Canada, the HE system is recognised for excellence at home and abroad. The country is involved in numerous multilateral organisations, and partnerships include the OECD and UNESCO. The EU and Canada have a longstanding education relationship, for example, the EU-Canada Programme for Co-operation in Higher Education, Training and Youth ran from 2006 to 2013 and supported various EU and Canadian post-secondary institutions in running joint study programmes, including faculty exchange and internships. Canada's International Education Strategy launched in 2014 marked a milestone and some crucial objectives—to double international student numbers to 450,000 by 2022 and increase the numbers of those choosing to remain in Canada as permanent residents after graduation.

JAPAN

Japan, with 128 million people, is seeing student numbers declining. Last year, universities enrolled 2,855,000 students, recruiting 14,000 fewer students than the previous year. In the 1980s the government launched a policy to boost international student numbers from 10,000 to 100,000 by 2000. Institutions got funds to develop international student services, accommodation services, and Japanese language training. A new fund in 2005 saw a budget of JPY10–40 million (US$81,700–326,700) per institution annually to 20 selected universities for five years for internationalisation. In 2013 international students numbered 135,519, or 4.7% of the overall college student population. These soared to 141,774 in 2010 but have since declined, despite a "300,000 international students" initiative in 2009. The reason for this decline may be linked to the Japanese earthquake in 2011 and the (mis)perceptions that Japan is radiation-contaminated.

MALAYSIA

In Malaysia, the internationalisation of HE is a major thrust of the country's national higher education policy. Private higher education particularly has seen enormous growth over the past 10 years: there are 20 public universities, 73 private universities and 403 private colleges. The numbers of Malaysians pursuing HE abroad has steadily risen—more than doubling between 2002 and 2011, with most students enrolling in HEIs in places like Australia, UK, the USA, New Zealand, and even Taiwan and Singapore. Malaysia's plan to become a highly developed country by 2020 has stimulated a boost in investment in human capital and policies, and a call for the private sector to deliver HE services via twinning programmes between Malaysian colleges and foreign universities. Education services are classified as one of the 12 National Key Economic Areas under the Economic Transformation Programme, bringing in some MYR27 billion (US$6.5 billion)—or 4% of Malaysia's Gross National Income in 2009.

SOUTH AFRICA

In South Africa, internationalisation isn't flourishing, with apartheid and the pre-1994 boycotts and isolation policies effectively blocking this. However, despite the government's lack of interest, progress has been made—mainly through HE institutions developing the process themselves, and through efforts of the International Education Association of South Africa, or IEASA. Without the IEASA leadership since its establishment in 1997, the concept of internationalisation of higher education would never have been implanted. IEASA provides guidance to a system with no national policy or strategy. Yet universities manage to include some form of internationalisation in their planning, seeing it as a means to enhance research and as a source of knowledge creation. International students have been accepted in the HE system since inception, numbers rising dramatically since 1994: from 7,031 contact students to 40,213 in 2013. This represents 7% of the total student population. Internationalisation is an evolving situation, and the education department has commissioned researchers to produce guidelines for the development of strategy to further guide internationalisation.

COLOMBIA

In Colombia, most institutions are privately funded and there are massive variations in the educational or research goals of establishments. The government plays a minor role in higher education, so internationalisation depends mainly on the capacities and goals of institutions themselves. Only after the Declaration of the Regional Conference on Higher Education in Cartagena in 2008 did Colombia's education ministry establish a committee for the internationalisation of higher education. Partially bridging academic divides are partnerships with HEIs in Spain, France, Germany, Italy, and Britain. Colombia's participation in programmes like Erasmus+ and Horizon 2020 has increased and there have also been opportunities for cooperation with agencies supporting academic exchange.

REFERENCE

de Wit, H., Hunter, F., Howard, L., & Egron-Polak, E. (2015). *Internationalization of higher education.* Brussels: European Parliament. Retrieved from http://www.europarl.europa.eu/RegData/etudes/STUD/2015/540370/IPOL_STU(2015)540370_EN.pdf

PHILIP G. ALTBACH AND HANS DE WIT

5. GLOBAL: INTERNATIONALIZATION AND GLOBAL TENSION: LESSONS FROM HISTORY

International Higher Education, Summer 2015, Number 81

At the start of the year 2015, after a year of increased political and military tension growing in several parts of the world, including Europe, as well as the fundamentalist attacks in Paris, it is relevant to look at its implications for higher education. The current global climate will inevitably affect international higher education. Increased nationalist, religious, and ideological conflicts challenge the original ideas of international cooperation and exchange in higher education as promoters of peace and mutual understanding and of global engagement. Since the end of the Cold War, we have not been used to this type of tension and turmoil on a global scale. What lessons can we learn from the past in how to act and react in this new environment?

THE WAR TO END ALL WARS

In medieval times one could speak of a kind of European higher education space, similar to the current one, with mobile scholars and students and a common language—Latin. Universities in the 18th and 19th centuries for the most part became less international as they adopted national languages, sometimes even prohibited study abroad, and focused on national priorities. One can speak of a nationalization and de-Europeanization of higher education in that period.

The end of World War I brought a burst of internationalism. It is worth looking at the internationalization of the past century, because it helped to shape contemporary realities. In the wake of the trauma of World War I, there was a strong belief that the academic community could help build international solidarity and contribute to peacebuilding. A century after the start of the Great War, it is particularly relevant to note the role and ultimate failure of academe in these idealistic efforts. Europe emerged from World War I, deeply traumatized. Intellectuals and academics on all sides wanted to build solidarity among the European nations as a contribution to peace. Most were horrified that the academic communities on all sides had been so easily drawn into fervent nationalism at the beginning of the conflict, easily giving up the veneer of Enlightenment ideals.

The creation of organizations—such as the Institute of International Education (IIE) in the United States in 1919, the German Academic Exchange Service

G. Mihut et al. (Eds.), Understanding Higher Education Internationalization, 21–24.

(Deutscher Akademischer Austauschdienst or DAAD) in Germany in 1925, and the British Council in the United Kingdom in 1934—are examples of political initiatives to stimulate peace and mutual understanding under the umbrella of the League of Nations. These efforts ultimately failed to stem the rise of fascism and Nazism in Europe or Japanese militarism in the Far East. Again, the goals of peace and cooperation were trumped by negative political forces. The most dramatic failure was in Nazi Germany, where the universities participated in Nazi ultranationalism.

A TRULY GLOBAL CONFLAGRATION AND ITS AFTERMATH

Those who lived through World War I could not imagine a similar conflagration—but just 21 years later, World War II broke out. When the war came to an end in 1945, a wave of idealism again arose, this time accompanied by the establishment of the United Nations, signaling a commitment to both global security and development. The dissolution of colonial empires also created new realities for higher education in the emerging Third World. Again, higher education cooperation was identified as a means of fostering the development of mutual understanding, and modest exchange programs were established or strengthened, the Fulbright Program being the most dramatic example.

In Europe, mobility of students and staff from the former colonial empires to western Europe were the main focus of international higher education activities, but they were rather fragmented and limited. At the national level, at least in Europe and North America, international cooperation and exchange were included as minor activities in bilateral agreements between nations and in development cooperation programs, driven by political rationales. Academic institutions were, in general, passive partners in these programs.

THE COLD WAR AND THE POLITICIZATION OF INTERNATIONALIZATION

Higher education, as well as cultural and intellectual life generally, became pawns as well as important fronts in the ideological struggles of the period. The era of "good feeling" lasted just a few years, as the struggle between the Soviet Bloc and the West started to develop as early as 1946—lasting until the collapse of the Soviet Union in 1989. Ideology and power politics were very much part of the Cold War, with the struggle between communism and capitalism, as well as the political contest between the great powers at the center.

Influenced by the Cold War, ideology more than idealism set the agenda in international education, especially between the United States and the Soviet Union. Europe was not much affected since the Third World was the battlefield of international educational cooperation—and struggle: continuing dominance of Western models and systems of higher education, the influence of the English language, the impact of foreign training, the dominance of Western scientific products, ideas, and structures. In other words, neocolonial and Western higher education hegemony were linked to much of international higher education relations during this period. The Soviet Union, for its part, was similarly engaged in expanding its influence. In Europe, the Iron Curtain that divided eastern and central Europe from the west prevented all but the most rudimentary higher education cooperation.

Only in the 1970s, when western Europe had sufficiently recovered from the impact of World War II and initiated its integration process, did a new type of academic cooperation and exchange emerge that was more focused on strengthening European cooperation and exchange within the countries of the emerging European Union. A modest warming in east-west relations opened doors for academic cooperation to some extent.

Western academic foreign policy, as in the case of the Soviet Union, was also directly linked to Cold War priorities. The former colonial powers—the United Kingdom, France, and to some extent the Netherlands—sought to maintain their influence in their former colonies through an array of scholarship programs, university collaborations, and other schemes. These initiatives also competed directly with the Soviet Union.

THE UNITED STATES, AS THE COUNTERWEIGHT TO THE SOVIET

Union in the Cold War, developed active and far-reaching higher education "soft power" initiatives, such as the Fulbright Program, established in 1946, the National Defense Education Act of 1958 (a direct reaction to the launch the year before of Sputnik I by the Soviet Union), and Title VI of the Higher Education Act of 1960 intended to stimulate the development of area studies and foreign language centers as well as programs for international studies and international affairs. Many academic partnership programs, funded through the US Agency for International Development and other organizations, linked American universities with those in many developing countries. These initiatives have to be seen in the context of attempts by the United States to become the leader of the noncommunist world in its Cold War with the Soviet Union.

AFTER THE COLD WAR: INCREASED INTERNATIONAL
COOPERATION AND EXCHANGE

In the 1980s, the first signs of increased academic cooperation between central and eastern Europe and western Europe as well as with the United States became manifest. Still, academic cooperation was mainly a political issue and little institutional and personal autonomy was possible. Only after the fall of the Iron Curtain at the end of the 1980s, did international cooperation in higher education increase rapidly. Both the European Commission and national governments developed programs to enhance the quality of the sector and stimulate cooperation and exchange. The Transnational European Mobility Program for University Studies scheme (TEMPUS) of the European Community, established in 1990 for Hungary and Poland, extended to the other central and eastern European countries over the years. An important example of a national initiative is CEEPUS, a program of the Austrian government. These initiatives formed the basis, not only for the inclusion of these countries in the regular European programs like the Framework Programs for Research and Development and ERASMUS, but also can be seen as a testing ground for the integration of these countries in the European Union. Without question, the impressive array of European Union sponsored exchange, research, and collaboration programs, both for the "core" EU community and a wider European audience, were related to the broader political and economic goals of the European Union.

THE COMBINATION OF POLITICS AND INTERNATIONAL HIGHER EDUCATION

Will we see again a de-Europeanization and nationalization of higher education in Europe emerging, in the light of greater criticism of European integration, the growth of nationalist populist movements, and tensions between Russia and western Europe and the United States?

In the 20th century, politics and global ideological struggles dominated the international agenda worldwide. Academic cooperation and exchange have been in many cases, including during the Cold War, the main relations between nations: they continued to take place and even were stimulated so as to pave the way for further contacts. We have to learn from these lessons. International higher education is substantially different from earlier historical periods, as well as from the Cold War. Its scope is also different, with increasing political and academic power influences from other regions of the world, especially Asia. But, even though we should be realistic that international cooperation and exchange are not guarantees for peace and mutual understanding, they continue to be essential mechanisms for keeping communication open and dialogue active. Will the increasingly widespread global conflicts—based on religious fundamentalism, resurgent nationalism, and other challenges—harm the impressive strides that have been made in international higher education cooperation?

HANS DE WIT AND FIONA HUNTER

6. EUROPE: THE FUTURE OF INTERNATIONALIZATION OF HIGHER EDUCATION IN EUROPE

International Higher Education, Special Issue 2015, Number 83

Internationalization of higher education (IoHE) is a relatively new phenomenon but, as a concept, it is one that is both broad and varied. Over the last 30 years, the European programs for research and education—in particular the ERASMUS program but also research programs like the Marie Curie Fellowships—have been the motor for a broader and more strategic approach to internationalization in higher education in Europe and have set an example for institutions, nations, and regions in other parts of the world. The internationalization of higher education has been influenced by the globalization of our economies and societies and the increased importance of knowledge. It is driven by a dynamic and constantly evolving combination of political, economic, sociocultural, and academic rationales. These rationales take different forms and dimensions in the different regions and countries, and in institutions and their programs. There is no one model that fits all. Regional and national differences are varied and constantly evolving, and the same is true within the institutions themselves.

In a study for the European Parliament—a project of the Centre for Higher Education Internationalisation (CHEI) at Università Cattolica del Sacro Cuore in partnership with the International Association of Universities (IAU) and the European Association for International Education (EAIE)—which includes 17 country reports (ten from Europe and seven from the rest of the world), we identify key trends in current national strategies and for the future of internationalization in Europe. Ten key developments for Europe and the rest of the world can be identified:

- The growing importance of internationalization at all levels (encompassing a broader range of activities, more strategic approaches, and emerging national strategies and ambitions);
- An increase in institutional strategies for internationalization—with accompanying risks, such as homogenization, and limitations, such as a focus on quantitative results only;
- The challenge of funding, everywhere;
- A trend toward increased privatization in IoHE, through revenue generation;

G. Mihut et al. (Eds.), Understanding Higher Education Internationalization, 25–28.

- The effects of the competitive pressures of globalization, with increasing convergence of aspirations, if not yet actions;
- An evident shift from (only) cooperation to (more) competition;
- Emerging regionalization, with Europe often seen as an example for other world regions;
- Rising numbers of stakeholders and participants involved in internationalization everywhere, with the resulting challenge of quantity versus quality;
- A lack of sufficient data for comparative analysis and decision-making;
- Notable emerging areas of focus, in particular internationalization of the curriculum, transnational education, and digital learning.

In Europe, it is apparent that internationalization as a strategic process began with ERASMUS. The program created common understandings and drivers for internationalization in most countries, and this was further reinforced by the Bologna Process. Internationalization is now becoming mainstream at the national and institutional levels in most countries of the world, and in particular in Europe. The rhetoric speaks of more comprehensive and strategic policies for internationalization, but in reality, there is still a long way to go in most cases. Even in Europe, seen around the world as a best-practice case for internationalization, there is still much to be done, and there is an uneven degree of accomplishment across the different countries, with significant challenges in Southern and, in particular, Central and Eastern Europe.

Two surveys on internationalization in Europe and the world, one by IAU and one by EAIE, draw a highly encouraging picture for Europe. Moreover, the IAU survey showed that Europe is the region most often prioritized in institutional internationalization activities in other parts of the world.

A SCENARIO FOR THE FUTURE

A Delphi Panel exercise among key experts in international higher education around the world confirmed this picture and resulted in a scenario for the future of internationalization of higher education in Europe. This scenario sees IoHE as a continually evolving response to globalization driven by a dynamic range of rationales and a growing number of stakeholders. While it expects mobility and cross-border delivery to continue to grow, it calls for a stronger focus on the curriculum and learning outcomes to ensure internationalization for all, and not just for the mobile few. It identifies partnerships and alliances in varying forms as becoming increasingly important for both education and research and recognizes the key role of the European Commission in supporting IoHE development.

Inevitably, there are barriers to overcome, linked mainly to funding and regulatory constraints, but also to institutional issues of language proficiency and the nature of academic engagement and reward. Equally, there are enablers such as technology, stronger (and more equal) collaboration, a greater focus on qualitative outcomes, the fostering of public-private initiatives, and greater alignment between education and research as well as between different levels of education. The scenario envisages that, if the barriers are removed and the enablers activated, a European higher education will emerge whose graduates will be able to contribute meaningfully as global citizens and global professionals in a Europe that is better placed not only to compete but also to cooperate.

REDEFINING INTERNATIONALIZATION

As an outcome of the Delphi Panel exercise, this study has revised Jane Knight's commonly accepted working definition for internationalization as "the intentional process of integrating an international, intercultural or global dimension into the purpose, functions and delivery of post-secondary education, in order to enhance the quality of education and research for all students and staff, and to make a meaningful contribution to society."

This definition reflects the increased awareness that internationalization has to become more inclusive and less elitist by not focusing predominantly on mobility but more on the curriculum and learning outcomes. The "abroad" component (mobility) needs to become an integral part of the internationalized curriculum to ensure internationalization for all, not only the mobile minority. It reemphasizes that internationalization is not a goal in itself, but a means to enhance quality, and that it should not focus solely on economic rationales.

Most national strategies, including in Europe, are still predominantly focused on mobility, short-term and/or long-term economic gains, recruitment and/or training of talented students and scholars, and international reputation and visibility. This implies that far greater efforts are still needed to incorporate these approaches into more comprehensive strategies, in which internationalization of the curriculum and learning outcomes as a means to enhance the quality of education and research receives more attention. The inclusion of "internationalization at home," as a third pillar in the internationalization strategy of the European Commission—European Higher Education in the World—as well as in several national strategies, is a good starting point, but it will require more concrete actions at the European, national, and, in particular, the institutional level for it to become reality.

The importance of the role of the European Union and the Bologna Process in the development of IoHE in Europe, but also around the globe, is undeniable and has to be built on even further. In this process, however, it is essential to focus on partnerships and collaboration that recognize and respect the differences in contexts, needs, goals, partner interests, and prevailing economic and cultural conditions. Europe can only be an example if it is willing to acknowledge that it can also learn from elsewhere; it offers an important model but not the only one for the modernization of higher education.

Summing up, we can say that the future of IoHE in Europe looks potentially bright, but its further positive development and impact will only take place if the

27

various stakeholders and participants maintain an open dialogue about rationales, benefits, means, opportunities, and obstacles in this ongoing process of change. We cannot ignore the fact that IoHE is also being challenged by increasingly profound social, economic, and cultural issues, such as the financial crisis, unfavorable demographic trends, immigration, and ethnic and religious tensions. While these challenges represent a threat, they also foster awareness of the importance of IoHE in developing a meaningful response.

GUILLAUME TRONCHET

7. FRANCE: LEARNING FROM THE PAST: HISTORICAL TRENDS IN INTERNATIONALIZATION OF FRENCH HIGHER EDUCATION

International Higher Education, Special Issue 2015, Number 83

For many policymakers in France, internationalization of higher education is a new subject. "Internationalization: It's time to invest," concludes a recent report presented in January 2015 by the French government. "It's a new challenge for France," said the organizers of the Congress of the French *Grandes Ecoles* already in 2010. People have short memories. They have forgotten—or simply do not know—that French universities were pioneers and leaders in internationalization between the end of the 19th and the middle of the 20th century, before being outshone by the United States and some other European countries. How can this be explained? And how can history help us understand some of the current trends in French higher education policy?

FROM LOCAL TO GLOBAL

During the 19th century, the global academic community was fascinated by the German university model. To counteract this influence, especially after the Franco-Prussian War, French elites of the new Third Republic decided to invest in higher education, in order to divert international students and scholars from Germany. By grouping together the existing faculties of arts, sciences, medicine, and law, 15 public universities were created in 1896, with a large autonomy of action in international academic affairs.

Local initiatives were then crucial. In order to increase the number of their students, and with the help of local actors—such as mayors, regional chambers of commerce, etc., who wanted to develop tourism and other economic opportunities for their cities—French universities launched what I call in my doctoral thesis "academic diplomacy." This entailed (among other things): marketing actions to promote French universities (handbooks, posters, advertisements in the international press); French language and culture courses for international students; international summer schools (the most famous was organized by the University of Grenoble in 1899); special degrees for international students; scholarships to study abroad; and new branch campuses abroad. In this final matter, the University of Lyon was very

G. Mihut et al. (Eds.), Understanding Higher Education Internationalization, 29–31.

active in the Middle East with the foundation of a law school in Beirut, while Paris turned to South America, Grenoble to Italy, Bordeaux and Toulouse to Spain. French cultural and scientific institutes were subsequently founded in Florence, Madrid, London, and Saint Petersburg in the early 20th century.

THE DEFEAT OF UNIVERSITY AUTONOMY

After World War I, as Philip Altbach and Hans de Wit stated in a recent issue of *IHE*, the development of international academic relations benefited from the rise of Geneva internationalism. France quickly took the leading position in the international student market: 17,000 students came to France in 1931—i.e., about 20 to 25 percent of the total number of internationally mobile students at this time—while only 9,000 international students went to the United States, about 7,000 to Germany, and 5,000 to the United Kingdom. The percentage of international students in French universities was up to 25 percent of the total number of students. In some universities, this rate even reached 80 percent—e.g., Rouen University in 1930.

At the same time, government administration became more present in the process. The Ministry of Education was first involved from the 1910s and gradually nationalized academic diplomacy. After 1920, the French Ministry of Foreign Affairs also came into play, developing its own "cultural diplomacy" to compete with other nations, especially the fascist countries. As I noted in my doctoral thesis, there were frequent conflicts between actors of academic diplomacy on the one hand, and of cultural diplomacy on the other. Universities tried to preserve their autonomy without success: the international academic policy of France gradually came under the control of governmental cultural diplomacy.

THE BURDEN OF HISTORY

The second part of the 20th century did not change this legacy. There were constant conflicts inside French administrations, between actors related either to higher education offices or to foreign affairs offices. The situation was complicated in the 1960s, first by the creation of a Ministry of Culture, which wanted to get involved in cultural diplomacy, and then after decolonization by the creation of a Ministry of Cooperation, which was in charge of relations with scholarship students from the former French colonial empire. Many reforms were then enacted before creating finally, in 2010, a unique national agency: Campus France was placed in charge of international student mobility and of the promotion of French higher education abroad. This could be translated into a new start for academic diplomacy.

The fact that the French government and higher education are both intrinsically linked to the Civil Service system is also significant. What kind of international autonomy can universities enjoy in this context? It is the government that sets down the rules for all public universities regarding scholar recruitments and student enrollments, and they do not always favor internationalization. For instance, in regards to scholar recruitments, no foreign scholar could be appointed to an ordinary teaching position in France, until the Edgar Faure Law in 1968; this is one of the reasons why French universities could not keep German scholars who fled Nazism in the 1930s. Even though the recruitment of foreign scholars in France recently increased to an average rate of 18 percent of the total number of new recruits each year, this is still not common: in 2004, according to Organisation for Economic Cooperation and Development figures, the percentage of foreign scholars in French higher education was 7.5, a long way from the United States (30 to 40 percent), Switzerland (35 percent), the United Kingdom (20 percent), and Norway (10.5 percent).

As for international student enrollments, the "republican consensus"—based on the principle of nondiscrimination between French and foreign students—has maintained equal tuition fees for French and international students since 1914, a fact that contributes to the international attractiveness of French higher education. Universities have nonetheless been deeply impacted by government immigration policy, which has at times closed the doors to foreign students, especially between the 1970s and the 1990s and again in 2011–2012. The effect has been such that a French political scientist talked about "the end of foreign students."

A centralized national government, numerous conflicts between elements of this government and, on occasions, enactment of restrictive immigration laws have led to a stifling of international innovation in French universities. The changing world order since the 1970s has also contributed to live down this historical tradition: the shift from internationalization to globalization has drawn public attention to private schools, especially business schools, which are more comfortable with globalization and are active in funding branch campuses abroad—according to the Cross-Border Education Research Team, about 90 percent of French branch campuses abroad are private school extensions. Instead of internationalization, which is clearly not a "new challenge," it is globalization that places French higher education today at the crossroads. Reclaiming its own history could be part of the solution.

PART 2

TRANSNATIONAL EDUCATION, BRANCH CAMPUSES, AND HUBS

INTRODUCTION

Transnational education, branch campuses, and hubs are a growing phenomenon in the field of higher education. This section introduces works that discuss the latest developments in this arena, as well as the rising awareness on associated challenges and concerns.

The first article in this section, written by William Lawton and Alex Katsomitros, discusses the increase in the numbers of international branch campuses globally. The article includes an overview of the significant players in this sphere. Next, Li Zhang, Kevin Kinser, and Yunyu Shi discuss their research on the relation between world economies and branch campuses, using the World Economic Forum global competitiveness index. Their research challenges the notion that international branch campuses flow exclusively from developed to developing countries.

The creation and running of a branch campus is often a difficult quest due to cultural, managerial, political, and financial reasons. In the third article presented, John Fielden discusses the intricate and not always profitable financial aspects of offshore educational activities and some of the ways in which translational ventures can be more successful. Using the criteria of ownership arrangements, Jason Lane and Kevin Kinser introduce a variety of models of international branch campuses, raising awareness of the associated risks and benefits. The following article, written by Jane Knight, discusses a phenomenon related to branch campuses—education hubs. Her contribution offers descriptions of key hubs around the world—Qatar, United Arab Emirates, Hong Kong, Botswana, Singapore, and Malaysia.

Jane Knight and John McNamara shift the conversation on transnational education by highlighting possible effects at the local level. Transnational education increases local access to higher education, but at the same time may not fully prepare students to meet community economic needs. The article also discusses some of the region-specific challenges faced by transnational education providers. Indeed, franchising and validation are emerging trends within the broader transnational education umbrella. Under such arrangements, one institution is responsible for day to day academic activities, while another is responsible for issuing degrees. Lukas Bischof offers an overview of the state of franchising, validation, and branch campuses in the European Union, with a particular focus on the legislative frameworks that enable and regulate such practices. The last article in this section, written by Esther Wilkinson, discusses the role of technology in transnational education and it may enable current UK global players to maintain their position.

The works featured in this section analyze the rise of and diversity of provision within transnational education. While some of the articles selected treat transnational education (uncritically) as a business opportunity, other offer a more skeptical view on the local impacts of transnational education.

G. Mihut et al. (Eds.), Understanding Higher Education Internationalization, 35.

WILLIAM LAWTON AND ALEX KATSOMITROS

8. GLOBAL: INTERNATIONAL BRANCH CAMPUSES EXPANDING, GEOPOLITICAL LANDSCAPE CHANGING

University World News, 22 January 2012, Issue 205

The number of international branch campuses for higher education continues to expand at a stately rate, rather than with a headlong rush. But the landscape is changing, in line with prevailing geopolitical currents. According to data collected by the Observatory on Borderless Education in the latter half of 2011, there are now 200 branch campuses around the world. This is an increase of 38, or 23%, since our September 2009 report, which identified 162 international branch campuses. That number, in turn, represented a larger increase of 43% over the total identified in our October 2006 report. The rate of increase has therefore slowed but given the narrower time frame between 2009 and 2011, it may not have slowed very much.

The research also shows that the rate of growth is likely to pick up again. There are 37 more international branch campuses currently being planned by universities. All but two are slated to open in 2012 or 2013. These numbers, of course, depend wholly on where the conceptual boundaries are drawn. Our report includes only degree-granting operations, while the 2009 report included 17 programmes at diploma and other pre-degree levels. This report also excludes some of the small international degree-granting operations established by higher education institutions that were included in the 2009 report. The ones excluded have no physical infrastructure for teaching in the host country and are therefore usually not considered to be campuses by the home institutions.

If all of the above exclusions had been retained, the total number of international branch campuses would now be at least 225 and probably higher, because there are likely also to be many more non-degree programmes of the type previously included. In common with its predecessors, however, this report also excludes the myriad of transnational education operations, from joint degrees to online learning, that constitute the vast bulk of international teaching activities. In India, for example, 631 foreign institutions were operating in 2010, of which 440 did so from their home campuses, 186 had twinning or some other arrangements with local institutions, and five had opened a campus in India.

When considered against this full spectrum, international branch campuses remain firmly a minority pursuit. This is not surprising when considering that they

G. Mihut et al. (Eds.), Understanding Higher Education Internationalization, 37–39.

represent a greater level of capital outlay and financial risk than other forms of transnational education (though not the greatest reputational risk—that distinction belongs to validation arrangements, in which the originating institution provides only brand marketing and the partner institution covers admissions, teaching, materials, curriculum and assessment). Having said that, many universities now considering branch campuses abroad are able to mitigate financial risk because prospective host governments are keen to cover the initial and operational costs. These governments see the provision of education by foreign universities as a core element of national economic strategies. In these cases, some or much financial risk is transferred from the foreign institutions to the host governments. Although significant overheads and resource investments for universities remain, external financial support could in many cases be the deciding factor when developing business plans.

SOME TRENDS

Some basic headline statistics remain unchanged. American universities still originate the greatest number of campuses abroad; this is unchanged at 78, although there have been additions and closures. The United Arab Emirates still host the greatest number (37), although this has in fact decreased by three. But the direction of travel under these numbers is more significant: the number of US-origin campuses had registered the fastest growth in the preceding interval (2006–09). Furthermore, there are no new international branch campuses planned for the UAE. The centre of gravity is clearly shifting eastwards from the Gulf.

The 2009 report showed 10 campuses on the Chinese mainland and five in Hong Kong. The number identified in China is now 17, but these include a few operations that existed before 2009. Hong Kong now has one fewer, with the withdrawal of the University of Northern Virginia. And surprisingly, there are no campuses planned in Hong Kong that we are aware of. In addition to the new campuses in mainland China, there are at least seven more currently in development—five from the US and two from the UK. This movement should not be surprising either: at a geopolitical level it reflects the shift in economic and political power towards China. But it also shows the responsiveness of Western institutions to Chinese determination to act on the world stage in higher education—a determination that is backed up with state funding. Of the 37 planned campuses identified, it is worth noting that 13 are from American universities and colleges, for destinations from China to Korea to Rwanda. It is therefore too soon to conclude that the US is losing interest in international branch campuses.

The expansion of international branch campuses worldwide therefore continues as an important element of higher education internationalisation. There is a great variety of models and approaches, although the motivations are fairly simple to state: international branch campuses extend the reach of institutions in such a way as to enhance their international profile and status. They provide greater access to an expanding student market, especially in Asia where demand for higher education is expected to continue to outstrip supply for another 20 years.

Many governments, especially in Asia and parts of Africa, see international branch campuses as preferable to the outward migration of young people and as essential components of their national economic and developmental goals, as expressed through the drive and support for education hubs. But building branch campuses will never supplant broader transnational education activities as a means of positioning universities with international aspirations. Long-term partnerships with mutual benefits for universities in different countries do not require new campuses. This is the case whether the primary motivating factor is securing a new sustainable revenue stream or securing a sustainable research relationship or broadening the institutional profile or providing more international mobility and development opportunities for staff and students. In all cases, the consolidation of enduring academic partnerships merely starts with the signing of memoranda of understanding. It requires the investment of a great amount of time and resources in relationship-building and in due diligence.

LI ZHANG, KEVIN KINSER AND YUNYU SHI

9. GLOBAL: WORLD ECONOMIES AND THE DISTRIBUTION OF INTERNATIONAL BRANCH CAMPUSES

International Higher Education, Fall 2014, Number 77

The international branch campus has become a symbol of higher education internationalization in recent years. Perhaps because the dominant exporting countries have been the United Kingdom, the United States, and Australia, many people assume that the higher education export flows from developed countries to developing countries, in a West-to-East fashion. However, using data from the Cross-Border Education Research Team (C-BERT) at the University at Albany, State University of New York alongside an economic framework provided by the World Economic Forum, we look at the distribution of international branch campuses around the world. There are distinct patterns between host and home countries and the interests countries have for establishing international branch campuses are connected to economic competitiveness.

WORLD ECONOMIC FORUM'S GLOBAL COMPETITIVE INDEX

Since its development in 2004, the World Economic Forum's global competitive index has been widely used to measure and compare countries' productivity and economic prosperity. It uses 12 competitive index measures, to categorize countries into three types of economies. The index measures are designed to describe economic competitiveness in a country more accurately than the controversial categories of developing or emerging countries.

The first four pillars—institutions, infrastructure, macroeconomic environment, and health and primary education—create factor-driven economies. Fifty-eight countries belong to this category where they use low wages and natural resources for competitive advantage. A second category of 53 efficiency-driven economies are determined by six different pillars: higher education and training, good-market efficiency, labor-market efficiency, financial market efficiency, technology readiness, and market size. These countries compete through the development of a skilled workforce and increased product quality. Finally, innovation-driven economies rely on the two pillars of business sophistication and innovation, to boost their economic development. Thirty-six countries are innovation-driven

G. Mihut et al. (Eds.), Understanding Higher Education Internationalization, 41–43.

economies that have advanced production processes and the capacity to create unique products.

Since higher education competitiveness is one indicator of a country's economic competitiveness, the former usually reflects the latter, but that is not always the case. For instance, Bahrain is listed as an innovation-driven economy, but its higher education competitiveness is ranked 53rd among the 147 countries. Barbados, Estonia, Lithuania, Costa Rica, Poland, Chile, and Latvia are efficiency-driven economies, but their higher education competitiveness is on par with that of innovation-driven economies. In the same vein, Saudi Arabia, Brunei, Sri Lanka, Philippines, Venezuela, and Armenia are factor-driven economies with more competitive higher education than many efficiency-driven economies.

INTERNATIONAL BRANCH CAMPUSES

C-BERT has identified 201 international branch campuses in operation worldwide. Using the World Economic Forum framework, we grouped these campuses into 9 categories based on the classification of the home and host countries, as either factor-, efficiency-, or innovation-driven economies.

There are a total of 12 international branch campuses established by 5 factor-driven economies—including India, Iran, Pakistan, Philippines, and Venezuela. All the factor-driven economies establish their branch campuses in innovation-driven economies, rather than factor-driven or efficiency-driven economies. United Arab Emirates (UAE) is the biggest importer, hosting eight of such international branch campuses, while India becomes the biggest factor-driven exporting economy, having 9 branch campuses worldwide, mainly in UAE.

Seven efficiency-driven economies have opened a total of 21 international branch campuses. These countries include China, Malaysia, Russia, Chile, Mexico, Lebanon, and Estonia. Unlike the factor-driven economies, such campuses from efficiency-driven economies are roughly evenly distributed among the three types of economies: 7 branch campuses are established in factor-driven economies, 8 in efficiency-driven economies, and 6 in innovation-driven economies. It is noteworthy that these efficiency-driven economies tend to establish the campuses in their neighboring countries or within the same region. For example, Russia has branch campuses in Armenia, Ukraine, Uzbekistan, Azerbaijan, Kazakhstan, and Tajikistan, which were part of the former Soviet Union. When neighboring countries have a less-competitive higher education sector and share similar culture and language, they are less risky as hosts compared to more far-flung locations.

The majority of international branch campuses, however, are established by innovation-driven economies: 168 out of a total of 201 such campuses worldwide. The innovation driven economies of the United States, United Kingdom, France, and Australia are the biggest exporters of higher education. United States alone has 77 branch campuses worldwide, more than the number established by the United Kingdom, France, and Australia combined. Only 11 of these international branch campuses are established in factor-driven economies, while 66 are established in efficiency-driven economies and 91 are established among innovation-driven economies. Among these branch campuses worldwide, export from innovation economy to innovation economy is therefore the most common form of them.

The United Arab Emirates, Singapore, and Qatar are the major innovation economies that host international branch campuses. These three countries aspire to become regional hubs by providing preferential policies for foreign institutions. China and Malaysia are the major efficiency-driven economies that import higher education from innovation countries. The Chinese government encourages the "bring in" of foreign education in order to improve its own higher education quality and plans to host another 5 to 10 international branch campuses in the following decade. Malaysia aspires to become a regional hub by inviting foreign institutions to open branch campuses in hubs at Iskandar and Kuala Lumpur Education City.

CONCLUSION

Our focus here is not on specific countries and their interests in the international branch campuses phenomenon, but the patterns suggested by this worldwide distribution under the World Economic Forum framework. The analysis presents a picture of institutional mobility, different from an outdated model that presumes flows are predominantly from developed to developing countries. The majority of international branch campuses have been established between innovation-driven economies, as well as some factor-driven and efficiency-driven economies extending their presence into innovation-driven economies. It is important to understand the myriad of reasons why emerging economies welcome such campuses, and how this might reflect national development agendas. Unmet demand for education and an emphasis on building a competitive workforce are often combined with regulatory incentives that encourage foreign investment in the direct provision of education. The multinational university may reflect the innovation economy's dominant entrepreneurial response to this scenario.

JOHN FIELDEN

10. GLOBAL: FINANCIAL ASPECTS OF OFFSHORE ACTIVITIES

International Higher Education, Summer 2013, Number 72

In April 2013, it was announced that the University of East London would close its new campus in Cyprus, after operating for only six months with an enrollment of just 17 students. In so doing, it joined the 11 closures of offshore campus ventures in the two years (2010–2012), recorded by the Observatory on Borderless Higher Education. These statistics emphasize the risky nature of offshore activities by universities and colleges. It is not just international branch campuses that are volatile; Australian transnational education operations have also fluctuated dramatically, falling from a peak of 1,569 programs delivered in other countries in 2003 to 889 in 2009. Despite these reverses, the growth in offshore provision continues remorselessly in some countries; in the United Kingdom, for example, in 2011/12 there were 571,000 international students studying for UK awards outside the United Kingdom, an increase of 40 percent on the figure two years before.

For members of university boards and senior managers the need for rigorous analysis of potential offshore activity has never been greater. They will be helped by a study from the United Kingdom's Higher Education International Unit—a guide to the financial aspects of UK offshore activities. This study sets out some of lessons learned by 24 universities in the United States, Australia, and the United Kingdom. Those interviewed were understandably reluctant to reveal too much about the financial consequences of their operations but were only too happy to pass on advice and recommendations to others. These have been encapsulated in the report under three headings: those at the early stage of entering into a Memorandum of Understanding; those when things are getting more serious and a legal agreement is required; and those at the operational stage when activities are underway.

SIGNING A MEMORANDUM OF UNDERSTANDING

The origins of these memorandums may hold the key to future success. Until recently they have been regarded by some as trophies collected at conferences or even a performance indicator of internationalization; some regard them as "a license to start talking," rather than any serious indication of collaboration. The interviews identified a trend to a more strategic approach. Major institutions are now investing

G. Mihut et al. (Eds.), Understanding Higher Education Internationalization, 45–47.

research effort in identifying favorable countries and suitable partner institutions within them. In some cases, this fits within a strategy of having a limited number of significant "deep partnerships" for research and teaching in a small number of countries. This has led to a new-growth industry, developing country profiles backed by extensive due diligence on their currency, regulatory frameworks, tax regimes and incentives, national quality-assurance agencies, and legal requirements for the operation of higher education institutions.

The word "values" is increasingly used when making decisions about foreign ventures. This applies particularly to the choice of partner. If the initiative comes from a government that will be the partner, this can be a sensitive issue; two major UK institutions—the University College London and the University of Westminster—have contracts for the delivery of higher education with the governments of Kazakhstan and Uzbekistan, which are not notable democracies. Both have taken great care to protect their reputation in their contracts. When choosing a commercial partner the problems are even greater, since many countries have financial and corporate accounting systems that are not very transparent. Commercial partners are often large conglomerates with property interests and see a university either as an attraction in a business development or as an emblem of corporate social responsibility. Even in such cases, however, the profit motive may not have gone away, and any difference of motive with the university can be a source of future discord.

DEVELOPING A BUSINESS CASE

The second stage of activity involves the development of a business case for the board and a subsequent legal agreement. It is at this stage that common values and motives are essential with early agreement on tuition-fee levels, scholarships, and a reasonable period of payback. Another key issue, once the technical studies are underway, is having a common language and understanding, since informal relationships in the operational phase will thrive if there is a personal positive chemistry between the partners' leading players. Whatever the legal agreements say, unexpected occurrences and midterm corrections will be inevitable. An American interviewee said "anyone who has low tolerance for surprises, ambiguity and frequent shifting shouldn't even think about offshore operations." Cultural difficulties often arise in the negotiation phase. In some countries, the final legal agreement is regarded as the starting point for negotiation, and key definitions of words such as "students" or "surplus" are particularly prone to misinterpretation. A "yes" can mean "I hear you," rather than "I agree."

Other major topics in negotiations are the percentage share in any local holding company that is created to operate an offshore campus and the terms of an exit strategy. Since few universities are able (for fiduciary or legislative reasons) to invest large sums in overseas operations, the most common role of a commercial partner is to provide the physical infrastructure and sometimes the equipment. The argument then centers on the financial value of the intellectual property and brand of the incoming university, which will be used to calculate its share of any surplus or deficit. This becomes a haggle and can even result in world-class institutions—such as, the University of Nottingham having to accept stakes of 37.1 percent and 29.1 percent in the associate companies running its two offshore campuses. In discussions, offshore providers have decided that it is essential to think early and hard about the terms of an exit strategy; in some cases, this is even considered at the Memorandum of Understanding stage in case it becomes a deal breaker.

MANAGING OFFSHORE ACTIVITIES

Once an offshore activity is up and running, the key question is where decisions are made and what is delegated to a local board or an academic partner. Most international branch campuses are owned by a local joint company with a board that takes the key decisions, while most transnational education operations have no local legal entity behind them and are managed by the home institution's academic structures. The most important decisions relate to admissions criteria (and consequential student numbers), local marketing strategies, and the level of tuition fees. This is when an early investment in building good personal relationships pays off. A commercial partner will be tempted to lower entry standards, adopt aggressive local marketing campaigns, and increase tuition fees, while the university will not.

Few offshore ventures make significant financial surpluses and many take between 5 to 10 years to see a return on investment. However, there are examples of reasonable financial benefits, and the research found that the most successful Australian universities claim to have average profit margins of 8 to 10 percent. But a key question is the cost base on which the 10 percent is calculated, since such a return is unlikely if all management and staff time is fully charged to the venture. Many of the universities in the sample claimed that it was not their aim to make financial surpluses but to promote their reputation in the region, to develop collaborative research with the partner or in the country, and to generate a flow of postgraduates back to the home campus.

Although the study has emphasized the importance of rigorous processes for due diligence and financial planning with comprehensive research about markets, a key conclusion is that these are not enough. Successful offshore operations demand good leadership and personal skills and mutually trusting relationships between the partners. If these exist, the unanticipated events and upheavals that will inevitably arise can be overcome.

JASON E. LANE AND KEVIN KINSER

11. GLOBAL: FIVE MODELS OF INTERNATIONAL BRANCH CAMPUS FACILITY OWNERSHIP

International Higher Education, Winter 2013, Number 70

Setting up an overseas campus can be a costly endeavor. One reason is the expense associated with building and maintaining a physical infrastructure in another country. In fact, mentioning an international branch campus (IBC) causes many people to think of small replicas of the home campus, set up in a foreign desert or jungle. However, only a handful of campuses are comprised of buildings and grounds that would be identifiable as a setting for higher learning. Even when they do have a full campus in the traditional sense, many do not actually own the facilities that they use. For example, the University of Nottingham's campuses in China and Malaysia have replicas of the iconic bell tower located on the UK campus; yet, they do not actually own those buildings.

Our many site visits to IBCs revealed a range of campus types. While some have many buildings, others have only a few rooms. Some are rented; others are fully owned by the home campus. Still others use space provided by partners, which is, however, not owned or rented by the home campus. However, information on this topic has remained largely anecdotal. So, when an international survey of IBCs was conducted, the ownership arrangements of their campus was specifically questioned.

SURVEY METHODS AND IBC DEFINITION

The survey, conducted in the fall of 2011, was distributed to 180 institutions that met the definition of an entity that is owned, at least in part, by a foreign education provider; operated in the name of the foreign education provider; engages in at least some face-to-face teaching; and provides access to an entire academic program that leads to a credential awarded by the foreign education provider. The only reference to the facilities is that there must be a physical location and space for face-to-face teaching. The mention of ownership in this definition refers to the corporate entity and does not necessarily mean ownership of the campus. Each respondent was asked to describe the ownership of their facilities, and then their written responses were analyzed.

Information on ownership was received from 50 international branch campuses. The findings revealed five basic types of ownership patterns: (1) wholly owned by the home campus, (2) rented from a private party, (3) owned by the local government, (4) owned by a private partner, or (5) owned by an educational partner.

G. Mihut et al. (Eds.), Understanding Higher Education Internationalization, 49–51.

WHOLLY OWNED

The most common ownership arrangement (14 IBCs; 28%) was for the home campus to wholly own the facilities of the IBC. This was somewhat surprising as the arrangement has the most financial risk associated with it. The development of a bricks and mortar campus can be quite costly; and should something go wrong (e.g., enrollments drop or the government changes the regulations), it may be difficult to recover the sunk costs if the campus operations are forced to close or be altered. However, it can also provide a level of stability as the home campus does not have to coordinate with a separate organization, in terms of the use or upkeep of the facilities. It also reduces the likelihood of a partner trying to leverage their ownership of campus to influence academic operations.

GOVERNMENT PARTNERS

After the wholly owned campus, the next most frequently cited arrangement (11 IBCs; 22%) was for the local government to subsidize the cost of, and thereby own, the local campus. This model seems to be most common, where governments see IBCs as part of their economic growth strategy and want to provide incentives to attract specific institutions. Depending on the country, ownership can be by either local or national governments. In Qatar, the development of Education City, and the building of campus facilities, is handled by the Qatar Foundation, which is sponsored by the national government. Whereas, in Australia, Malaysia, and Europe, there are examples of local and state governments, investing in the facilities as a way to attract foreign institutions—which would help support local economic growth. In fact, at least two examples were found of local governments stepping up to build facilities for IBCs after the national government refused to support the development of a new public university in their region.

PRIVATE INVESTORS

A third ownership structure is found when a foreign academic institution (10 IBCs; 20%) partners with a local private partner, usually an investment firm or property developer, to build the campus. In these cases, the private partner sometimes receives a stake in the revenues produced by the IBC, or they use the IBC as an "amenity" to help sell other property they own in the immediate vicinity.

RENTING

Nine (18%) of the institutions rent their campus space. A couple of the rented facilities were located in Europe, but most of these institutions were located in Dubai Knowledge Village or Dubai International Academic City, which were designed primarily as a real estate development for foreign institutions to rent space. In this model, multiple institutions rent similar space in the same buildings or nearby buildings, creating a sort of shopping mall effect, whereby students have many academic options available to choose from. One of the more costly aspects of this endeavor is that the campuses had to pay for the furnishing and fixtures in addition to renting the space. In some instances, renting seems to be a transitional phase, as some institutions later build their own stand-alone campus buildings, moving out of the nearby rental facilities.

ACADEMIC PARTNERS

Finally, in a very interesting arrangement, the IBC (6 IBCs; 12%) is housed within the academic facilities of another campus. This partnership, of which examples were found in Asia and the Middle East, does not count as a dual or joint-degree program, as there is no academic partnership in place. Instead, the IBC uses the facilities to offer stand-alone academic programs. It is located in facilities owned by another college or university but operates separately from the other institution.

CONCLUSIONS

While the label "international branch campus" can imply that the ownership or condition of facilities is important in the model, most operating definitions only require that there be a physical presence in a foreign country. The research has revealed that IBCs actually come in many shapes and sizes, ranging from rented storefronts to government subsidized architectural wonders. These data reveal five models that universities use when seeking to establish an IBC's physical plant. It is important to note, however, that the use of these models will be limited, based on local regulations (e.g., some countries do not allow foreign ownership of facilities), as well as the ability to find a willing government, private, or academic partner to provide the space. Each arrangement comes with its own set of opportunities and obstacles. Wholly owned endeavors provide some stability and freedom from external interference but also pose a financial risk, should the enrollments not meet projections or government hospitality lapse. Partnering reduces the financial risks, but could lead to outside interference in academic affairs. While the models of facility ownership have been identified, more research is needed to understand their operational implications.

JANE KNIGHT

12. GLOBAL: FINANCING OF EDUCATION HUBS: WHO ARE THE INVESTORS?

International Higher Education, Winter 2015, Number 79

International education hubs are the latest development in the international higher education landscape. A country-level education hub is a planned effort to build a critical mass of local and international actors—higher education institutions and providers, students, research and development centers, and knowledge industries—who work collaboratively on education, training, and knowledge production/innovation. To date, six countries—Qatar, United Arab Emirates, Singapore, Malaysia, Hong Kong, and Botswana—claim to be education hubs. But how are they financed? Are the investors public or private? Are they local or foreign based? Are the current-funding models sustainable? These are important questions worthy of closer examination.

QATAR

Each country has its own capacity and strategies to fund education hub initiatives. Qatar is an interesting but unique model. All physical infrastructure and facilities are provided for foreign-branch campuses and companies located in Education City and the Science and Technology Park. Furthermore, 100 percent of the sizable operating costs for the 10 branch campuses and the new graduate-level university, Hammid bin Khalifa University, are covered by the Qatar Foundation. The annual operating costs to support Education City, Science and Technology Park and the extensive array of research programs and grants is the responsibility of the Qatar government and is extremely high. Is this government supported full funding model sustainable and is it optimal? In essence, Qatar is importing and purchasing the majority of education programs, services, and research for the education hub activities. A pivotal question is how long should a country attempt to build and strengthen domestic capacity by purchasing and importing foreign expertise. It has been 17 years since Qatar first started its work on inviting select foreign universities to establish specific programs in Education City. Is this the first phase of Qatar's long-term plan to develop more domestic human resource capacity as it loosens its reliance on natural gas and foreign expatriate talent, or is this becoming modus operandi? If so, is it a sustainable and effective model? If not, what will be the second phase?

G. Mihut et al. (Eds.), Understanding Higher Education Internationalization, 53–55.

UNITED ARAB EMIRATES

The United Arab Emirates (UAE) offers a completely different set of circumstances in terms of funding, investments, and revenue generation. Each emirate has developed its own approach to making UAE an education hub. Abu Dhabi has invited world renowned institutions, such as New York University and the Sorbonne, to set up branch campuses in customized facilities provided by Abu Dhabi Government. In addition, the Massachusetts Institute of Technology was invited to help develop and advise on the development of Masdar Institute of Technology and Masdar City, the first carbon free zone in the world. Masdar City hosts world-class research facilities, scientists, and graduate programs—all of which are supported by the Abu Dhabi government. This represents an enormous domestic public investment.

Dubai is a different story. Dubai's Strategic Plan called for the establishment of several theme-based economic free zones. Two of these are education focused— Knowledge Village and Dubai International Academic City. The investment arm of the Dubai government (TECOM) is mandated to build the physical infrastructure and facilities for these zones and recruit reputable foreign institutions and training companies. The tenants in these zones enjoy attractive tax and regulatory incentives to offer their education and training programs. Unlike the situation in Qatar and Abu Dhabi, the foreign institutions and providers do not have their operating costs subsidized, and they pay rent for the use of their facilities. It is estimated that in Dubai's two economic free education zones, the public domestic investment is about 80 percent in terms of land, infrastructure, services, and private foreign investment from the tenants is about 20 percent. The amount of revenue generated from facility rentals for TECOM and from tuition fees for branch campuses/private training companies is not available; but given that these zones are relatively stable and operating at full capacity the funding formula seems to be working; and increased education opportunities are being offered to primarily expatriate students living in UAE (60% of enrollments), international offshore students (32%), and some UAE citizens (8%).

HONG KONG, BOTSWANA, AND SINGAPORE

Hong Kong presents yet another scenario. The government has made limited public investment into hub development, since its first announcement in 2004. The primary public investment by Hong Kong has been in the form of scholarships to attract international students, most of who come from China. Recently, a plot of land was made available to attract branch campuses of local or international universities; but there is not information as to whether facilities will be built and available for rent or whether the institution has to invest in building their own infrastructure. Similarly, the public investment of the Botswana government, beyond engaging in a sophisticated planning and consultation process for hub development, appears to be limited. Botswana hub plans are still on track but have been negatively impacted by the 2008 and 2012 economic crisis. Their investment to date has been scholarships for international students and the establishment of a new university—Botswana International University of Science and Technology.

The financial investments in Singapore's hub building activities since 1998 are impossible to track, due to the lack of any published information on public/private or domestic/foreign funding sources. No conclusions can be drawn but worth noting is that the Singapore government has been referred to as the "venture capitalist" in terms of its significant and generous role in bankrolling the education hub efforts.

MALAYSIA

The situation in Malaysia is complex, given the number of different components to the hub strategy. Malaysia is home to seven branch campuses and more are planned. Both private foreign and domestic funds were used to fund these initiatives. Yet, with the establishment of an economic free zone in the form of Educity@Iskandar, there has been major financing provided by the public investment arm of the government, Khazanah Nasional. It has funded the building of infrastructure and education facilities to attract international institutions. Overall in Malaysia, it is estimated that public domestic investment represents 50 percent of the funding for education hub activities, complemented by 40 percent of domestic private investment. The remaining 10 percent is made up of foreign private investment and other sources.

CONCLUSION

These case studies demonstrate that public domestic investment is critical to the development of education hubs. While, hub building also requires private investment from domestic and foreign sources, the importance of local government support to kick start and leverage other sources of financing should not be underestimated. The UAE and Malaysia are examples where initial public investment has paid off and attracted other streams of private funding. Singapore and Qatar present other models where financing of education hub activities has been done primarily by the government (or ruling family) and over the last 15 years much has been accomplished. However, the sustainability of such funding and the ability to replicate this model in other nations remain as two unanswered questions.

JANE KNIGHT AND JOHN MCNAMARA

13. GLOBAL: THE IMPACT OF TRANSNATIONAL EDUCATION IN RECEIVING COUNTRIES

International Higher Education, Fall 2015, Number 82

For many years, transnational education (TNE), also known as cross border mobility of academic programs and providers, has provided new modes of study for students; opportunities for provider institutions to broaden their reach; and alternative strategies for host countries and institutions to widen access to higher education. There is no question that more and more students across the world are choosing to study international higher education programs, without moving to the country that awards the qualification. This growing phenomenon is facilitated by higher education institutions establishing branch campuses or delivering their programs in foreign host/receiving countries alone or in collaboration with local partners.

To date, the majority of research, discussion, and debate on TNE has been from the sending/home country perspective. Given the criticism that TNE is for revenue and status building purposes by sending institutions, a frequently heard phrase these days is that "TNE is a win-win situation." This may be correct, but to examine the true impact of TNE on receiving/host countries it is necessary to get their opinions and understand their views. To that end, a major survey study was undertaken by the British Council and the German Academic Exchange Service, with collaboration from Australian International Education, and in association with Campus France and the Institute for Education in London. Customized surveys were sent to eight different target groups—TNE students, TNE faculty members, senior TNE institutional leaders, higher education experts, government agencies, employees as well as non-TNE students, and non-TNE faculty in 10 TNE active countries in all regions of the world. The analysis of the 1,906 responses yielded some fascinating insights.

TNE IS REACHING A DIFFERENT PROFILE OF STUDENTS

An interesting and helpful outcome of the research is insight into the profile of TNE students. While there is no typical TNE student, the data suggest that TNE students are generally older than the traditional secondary school leaver entering higher education. The proportion of TNE students with previous employment

G. Mihut et al. (Eds.), Understanding Higher Education Internationalization, 57–60.

experience, as well as the high numbers studying master's and PhD level programs, also point to a relatively older student cohort. Worth noting is the high proportion of students working full-time during their studies, facilitated by modules delivered over concentrated time periods during the evenings or weekends. The flexibly of TNE clearly has appeal for students with requirements to balance work, study, and other life demands.

"CAREER DEVELOPMENT" IS THE MAIN MOTIVATION FOR CHOOSING TNE

Understanding why students chose their TNE program is fundamental to understanding their expectations and objectives. A clear message from students is that TNE is perceived as a way to improve their professional skills, thereby improving their career prospects. TNE students also believe that employers perceive TNE to be advantageous when selecting job candidates. The two main reasons cited for this were: (1) prestige and status of the foreign institution/ education system; (2) the international outlook and multicultural experience of TNE graduates relative to local non-TNE graduates. While students perceive that employers are predisposed to TNE graduates, more research is needed to ascertain employers' awareness level of TNE, their perceptions of its value, and their support for further education through TNE programs.

COST OF TNE—POSITIVE AND NEGATIVE

The affordability of TNE relative to study abroad represents the most positive attribute of TNE for students. This provides evidence that increasing demand for international education can be partially met through program and provider mobility and also highlights the extent to which the lines between TNE and traditional student mobility have become blurred. On the other hand, the high cost of TNE compared with local academic programs represents a main negative attribute of TNE. Issues about pricing, affordability, and how TNE tuition fees compare with local education options are important to students and institutions alike. In studying the costs and benefits of TNE, more attention needs to be given to differentiating between the various modes of TNE, such as branch campuses, franchise/twinning, distance education (including MOOCs—massive open online courses), and joint/double degree programs.

INCREASED ACCESS: A TOP BENEFIT

Feedback from senior TNE leaders, higher education experts, government agencies, and employers suggest that TNE is having the greatest impact by "providing increased access to higher education for local students" and "improving the overall quality of higher education provision." The findings also show that TNE, in general, is not providing different programs to those offered locally, which somewhat dispels the myth that TNE offers specialized niche programs not available in the host country. For the most part, TNE programs appear to be responding to student demand.

LACK OF AWARENESS OF TNE

A surprising finding is an overall lack of awareness about TNE programs in the host country. The majority of non-TNE students and non-TNE faculty surveyed were not aware of the TNE opportunities in their country and sometimes in their own institution. Surveyed employers often expressed a lack of understanding or confusion about what actually constitutes a TNE experience. This revealing finding suggests that the full potential of these programs is not being realized and that much work is needed to publicize TNE opportunities in the host country.

TNE GRADUATES HIGHLY SKILLED BUT NOT NECESSARILY IN LINE WITH LOCAL NEEDS

All target groups believed that TNE graduates are better equipped than locally educated graduates across a varied set of specific skills—such as problem solving, critical thinking, and international outlook. Thus, while TNE graduates are perceived as relatively skilled, the research suggests that TNE may be only "moderately" addressing skills gaps in the local labor market. Specialized TNE courses covering niche topics were felt to have a positive impact on addressing local skills gaps, but overall, many TNE providers are offering programs already available locally.

OUTLOOK FOR TNE

Respondents were generally optimistic about the outlook for TNE and indicated that both the number of new programs and the capacity of existing programs will continue to grow over the medium term. In terms of helping to build the local knowledge economy and producing collaborative research output, TNE looks well placed to play an increasing role in the host country. Economic considerations, such as the capacity of TNE to attracting foreign-direct investment and improve local infrastructure, appear less pronounced and will largely depend on host country government policy and country specific circumstances.

The results paint an overall positive picture of the impact of TNE in host countries, especially in terms of TNE providing increased access for local students to higher education. But, there is very little concrete evidence to back up these opinions, as few TNE receiving countries have the capacity or will to gather enrollment data on all TNE operations in their country. An important challenge is the collection of data by host countries on the number and type of TNE operations in their country and the aggregate enrollment of local students, expatriate students living in the country, and international students enrolled in all TNE operations. For further information, see: British Council and DAAD (2014. Impacts of transnational education on host countries).

LUKAS BISCHOF

14. EUROPE: FRANCHISING, VALIDATION, AND BRANCH CAMPUSES IN THE EUROPEAN UNION

International Higher Education, Winter 2014, Number 74

The Bologna process aims at creating a European higher education area with more comparable, compatible, and coherent higher education systems in Europe. Indeed, students, staff, and research teams are increasingly mobile within that area. In addition, a growing number of institutions are offering their study programs across borders. The most common form of such cross-border provision of higher education (CBHE) are joint or double degrees. Branch campuses, franchising or validation arrangements are less frequent but have lately stirred controversy in European higher education.

EUROPEAN LEGISLATION HAS CREATED A COMMON MARKET

The European common market guarantees that European citizens have their qualifications recognized in any EU member state in the same way they would be recognized in their own country. At the same time, it allows any European business to offer their services in any other EU member state. A holder of a Spanish diploma is therefore allowed to work in their profession in Germany or any other EU country, and a company from Poland is allowed to offer its services in Ireland. No member state is allowed to infringe on these rights.

Education on the other hand has always been the exclusive domain of each EU member state. In 2008, however, in a series of recent landmark rulings, the Court of Justice of the European Union has established that franchised or validated study programs fall within the responsibilities of the member state in which the diploma-granting institution is established, irrespective of where the course took place. This ruling now effectively allows a British university to allow a non-accredited institution (or company) based in another EU country (e.g., Greece) the right to issue British degrees, in spite of the receiving country's exclusive responsibility for education. The receiving country must therefore accept these degrees as any other EU degree. Quality assurance of such degrees is the sole responsibility of the exporting country, although to many observers it is not clear how or whether franchised or validated degrees are quality assured by their degree-granting institutions.

G. Mihut et al. (Eds.), Understanding Higher Education Internationalization, 61–63.

THE EUROPEAN MAPPING OF CROSS-BORDER HIGHER EDUCATION

Given the potential implications for consumer protection, transparency, and the general trustworthiness of European higher education, surprisingly until recently there was very little information about the extent and quality assurance of such cross-border provision of higher education. On behalf of the European Commission (the executive branch of the European Union), CHE Consult has now published the first systematic research and comprehensive overview on branch campuses, franchising, and validation activities in the European Union, as well as a comparative overview of national legislation governing their establishment in the European Union. By collecting and verifying data from ministries, quality-assurance agencies, rectors' conferences, CBHE providers, and recognition organizations in all 27 member states, we were able to identify 253 instances of branch campuses, franchising, and validation activities that are currently going on in the European Union.

The results confirm earlier research on cross-border higher education. Firstly, Anglophone countries are major providers of higher education services. Second, economically stronger countries serve as "exporters" of degrees, while economically weaker countries tend to be recipients. The study identified Great Britain, the United States, France, and Poland as the main providers of CBHE arrangements in EU member states, whereas Greece, Spain, and Hungary are the main receivers. More interestingly, we were able to demonstrate that the number of such received activities in a country shows a strong statistical relationship to the percentage of its students leaving to study abroad.

LEGISLATION IS OFTEN INCONSISTENT

Since it is in the exclusive domain of EU member states, legislation on higher education is highly diverse in the European Union. Some member states do not have a policy on CBHE. Of those who do have a policy, it may range from compulsory registration as a means to monitor activities to the outright ban of certain forms of provision. Some member states require proof of accreditation of the exporting country, others require institutions to be authorized by national authorities. In some cases, member states require foreign providers to undergo an additional accreditation, effectively forcing them to become part of the national higher education system, which seems to be a clear violation of the EU Court rulings. Short of outright banning CBHE activity, member states sometimes impede the operations of foreign CBHE providers by denying holders of their degrees access to the national education system; excluding them from access to state-regulated professions or government employment (which might be in contradiction of EU law); while at the same time barring foreign providers from seeking national accreditation. The study contains a detailed description of the various member states' legislation on provider mobility.

LOOPHOLES IN QUALITY ASSURANCE

Our research also identified inconsistencies and potential loopholes in current European legislation of CBHE activities. On the European level, the European Union strictly enforces the common market and guarantees the recognition of certificates and diplomas in different member states. At the same time, the responsibility for quality assurance lies with the individual member states. Because of highly heterogeneous registration requirements and the absence of a joint register of "white-listed" providers and programs, rogue providers have been known to take advantage of the system. The validation activities of the University of Wales (UK) provide an interesting example of how structural and contingent factors can interact in the CBHE field. The University of Wales was unusual in being a federal institution awarding degrees but not directly running any of its constituent universities. During the 1990s and the 1st decade of the current century, it found itself losing constituent institutions and turned to validation both as a means of securing a role and generating income. By 2009/10 its international validation activities were taking place in 140 collaborative centers in 30 countries and accounted for two thirds of its income.

Only in late 2011, after the quality of its validation processes was being put into question of a critical report by the British quality-assurance agency, it was announced that only programs it designed itself and controlled would be available internationally. The fact that the university was able to operate in this way reflects the high level of autonomy in the UK higher education system, the popularity of international activities, the need to generate income, and the lack of formal powers of the main quality-assurance body to correct or curtail them. However, within the European Union, no other member state would have had the right to refuse to recognize the University of Wales' degrees.

TOWARDS QUALITY ASSURANCE AND TRANSPARENCY

Our research into the prevalence and regulation of franchising, validation, and branch campuses has made it clear that a converging European higher education area with guaranteed recognition of degrees and freedom of establishment needs corresponding mechanisms of transparency and quality assurance. Such a quality-assurance framework should include a joint European register of recognized, quality-assured higher education institutions and programs. Commonly agreed-upon standards and a white list of institutions adhering to them would help to ensure transparency and develop trust in the cross-border education, provided within the European higher education area.

ESTHER WILKINSON

15. UNITED KINGDOM: TECHNOLOGY: THE SILENT PARTNER IN TRANSNATIONAL EDUCATION?

University World News, 13 February 2015, Issue 354

It may sound counterintuitive that creating opportunities for foreign students to remain in their countries and access UK qualifications overseas is an effective driver for economic growth, but that's the very real proposition of transnational education. Already generating a significant amount of income from overseas sources—an estimated £496 million (US$756 million) in 2012–13 alone, according to the Department for Business, Innovation and Skills—there's huge potential for more, being driven both by overall demand for higher education and international student mobility. Its importance as a growth enabler has even been recognised by government, having been named as a key policy strand for education in its industrial strategy. The question, then, is how can individual organisations take advantage of the opportunities before them and help the UK retain its position as a global leader?

LACK OF IT INFRASTRUCTURE

Last year Jisc carried out a survey with the Observatory on Borderless Higher Education, or OBHE, in order to answer this question by looking into how higher education institutions are approaching transnational education. We heard from 84 distinct Universities UK or GuildHE member institutions, across two distinct groups that are important in pushing forward the transnational education agenda: international offices, of course, and IT departments.

Technology and internet network provision is clearly a vital pin in organisations being able to offer education and qualifications to students in other countries, but our research showed that information technology, or IT, infrastructure is not always front of mind in transnational education planning and delivery. In our conversations with IT staff we found that many were in the dark when it comes to the transnational education efforts within their own institution. Almost half (45%) were not aware of current transnational education activities, and even fewer were involved in the actual decision-making, with just 27% of IT staff involved in institutional development plans, and a low 1% who said they were involved in planning.

G. Mihut et al. (Eds.), Understanding Higher Education Internationalization, 65–67.

This lack of awareness runs through to IT service management. About half (52%) of those we spoke to were unaware of whether their institution had run into any data-related problems through their transnational education activities and around the same amount (57%) were unable to say if their institutional risk assessments included IT infrastructure. Of course, the inclusion of an institution's IT staff in transnational education operations will often be down to how these relationships are managed internationally. For example, in a partnership model the organisation of the network will often be left to the overseas institution to arrange—as 34% of the people we spoke to claimed—so there's clearly less of an impetus to bring in colleagues from your own institution, although that's not to say they shouldn't be involved.

APPETITE FOR MORE TRANSNATIONAL EDUCATION

So why are they finding themselves absent? Well, the booming trend for transnational education has meant a lot of institutions have quite quickly had to put their own programmes into place and doing so has meant they haven't always been able to fully consider their methods of delivery, including IT infrastructure. It's an issue that will only increase as transnational education's popularity does. And there's clearly appetite from international offices staff to increase transnational education activity. A huge 82% confirmed they do have plans for new transnational education activities in the next five years. Pleasingly, there's also a desire to improve the provision that already exists. One quarter of these staff responded that they would like to see changes to delivery mechanisms, with many quoting they would like to shift to real-time online teaching.

This finding is particularly interesting, as the view follows that if local network infrastructure were sufficient, this would allow more live video streaming, webinars, and peer-group workshops to be employed—both valuable to students and more cost efficient than alternatives, such as flying in UK lecturers. The shift seems to represent a new desire to move to a more "blended" approach to transnational education, reflecting a mix in modes of delivery.

CLEAR COMMUNICATION

The consequence is, if you want to improve transnational education you first need to bolster the IT infrastructure (including network connectivity) underpinning your activity. Bringing in your own institutions' IT department, whether that's to lead the programme or support it, can be crucial in achieving this goal. Just knowing who is responsible for what is actually half the battle.

To do this there needs to be clear communication. IT staff need to be made aware of the important role they can and should be playing to help boost the institution's transnational education offer. Encouragement and involvement by international staff will go a long way towards bridging the gap. One of the key actions that Jisc is taking forward from the report is beginning an engagement campaign to encourage dialogue between the groups and create a landscape for sharing best practice. We will also be working to support the sector's needs in delivering world-class connectivity and services, including the digital architecture where needed.

PART 3

COMMERCIALIZATION OF INTERNATIONALIZATION

INTRODUCTION

Internationalization of higher education has been problematized by scholars and practitioners alike. Disequilibria in power relations and neo-colonial practices are sometimes replicated through transnational and international education. This section brings together articles that engage with one of the widely-discussed elements of internationalization: commercialization.

As part of the first article included in this section, Peter Scott analyzes the "neo-liberal turn" that globalization has taken in recent years and the related impacts on international higher education. His analysis differentiates between neo-liberal impacts and impacts caused by technological developments. The next article, written by Nic Mitchell, provides an overview of the growing global market for pathway programs to study abroad, such as non-degree language training programs. In a related work, Hans de Wit discusses an alternative to massive open online trainings that can be appropriated to facilitate access to internationalization: collaborative online international learning (COIL). COIL represents a cost-effective alternative that may advance learning and intercultural understanding, as well increase access to international opportunities in a commercialized internationalization landscape.

The increased presence of commissioned agents to recruit international students is one of the most controversial topics within the broader commercialization debate. Rahul Choudaha offers a balanced analysis of the role of agents, as well as some of the measures that higher education institutions may take to improve the function of agents and increase transparency. Also featured prominently in the commercialization debate, Nordic countries have recently introduced tuition fees for international students. Jan Petter Myklebust offers an insightful take on the developments in the region and the different realities in Nordic countries associated with this new tuition structure. In a complementary article, Ariane de Gayardon offers an analysis of France's national debates on international student fees, where reflections on the country's colonial past are highly relevant.

The commercialization of internationalization is best understood as an extension of the commercialization of higher education more broadly. It can be difficult to differentiate the recent trends of treating international students as a source of profit as well as the use of exploitative practices from principled, system-level questions about who should pay for higher education. Section three seeks to offer insight into the broad debates that govern this topic.

G. Mihut et al. (Eds.), Understanding Higher Education Internationalization, 71.

PETER SCOTT

16. GLOBAL: INTERNATIONAL HIGHER EDUCATION AND THE "NEO-LIBERAL TURN"

International Higher Education, Winter 2016, Number 84

In its original form, international higher education, which emphasized staff and student mobility and collaboration between universities across national frontiers, was one of the most idealistic, even altruistic, aspects of higher education. The myth-ideal of the wandering scholar in the Middle Ages was reinforced by the role played by imperial universities in educating colonial (and, ultimately, post-colonial) elites and also the role played by modern higher education systems in these countries in terms of aid and capacity building as well as the continued training of elites in the developing world. Today, international education is perhaps the aspect of higher education most associated with markets and competition; its language is now dominated by talk of market shares of international students and global league tables. So complete has been this reversal of perceptions of, and practices in, international higher education, that it passes almost without comment.

The major reason for this reversal has been the impact on higher education of the so-called "neo-liberal turn," the drift away from the social markets and welfare states developed in the 20th century as a response to recession, depression, and world wars—and which, remarkably, survived the shocks of the 2008 financial crisis and subsequent global recession. In the United Kingdom, there is now a strong, if contestable, belief that the ideals of mass higher education—democracy, social justice, individual "improvement" in a still recognizable Victorian sense—are out of sync, out of sympathy, with the dominant ideas of our age: wealth generation, growth, and competitiveness. In a global setting the same has happened. The older ideals of international education—solidarity, development, mutual understanding—have been replaced by new market imperatives summed up in a much over-used word globalization.

THREE SHIFTS

The "neo-liberal turn" has many guises, from the rigidly ideological to the flexibly pragmatic. It is a broad church composed of true believers and outwardly conforming agnostics. For some, it must be embraced by higher education as the major, or perhaps only, driver of future development; for others, it must be accommodated as

G. Mihut et al. (Eds.), Understanding Higher Education Internationalization, 73–75.

an inescapable but contingent set of circumstances. Reductionist definitions of the "neo-liberal turn," therefore, are dangerous. But three big trends stand out.

The first is the shift from the post-war "welfare state," forged in the shared memories and solidarities of world war and economic depression, to the so-called "market state." This has comprised both structural and cultural changes. The first include the retreat from high levels of personal taxation and the consequent increase in state borrowing (and the impact of that borrowing on financial markets) and the shrinking of publicly funded services. The second include the redefinition of the core purposes of the state that have seen a shift from the traditional sense of the state as embodying the public good to the idea of the state as both a "regulator" and also "customer."

The second aspect of the "neo-liberal turn" is globalization (actually much older and more complex than is often suggested by contemporary, over-excited accounts). It is older because "world societies" have existed in past history and also because global markets have existed for at least half a millennium. It is more complex is because the interactions between global brands and local cultures are highly nuanced and also because there are many forms of globalizations. Some of these "other" globalizations are at odds with the apparently hegemonic free-market geopolitical forms, violently so in the case of fundamentalism and terrorism (which, in turn, have legitimated the frightening contemporary phenomena of the "national security state"). One of the impacts of the discourse about globalization has been to regard not only all goods but also services as tradable "commodities." Although the debate about the incorporation of higher education within the General Agreement on Trade in Services (GATS) accords is currently muted, it is surely only a matter of time before higher education surfaces in the debate about the Transatlantic Trade and Investment Partnership (TTIP) between the United States and the European Union, and a related trans-Pacific trade treaty.

The third aspect is the revolution in communications—or, more broadly, communicative cultures. This contains many strands—the rise of social networking but also the mediatization of politics as "celebrity" and "brand"; the erosion of traditional print-based "literacies" (pessimists would go further, and lament the death of "logos"); the creation of "virtual" communities (highly beneficial in the case of science, less so in the context of cyber-sex or cyber-crime); the "hollowing out" of traditional institutions (such as political parties or trade unions), the replacement of traditional top-down hierarchies by "flat" and "instant" linkages (courtesy of Google et al.,).

IMPACT ON HIGHER EDUCATION

As a result, higher education, international and domestic, now has to operate in very different social, political, economic, and cultural environments than those taken for granted when our contemporary mass systems were first created almost half a century ago. But the impact of these new environments has been more than simply a drive to monolithic markets.

Changes in the nature of the state have certainly weakened its ability to maintain public systems of higher education. Both ideas—of the "public" and of "systems"—have been eroded; the former because it seems to imply publicly provided or funded services, and the latter because it appears to require a degree of top-down "planning" at odds with the free play of "markets." But the inexorable advance of high-fee funding regimes is far from assured, as countries as different as Chile and Germany have demonstrated by rejecting fees. In addition, the power of the state over higher education has reemerged in the form of more intrusive regulation.

Globalization has multiple and ambiguous impacts. It has produced great opportunities—for example, in terms of cross-cultural learning or transnational education. But it has created new barriers—most notably, in the context of immigration controls. Although free-market globalization is currently its dominant form, other forms exist—actual and potential. New globalizations of resistance to the "neo-liberal" turn or of solidarity built round environmental, equity and ethical concerns are already emerging.

Finally, changes in communicative cultures have radically shaped student expectations and their patterns of learning—as well as problematized the traditional structures of higher education. At present our understanding of this transformation is dominated by Massive Online Open Courses (MOOCs) and the power of IT-powered diagnostics and analytics to fine-tune higher education to "satisfy" student-customer needs; the mechanics of e-learning and e-assessment; and worries about Twitter-ish triviality. But there are other aspects of the communications revolution—for example, open-source and "instant" publication, the potential for global research alliances or for more intense engagement with "user" communities—with more collectivist than commercial implications.

NIC MITCHELL

17. GLOBAL: GROWING PATHWAYS TO STUDY ABROAD

University World News, 9 October 2015, Issue 385

A new study predicts growth in English-language foundation programmes for international students, particularly in continental Europe, which has seen the number of English-medium degrees triple in the last seven years. The report *New Routes to Higher Education: The global rise of foundation programmes* from Dutch-based StudyPortals and Cambridge English also predicts a slowing down of outbound students from China going to the United States, Japan, and the United Kingdom. In contrast, India is forecast to be the largest growth area followed by Nigeria, Malaysia, Nepal, Pakistan, Saudi Arabia, and Turkey.

The study claims to be the first global overview of foundation, or pathway preparation programmes, which help international students to bridge gaps in their academic knowledge, language proficiency and study skills, and ultimately, win a place on an English-language degree course. The programmes usually last one year and offer a route into some of the West's leading universities for students whose lack of English proficiency or academic qualifications prevents them from immediate direct entry to the first year of a degree course. Most programmes are provided by universities or by corporate provider–university partnerships. The five biggest corporate providers—Cambridge Education Group, INTO University Partnerships, Kaplan International Colleges, Navitas and Study Group—provide almost half of the programmes worldwide.

GLOBAL VALUE $825 MILLION IN FEES

The global value of tuition fees alone from foundation programmes is estimated at US$825 million per annum, says the report. Worldwide, StudyPortals listed 1,192 English-medium foundation programmes on its site in January this year when data was collected. Since then the number has grown by 20%, to 1,427. Britain currently dominates the market, with 748, or 63% of the programmes on offer. Oceania had 193 programmes—a 16% share—followed by North America with 145 programmes, Europe with 75 and 29 in Asia. But this may not reflect actual student numbers as some UK programmes have small cohorts of 10 to 15 students, said Carmen Neghina, education intelligence specialist at Study Portals and one of the authors of

G. Mihut et al. (Eds.), Understanding Higher Education Internationalization, 77–81.

the report. She told University World News: "It is difficult to know whether the total number of international students on UK foundation programmes is going up or down as the data is not collected by the Higher Education Statistics Agency, or HESA. But we do know there are more choices opening up worldwide for students needing these courses, particularly from Australia, and more recently from continental Europe."

EUROPE SET FOR PATHWAY GROWTH

The report says growth in English-medium degree programmes in mainland Europe has accelerated in recent years—rising from 725 courses in 2001, to 2,389 in 2007, and 8,039 in 2014. In absolute terms, the largest number of English-language undergraduate and master's degrees is in the Netherlands (1,078), followed by Germany (1,030), and Sweden with 822. Neghina said the Netherlands was leading the way in expanding its English-language undergraduate provision to help internationalise its higher education system and more universities are interested in offering foundation programmes. Study Group opened an international study centre in Holland in 2013 to prepare international students for progression to seven Dutch higher education institutions. Among them is Groningen University, where Rieks Bos, director of international affairs in the faculty of economics and business, told University World News that working with Study Group enables them to benefit from its international market reach. "The foundation programme enables us to diversify our international student inflow. We've actually asked Study Group to limit the number of Chinese students in the foundation year so we can have a good mix of nationalities, with no one nationality accounting for more than 20% of the international student population. The foundation year enables us to get more students from countries like South Korea, Azerbaijan, and Russia."

QUALITY BEFORE QUANTITY

Bos said: "Bringing in students from different cultural backgrounds to our classroom enhances the intercultural learning experience, but we always put quality before quantity and only invite those candidates on to our programmes who have the required prior knowledge and experience to be successful." "The quickest way to lose institutional commitment to internationalisation is to confront lecturers with students who are insufficiently prepared," Bos said. "The Study Group foundation year gives us a pretty good idea of the scope and level of knowledge of the students and we can influence the curriculum and ensure that students are socially and culturally prepared for the "Dutch-style" of teaching in higher education."

US EXPANSION

The US is also expanding its pathway provision, says the StudyPortals research. At present it only has a 12% share of foundation programmes on offer. Tim O'Brien, vice-president of global business intelligence and development at INTO University Partnerships, and an expert adviser for the StudyPortals-Cambridge English report, said most US universities realise they need to become more international for their own students to compete in the global economy. He pointed to Oregon State University as a good example of an institution that has gone from largely serving its local community to having a worldwide reach through partnering with INTO. "They have gone from 4% international students to 11% in a matter of seven years, boosting their income from international tuition to US$100 million a year and going from having 970 international students to over 4,000," he told University World News.

BRITAIN COULD LOSE MARKET SHARE

Industry experts in the UK estimate that nearly 40% of international students studying in British universities took a foundation or pathway preparation programme before starting their first-degree course. But this well-trodden route into British higher education is under threat from increased competition from abroad and mixed messages from the UK government, said Janet Ilieva, director of Education Insight and a former market analyst with the Higher Education Funding Council for England, or HEFCE, and the British Council.

Visa restrictions for students wanting to study in the UK have been tightened in recent years, particularly at pre-degree level, and Home Secretary Theresa May used her speech at last week's Conservative Party conference in Manchester to warn universities that rules must be enforced in relation to international students returning to their home countries after the expiry of their visas. The UK welcomed the brightest students from around the world, May told the Conservative conference. "But the fact is too many are not returning home as soon as their visas run out. "I don't care what the university lobbyists say. The rules must be enforced. Students, yes; over-stayers, no."

In response, Nicola Dandridge, chief executive of Universities UK, agreed care must be taken to ensure students are genuine and that there must be mechanisms to ensure that individuals do not overstay. But she warned: "While genuine international students in the UK continue to be caught up in efforts to bear down on immigration, it will feed the perception internationally that the UK is closed for business and does not welcome students. "As the Foreign Secretary suggested last month, one step the government could take would be to remove international students from their net migration target."

Governments overseas are becoming increasingly aware of the value that international students bring in both the short and long term, she said. "This is why the United States, Australia, Canada, Germany, France, China and others are implementing strategies and targets to increase the number of international students going to their universities."

FOUNDATION STUDENTS COULD BE CAUGHT IN CROSSFIRE

O'Brien said that INTO and the four other big corporate providers have around 18,000 students on their foundation programmes in the UK. "There is also homegrown provision by universities, such as Nottingham and Warwick, and a sizeable number of international students on different types of "pathway" courses at independent schools doing A levels and further education colleges," he said. Ilieva and O'Brien fear that pathway preparation students could find themselves increasingly caught in the crossfire as the Conservative cabinet colleagues battle over whether further restrictions are needed to ensure international students are genuine, with a possible tightening of language requirements under consideration.

Most foundation programmes require minimum International English Language Testing System, or IELTS, scores of 4.5–5.5, says the StudyPortals report, whereas many UK undergraduate programmes require scores of 6.0–7.0. O'Brien told University World News: "US pathway numbers are growing rapidly, while we are up around 8% so far this year in the UK despite constant changes to visa guidance that have undoubtedly unsettled students and recruitment agents. "There is enormous historical goodwill to the UK but this has been severely tested and there is a danger that we could reach a tipping point."

CHINESE STUDENTS COULD BE HIT HARDEST

O'Brien also warned that any British clampdown on non-degree international students was likely to hit exactly the wrong target—with Chinese students being the most likely to suffer from a tightening on the rules for English-language proficiency. "We are all in favour of getting rid of the rogue operators, but the blunt instruments being used by the Home Office will cause massive collateral damage to the very people we are trying to build bridges and better understanding with. "About 40% of our pathway students are from China; and one of the reasons so many of them come on pathway programmes first is to improve their level of English. "Chinese students are the least likely to want to stay in the UK after graduating and yet raising the language requirements will hit them harder than say Malaysian, Nigerian, or students from other Commonwealth countries."

GROWING FOUNDATIONS IN ASIA

O'Brien predicts future growth in pathway programmes in Asia to meet increasing middle class demand for lower cost options and points to regional hubs such as Singapore, which for years has been home to international students from Myanmar, Cambodia, Vietnam and elsewhere preparing for further study overseas. A good example for students wanting a British higher education is the Northern Consortium UK, or NCUK, partnership. It handles around 3,000 students annually, delivering foundation programmes in the students' home country. On completion, and with their

English language skills upgraded, the students can study at one of the 11 universities in northern England, including leading universities like Manchester, Leeds, and Liverpool. Ilieva said she expected to see a greater shift towards pathway study via the home country route as it is significantly cheaper than an extra year abroad.

HANS DE WIT

18. GLOBAL: COIL—VIRTUAL MOBILITY WITHOUT COMMERCIALISATION

University World News, 1 June 2013, Issue 274

Much, if not all, of the debate in higher education seems to be focused these days on massive open online courses, or MOOCs, which according to several people should be considered nothing less than a revolutionary new model for higher education teaching and learning. In the meantime, a slower burning addition to international teaching and learning is already taking place with much less attention—"virtual mobility," as it is called in Europe, or "collaborative online international learning" (COIL), as it is more correctly referred to in the United States. While in MOOCs the teaching stays more or less traditional, using modern technology for a global form of delivery, in COIL the technology is used to develop a more interactive and collaborative way of international teaching and learning. If one follows the divide between globalisation and internationalisation in higher education, MOOCs fall more into the former category and COIL into the latter, with a strong focus on the internationalisation of the curriculum and of teaching and learning. And while at first glance MOOCs present this idea of being free of charge but increasingly seem to have become part of the wider commercialisation of higher education, COIL has more in common with the non-commercial, cooperative, international dimension of higher education.

VIRTUAL MOBILITY AND COIL

The term "virtual mobility" has emerged from documents from the European Commission as well as from other European entities and institutions of higher education over the past few years. It relates to the increasing attention being paid to forms of mobility other than physical mobility, exchange and/or study abroad. It is connected to a desire to focus on the large majority of students who are not mobile, the "internationalisation at home" movement. In other words: how to make it possible for non-mobile students to develop an international dimension to their teaching and learning. Others see it more as a way to realise international, collaborative experiences. This focus on the mobility dimension of online learning, as expressed in the name of "virtual mobility," in my view ignores the potential

G. Mihut et al. (Eds.), Understanding Higher Education Internationalization, 83–85.

of international online learning as an integral part of the internationalisation of university curricula and teaching and learning.

The term "collaborative online international learning" combines the four essential dimensions of real virtual mobility: it is a collaborative exercise of teachers and students; it makes use of online technology and interaction; it has potential international dimensions; and it is integrated into the learning process. The COIL movement in the US started some five to six years ago in a small way, with a one-day conference in 2007 at Purchase College in Westchester, and since 2010 it has become integrated into the international mission of the State University of New York (SUNY) and linked as a unit to the SUNY Office of Global Affairs. Its annual conference attracts an increasing number of participants from all over the US and abroad. Participation is still very small compared to other international education conferences, but I am sure that it will expand and that we will see an increase in the number of sessions dealing with this subject at major international education events around the world.

WHY COIL IS IMPORTANT

What makes COIL such an important addition to the many forms of physical mobility and to the internationalisation of curricula and teaching and learning? In the first place, it provides opportunities for students (for instance, part-time students) who cannot or do not want to go abroad for a semester or longer, but would like to have an international teaching and learning experience. Through interaction with students and teachers from other countries they receive different perspectives on their subject and on learning and teaching, which they would find it hard to obtain otherwise. In the second place, COIL offers the opportunity and makes it necessary for students and teachers to work closely together—an opportunity that in many cases is missed in physical mobility, where students and teachers do not collaborate inside and outside the classroom.

To give an example, in a one-semester joint minor programme between the school of economics and management at the Amsterdam University of Applied Sciences and universities in Paris and Barcelona, students work on real-life projects for businesses and organisations in the three cities—for instance, on how to increase younger people's access to museums or how to improve student accommodation in the cities. Students start the programme with a one-week visit to Amsterdam, where they get to know one another (including staying in fellow students' homes), their teachers and the companies. Then they work together via social media in small online groups on the assignments and at the end come together again for a week to discuss their results and compete for the best analysis. Students, teachers and companies are excited about the results and the interaction. And the whole process combines short study abroad with online learning. In the third place, COIL draws attention to the specific national and cultural approach to a subject as well as to the way it is taught and learned.

To give another example, in an online course on sports management between my school in Amsterdam and one at SUNY Cortland, the different approach to sport in the US and Europe, as well as the different way the subject is taught, become clear and make students think differently about the subject. It is positive to see that both in practice and in policies there is increasing attention being paid to virtual mobility, or collaborative online international learning. As the COIL conferences show, there is still a lot to learn and several models are possible. But in a less headline-grabbing way than MOOCs, and one that is more integrated in the teaching and learning process, an important new dimension to internationalisation is evolving and should receive similar attention to MOOCs.

RAHUL CHOUDAHA

19. GLOBAL: IN SEARCH OF SOLUTIONS FOR THE AGENT DEBATE

International Higher Education, Fall 2013, Number 73

The use of commissioned agents for recruiting internsational students had been a divisive debate, with some strong viewpoints and weak action points. The recent report by National Association of College Admissions Counseling (NACAC), on the practice of commission-based international student recruiters, attempted to bring clarity to this debate through a comprehensive and inclusive process. Although it has something for everyone to justify their arguments for or against the use of commission-based agents, it left most of us searching for solutions. At the same time, the report aptly addressed two critical pieces, often overlooked in the debate and have implications for future directions—diversity and transparency.

DIVERSITY OF INSTITUTIONS, STUDENTS, AND AGENTS

The NACAC report rightfully acknowledges that just because commission-based agents are used in other countries, they are suitable in the US context. In the United States, international students are highly concentrated in research universities. Of nearly 4,500 postsecondary degree-granting institutions in the United States, just 108 universities classified as "Research Universities (very high research activity)" by Carnegie Classification, enrolled nearly two-fifth of all international students. Most of these universities are not engaged with the agent debate, as they have a strong brand visibility among prospective international students and also perceive the use of agents as a risk to delegate their brand presence with a third party. Granted, there are exceptions like the University of Cincinnati, which was an early adopter of the agent model.

The discourse on the use of agents in general and the NACAC report in particular, has implications primarily on institutions beyond these 108 research universities (very high research activity). Within this segment, public universities are increasingly interested in recruiting international undergraduate students. Diminishing state support renders undergraduate international student enrollment an important revenue stream, and agents are being positioned as a cost-effective measure for finding them. This is where some institutions have hastily started using agents without considering the fit with the type of students they want and how those students make choices.

G. Mihut et al. (Eds.), Understanding Higher Education Internationalization, 87–89.

A report by World Education Services—*Not All International Students Are the Same*—addressed this information gap to better understand students. The report identified four segments of international students—explorers, strivers, strugglers, and highflyers—based on financial resources and academic preparedness. These segments have diverse information needs; and this shapes not only whether or not they use agents but also why they use them. For example, 24 percent of explorers (high financial resources and low academic preparedness) reported use of agents as compared to 9 percent of strivers (low financial resources and high-academic preparedness).

The quality of agents, in terms of their reliability and ethical behavior, is equally diverse. A segment of students and institutions may still want to work with agents, due to a variety of constraints related to market intelligence, resources, and capacity. Any kind of outright ban from NACAC would have been impractical and unfair, as it would have ignored these diverse institutional needs. At the same time, claiming that commission-based agents are a good fit for all segments of institutions is an overstatement.

INSTITUTIONAL RESPONSIBILITY

Decisions of whether to use commission-based agents, or not, depend on the institutional context and needs. There is nothing prima facie unethical or illegal about such conclusions; however, based on autonomy professional responsibility must uphold the highest standards. This is where a commission-based agency model increases the risks and may result in actions by agents that are not in the best interest of students and even the institutions paying commission. At the end of the day, for agents, if there is no admission, there is no commission.

Consider the case of lack of transparency in an agent-student relationship. A forthcoming research report by World Education Services surveyed international students and asked them "Has your educational consultant shared with you whether he or she receives a commission from colleges/universities for each student recruited?" Only 14 percent of prospective international students who reported to use education consultants were informed that the agent would receive commission from institutions, 43 percent were unaware, and 45 percent reported "don't know/ can't say."

The finding highlights that the issue of information asymmetry—where one party in the transaction has more information than the other—provides an unfair advantage to the commission-based agents, often at the expense of the institutional brand. At the same time, it is nearly impossible to manage or enforce the "code of conduct" on agents and their network of subagents in other countries.

This is where institutions' responsibility of setting standards of transparency at their end becomes even more important. The NACAC report recommends "providing clear and conspicuous disclosure of arrangements by agents with institutions for students and families." Higher education institutions using commission-based agents should come forward and explicitly state on their Web sites if they work with agents, what commissions they pay, and make this information available to prospective students. For example, the University of Nottingham transparently offers this information to students and also publishes how much commission it pays to agents.

The acid test for institutions that are using commission-based agents is in their proactive enforcement of transparency in engagements between themselves, agents, and prospective students. If they are confident about their practices, what do they need to disclose? This emphasis on transparency will bridge the information asymmetry and will set the standard from institutions that there is nothing secretive about the use of commission-based agents.

CONCLUSIONS

Many are in search of guidelines, however, in the context of seeking solutions to their increasing problems in recruiting international students proactively and quickly. This is where a global industry of agent networks has positioned itself as the panacea for all institutions. The fact remains that the quick-fix solution of using commission-based agents to ramp up international student numbers may increase the risk to the institutional brand, admissions standards, and even the quality of students admitted.

In this context, the NACAC report attempted to investigate and highlight several issues related to the use of agents—including, institutional accountability, transparency, and integrity. At the same time, it did not resolve the core issues related to incentive payments as "the Commission was unable to achieve unanimous consensus." This puts even more onus on universities using or considering the use of commission-based agents to assess the segments of students they wish to recruit, their decision-making processes, and institutional readiness to retain them. In addition, institutions need to take proactive steps in setting standards of transparency to break the ills of secretive practices and information asymmetry.

JAN PETTER MYKLEBUST

20. EUROPE: FEES AND INTERNATIONAL STUDENTS IN NORDIC NATIONS

University World News, 4 May 2013, Issue 270

In 2010 there were 68,256 foreign students in the five Nordic countries of Denmark, Finland, Iceland, Norway, and Sweden. Foreign student numbers were up by 117% from 2005 and they comprised 5.8% of the total Nordic student population of 1.18 million, according to a recent study. Denmark had the highest proportion of foreign students—8.6% of all students—and Sweden had the highest number—27,859— among the five nations, which have a combined general population of nearly 26 million. The Copenhagen-based Nordic Council of Ministers commissioned Oxford Research to undertake a study on *Tuition Fees for International Students—Nordic Practice*. The study's foreword said that Nordic higher education was now competing "in a truly global market, where competition is tough and institutions work hard to attract the best students."

HIGHER EDUCATION NO LONGER FREE

Until a few years ago, Nordic countries had a long tradition of free higher education financed by taxpayers. The situation has changed. Denmark was the first to introduce tuition fees in 2006. Finland launched a five-year trial period running from 2010–2014, while Sweden brought in tuition fees from 2011. Only Iceland and Norway did not charge at all. The report questioned the effects of the introduction of tuition fees, and how fee systems were constructed and applied in different countries. It also queried the existence of scholarship schemes and how they worked. The aim of the study was to provide a knowledge base for further cooperation within the Nordic region. It focused on national practices concerning international students, defined as students coming from outside the European Union-European Economic Area (EU-EEA)—except Switzerland, Norway, Iceland and Lichtenstein. It also examined the introduction of fees and the number of international students, and discussed future perspectives, notably arguments for and against tuition fees. The researchers interviewed around 40 people from public agencies and staff at Nordic educational institutions and organisations, and also compared the effects of tuition fees in the UK and the Netherlands.

G. Mihut et al. (Eds.), Understanding Higher Education Internationalization, 91–93.

SWEDEN

The study showed a significant increase in international student numbers in Sweden, notably from outside the EU-EEA, until 2010. After fees were introduced, there was a dramatic fall in in the number of non-EU-EEA students—from 8,000 to 2,000 from 2010–2011—as previously reported by University World News. Living costs and fees deter foreign students, and the study looked at which students were deterred. Bachelor and master's programmes were now demanding fees, but doctoral programmes were excluded. The report compared fees in universities and polytechnics for different study programmes. They ranged from SEK65,000 (US$9,972) in Sweden to €5,000-€12,000 (US$6,550-US$15,720) in Finland, to €6,200-€13,100 in Denmark. When introducing tuition fees in 2011, Swedish institutions initiated measures to strengthen the country's competitive position, in order to compensate for the fees. An application fee was also introduced. Legislation stipulated that the fees should cover full costs. In both Sweden and Finland, until 2010 most non-EU-EEA students were from Asia. These statistics also declined after fees were introduced. The report attributed this to the "shock effect" when going from no payment to full costs.

FINLAND

The increase in non-EU-EEA students in Finland from 2005–2010 was 102% at universities and 137% at polytechnics, against 23% and 27% for EU-EEA students. In Finland, 41 programmess out of 399 at nine universities and 10 polytechnics were fee-charging. Institutions within the fee pilot scheme must offer master's programmes and scholarships, and the medium of instruction must be English.

NORWAY

The study found a "marked increase" in the proportion of international students and universities and scientific colleges in Norway from 2005–2012—their numbers grew by 56%. There were nearly 16,000 international students in 2012, some 8,700 from the EU-EFA and 7,260 from outside Europe. Between 2005 and 2012, EU-EFA international student numbers grew by 89% while non-European numbers rose by 29%. In Norway, students generally do not pay for education. Several people told University World News that free education for all might come under pressure within the next five to 10 years. One stakeholder said that if Norwegian students were unable to find places on courses due to international students, this would increase incentives to introduce tuition fees. The issue will not be raised under the current government. But if a conservative-led coalition government were elected this autumn, the subject might resurface during the next four years. Currently, the polls show a clear majority for a conservative coalition government.

ICELAND

Icelandic universities said they had seen significant increase in international students, including "more students from developing countries who cannot afford to study in countries with tuition fees." The numbers of international students were small in low-population Iceland's higher education system—852 from the EU-EFA and 281 non-European students in 2010—but in the five years from 2005 there had been increases of 45% and 86% respectively.

DENMARK

In Denmark, universities can set tuition fees that are higher than costs, but the surplus they generate must be used for scholarship schemes. There is an application fee of €105-€150 to some institutions. From 2005–2010, there was a 154% increase in students from the EU-EEA, in particular to business academies (up 421%) but a reduction in foreign non-EU-EEA students of 31% at universities and 8% at university colleges. There was also an increase in non-EU-EEA students at the business colleges, which did not introduce tuition fees before 1 January 2008. One Danish stakeholder said: "The fact that prices are at taximeter level [full cost] means it costs the same to study engineering in Denmark as at the best American universities and considerably more than in other European countries, while the social sciences courses are relatively cheap in Denmark compared with other countries."

ARIANE DE GAYARDON

21. FRANCE: FRANCE DEBATES INTERNATIONAL STUDENT FEES

International Higher Education, Winter 2016, Number 84

With 4 million students studying abroad in 2012, student mobility has become one of the most prominent features of the internationalization of higher education. But host countries receiving an ever-increasing number of international students are starting to think over their funding strategy. In an age of global austerity, it is legitimate to question whether international students' education should be as subsidized as domestic students' education.

This question was under scrutiny in France during the first half of 2015, as a report by France Stratégie—a think tank working for the prime minister—suggested the introduction of international tuition fees. France is not the first country to face this debate and will not be the last, but it takes special significance in the third most attractive country in the world and in a country where half the international students come from Africa.

WELFARE STATES

European welfare states have proven particularly vulnerable to the debate around the financing of higher education for non-domestic students, as they subsidize heavily higher education, which is conceived as a right. In a time of financial hardship for higher education globally, the welfare states are questioning whether they should continue to accept international students under these lenient financial conditions. The fact that such debates have been omnipresent in the Nordic countries, the archetypes of welfare states, in the past decade shows how prevalent this question has become. Denmark and Sweden now charge tuition fees to international students, and Finland will likely start doing so in 2016 despite mixed reviews of the trial period and resistance from student unions.

THE STATE OF FRENCH HIGHER EDUCATION

France is without doubt a welfare state, with a very low-tuition higher education system. In 2014–2015, the tuition fees were at about US$210 annually for undergraduate students—domestic or foreign. Indeed, according to OECD, the French government was funding 80.8 percent of public higher education expenditures

G. Mihut et al. (Eds.), Understanding Higher Education Internationalization, 95–97.

in 2011. It was estimated that the government funding of tertiary education exceeded US$12,500 per student per year, up from US$7,700 in the 1980s. This trend parallels a continuous increase in the number of students. It is in this context, unsurprisingly, that the question of who should be subsidized arose.

In 2015, a report entitled Investing in the Internationalization of Higher Education was published by the French Prime Minister's think tank. It suggested the introduction of tuition fees covering the full cost of higher education for international students. The fund thus saved would be used to foster the internationalization of universities. But the French context includes specificities that make this debate particularly compelling.

ATTRACTIVE TO WHOM?

France is a unique country because of the position it holds as a host country for mobile students. It was ranked the third most attractive country by UNESCO in 2012, drawing as much as 7 percent of the 4 million international students. Interestingly, the ranking is dominated by countries that charge international students high tuition fees—including the United States, the United Kingdom, and Australia.

The issue of international student fees in France sparked acute debate at least in part because of the origin of its students. Nearly half of the international students studying in France come from Africa, a heritage from France's colonial past. Morocco, Algeria, Tunisia, Senegal, and Cameroon are in the top 10 countries of origin. It is very unlikely that these students can afford more than US$12,500 of tuition fees. Actually, in the present circumstances—i.e., with very low tuition—82 percent of international students in France declared in a survey that studying in France constitutes a financial strain for them and their families. In these conditions, it is impossible to contemplate such an increase in tuition fee without considering the consequences for these students who want and need to get access to a good higher education system. Additionally, the question of the public good needs to be raised, as France is currently helping countries that are in less fortunate economic conditions, by providing them with the skilled labor that is essential in today's economy.

From France's point of view, however, the trade-off is in the quantity and diversity of international students in the system. There is no question that an increase in international tuition fees would have an impact on the number of mobile students coming to France. The 2015 report forecasts a 40 percent decrease, a number that will be hard to gain back. Replacing the international students that will be put off by tuition fees would indeed be extremely difficult, as France does not have the capacity to attract the students that can and are ready to pay—especially when one considers the language barrier and the competition of the United States, the United Kingdom, and Australia among others.

Last but not least, this question needs to be properly examined economically. In 2014, economic benefits from the presence of international students in France were estimated at nearly US$5 billion with a positive balance of US$1.6 billion once the cost of tuition was removed. This far exceeds the US$930 million the 2015 report estimates would be saved from moving to full cost tuition fees. The economic benefits of having international students participate in the economy might very well be worth the investment in their education.

CONCLUSION

In July 2015, the French government put an end to the debate about international tuition fees by stating that international students will continue to pay the same tuition fees as domestic and European ones. But the debate itself opened the door to the possibility of establishing higher tuition fees for international students in the future. Finland, for instance, resisted the trend for a few years but is now set to introduce such fees in September 2016. When the debate resurfaces, France will once again need to consider the role of international students in the system, but also its role as a developed nation in educating foreign students. Therefore, the debate should not stop at mere economic arguments, but also focus on the diversity in the system, the global and national public good, and even foreign affairs.

PART 4

QUALITY ASSURANCE OF INTERNATIONALIZATION

INTRODUCTION

As internationalization of higher education grows in complexity, there is an increasing need to implement quality assurance regulations for international education. This section includes articles that elaborate on some of the quality concerns impacting international education, such as accreditation, quality of teaching and training, and recognition procedures, as well as some of the efforts to address them.

The first article in this section, written by Philip Altbach and Liz Reisberg, offers an overview of visa and immigration fraud cases associated with international students, international staff, and their host institutions. Their summary includes an analysis of the government and regulatory response to such cases, but also elaborates on how these responses fit into broader trends such as anti-immigration policies. In the next article, Philip Altbach discusses the surge in private providers aiming to profit from the internationalization process. The article also addresses the effects that severe corruption practices such as falsifying standardized test results, accreditation mills, and the used of payed agents have on educational provision.

Jane Knight raises critical questions about the value and challenges of double and multiple degrees, including issues around accreditation and recognition regulations. The next article in this section also considers aspects of joint and dual degrees. Claire Morel draws lessons from the former Erasmus Mundus program financed by the European Commission, in order to suggest improvements to the program quality of the newer Erasmus + scheme. In an article that touches on the realities of the quality and transferability of international education, Chrissie Long brings attention to the case of Cuba-trained doctors who have failed the medical license exam in Costa Rica. In a similar vein, Suvendrini Kakuchi's article offers an overview of the regulatory state of foreign universities interested in opening and operating a branch campus in Japan.

The articles in this section illustrate that the frameworks of international and transnational education are still very much in development. As such, regulatory and quality assurance standards are still being debated and refined. While it is important to guard against fraud, corruption, and poor quality, punitive measures enacted by various national governments and targeting international programs need to be transparent and acknowledge the diversity of needs among various providers.

G. Mihut et al. (Eds.), Understanding Higher Education Internationalization, 101.

PHILIP G. ALTBACH AND LIZ REISBERG

22. GLOBAL: ANOTHER WEEK, ANOTHER SCANDAL: IMMIGRATION DILEMMAS AND POLITICAL CONFUSION

International Higher Education, Winter 2013, Number 70

Immigration regulations for international students seem to be changing somewhat unpredictably of late, in major receiving countries. In several English-speaking nations, immigration regulation has become a significant policy issue, and international students are the frequent focus of recent crackdowns. These changes have the potential for altering the landscape of global student flows and might even slow the increases in student numbers of the past two decades. In this context, the expansion of recent years might actually have been a temporary "bubble."

RECENT SCANDALS

The latest crisis involved London Metropolitan University (LMU), an institution with one of the largest enrollments of international students in the United Kingdom. The UK Border Authority withdrew its "highly trusted sponsor" status from the university, after an audit revealed that a significant number of international students did not have appropriate or adequate documentation to remain in the United Kingdom, adequate English-language skills, or had not registered for classes. Some of these students may need to return to their home countries. Other international students, legitimately enrolled, are panicked. A large percentage of London Metropolitan University's international students come from India. As explained by the manager of a firm that places students at UK universities (quoted recently in the Guardian newspaper): "We divide the market into two categories: the university market for genuine students and the immigration market." The challenge for immigration authorities is how to distinguish the two groups, when both arrive with student visas. Many observers see the LMU case as the tip of the iceberg of questionable admissions and recruiting practices in the United Kingdom.

Scandals have made national headlines in the United States, as well. In August 2012, the head of Herguan University in California was arrested on charges of visa fraud. This follows the similar case of Tri-Valley University, and both serve mainly Indian students with little intention of studying. Both appear to have operated

G. Mihut et al. (Eds.), Understanding Higher Education Internationalization, 103–106.

profitably as "visa mills." As neither institution is duly accredited, one has to wonder why these were authorized to issue student visas at all.

But there are different levels of misdeeds, and not all merit an immediate and draconian response. The US State Department caused mayhem last May after determining that 600 instructors, attached to Chinese government – sponsored Confucius Institutes, were inappropriately documented and would have to leave the country immediately and then reapply for visas in order to return. In this case there was no subterfuge, only a seemingly innocent misunderstanding of confusing visa regulations. In the end, no instructors were deported, but the way the State Department handled the incident came close to causing a major diplomatic tangle with the Chinese government.

POLITICAL PRESSURE AND POLITICAL RESPONSE

It seems that there is a "perfect storm" of concern over the movement of individuals across borders. In North America, Europe, and Australia, the issue of immigration is increasingly present in political discourse. Perhaps reacting to job losses due to the economic recession and a general conservative trend in many countries, immigration has become a political "hot button." The United Kingdom, for example, has a policy goal to reduce immigration into the country. In many other European countries, immigration is politically sensitive, often used by populists on the extreme right as a central and provocative theme. Many US states have made illegal immigration a political focus.

Australia seems to vacillate between wanting more and wanting less immigration. In a move earlier this year, graduating international students will now be allowed to remain to work for two to four years (up from a previous limit of 18 months) without any restrictions on the type of employment. Malaysia wants more foreign students but recently introduced new restrictions to constrain the flow. The government now requires students to demonstrate that they have been accepted to a higher education institution before entering the country, also that international students study Bahasa Malaysia during their first year and that they buy medical insurance. These new measures are indicative of an international trend toward greater regulation.

More governments are concerned that the flow of international students needs more oversight and controls. In the past, academic institutions have been given considerable leeway over the admission of international students and the subsequent granting of study visas. Immigration authorities relied on academic institutions to ensure that only qualified, legitimate students are recommended for visas. Recent events indicate that a segment of educational institutions, typically those highly dependent on income from international students, may be taking advantage of their freedom as gatekeepers and not behaving "in the spirit of the law."

PROTECTION FOR WHOM?

International students are easy targets in this rarified environment. As a transient group they are not well-positioned to become a political force or to create a lobby to speak for them. But importantly, they are less of a threat than other temporary visitors. Unlike tourists who enter countries and are impossible to track afterwards, international students are registered at an educational institution and entered into immigration databases.

International students are also particularly vulnerable to exploitation. They are subject to confusing and changing laws that they can only barely comprehend, evidenced in the debacle with the instructors of the Confucius Institutes. These students and scholars are likely to accept (and often pay for!) advice from others, who may not have the student's best interest at heart. They are also less likely to know the rights and protection available to them in another country, raising concerns in Australia that the new work privileges will encourage unscrupulous employers to exploit this new class of foreign workers. Much as governments need to protect visas programs from abuse, so do students need to be protected from abusers.

THE NEW ETHOS

The landscape of international higher education has changed in recent years and this contributes to the necessity of screening students more carefully. Some academic institutions rely on international students to balance the budget. At these institutions, international students have become a "cash cow." Australia is the best example—with government policy for several decades encouraging earning revenue through international endeavors. While the United States has no national policy concerning international ventures, several states—notably, New York and Washington—have determined that income from international students should be an important part of a public institution's financial strategy. At some institutions, international students now represent the difference between enrollment shortfalls and survival, due to changing demographics in their traditional student market.

It is worth noting that some receiving countries welcome international students without the same degree of "commercialization." Canada, for example, while it does charge international students higher fees, permits highly skilled graduates from abroad to remain in the country after completing their studies. In the Canadian case, international students promise an influx of talent as well as additional revenue. Germany, Norway, and several other European countries do not charge fees to international students.

Internationalization has presented new opportunities for commercialization in countries where institutions have a long history of autonomy. Institutional leaders who represent a new ethos, more attentive to revenue than to educational integrity or quality, are free to subsume various dimensions of the academic enterprise—including admissions, student supervision, degree qualifications—to the bottom line.

This new ethos is evident where universities have outsourced overseas, recruiting to agents and recruiters who are paid commissions for delivering applications and enrolling international students. Of course, the introduction of third-party recruiter adds another level of interaction between the university and the student giving immigration authorities additional reason for concern about how students are screened for admission and visas.

ADDRESSING THE PROBLEM

The general reaction from the academic community has been negative to the imposition of additional governmental restrictions concerning overseas students and other aspects of international higher education. Few people acknowledge the seriousness of the problem and express concern that stricter immigration policies will reduce international enrollments and contribute to an "unwelcoming" image overseas.

The problem is that immigration and border enforcement agencies tend to respond, by applying legal and bureaucratic rules that lack nuance. Considering that the majority of the millions of internationally mobile students are qualified for the programs, where they are enrolled, and that they contribute intellectually as well as economically to the institutions that host them, dramatic changes in immigration should be contemplated carefully. When individuals enter a country in violation of immigration regulations, they are (and should be) subjected to sanctions. When institutions ignore rules or admit unqualified students, they should be subjected to penalties or legal action. In some cases, they are closed down. This is inevitable. In fact, governments do need to bring some additional discipline to the management of international higher education, particularly where financial interests may determine institutional policy and practice. But this needs to be done in a way that does not penalize everyone.

PHILIP G. ALTBACH

23. GLOBAL: CORRUPTION: A KEY CHALLENGE TO INTERNATIONALIZATION

International Higher Education, Fall 2012, Number 69

A specter of corruption is haunting the global campaign toward higher education internationalization. An overseas degree is increasingly valuable, so it is not surprising that commercial ventures have found opportunities on the internationalization landscape. New private actors have entered the sector, with the sole goal of making money. Some of them are less than honorable. Some universities look at internationalization as a contribution to the financial "bottom line," in an era of financial cutbacks. The rapidly expanding private higher education sector globally is largely for-profit. In a few cases, such as Australia and increasingly the United Kingdom, national policies concerning higher education internationalization tilt toward earning income for the system.

Countries whose academic systems suffer from elements of corruption are increasingly involved in international higher education—sending large numbers of students abroad, establishing relationships with overseas universities, and other activities. Corruption is not limited to countries that may have a reputation for less than fully circumspect academic practices, but that problem occurs globally. Several scandals have recently been widely reported in the United States, including the private unaccredited "Tri-Valley University," a sham institution that admitted and collected tuition from foreign students. That institution did not require them to attend class, but rather funneled them into the labor market, under the noses of US immigration authorities. In addition, several public universities have been caught admitting students, with substandard academic qualifications. Quality-assurance agencies in the United Kingdom have uncovered problems with "franchised" British-degree programs, and similar scandals have occurred in Australia. A prominent example is the University of Wales, which was the second-largest university in the United Kingdom, with 70,000 students enrolled in 130 colleges around the world. It had to close its highly profitable degree validation program, which accounted for nearly two-thirds of institutional revenue.

With international higher education now a multibillion dollar industry around the world, individuals, countries, and institutions depending on income, prestige, and access—it is not surprising that corruption is a growing problem. If something is not done to ensure probity in international relationships in higher education, an

G. Mihut et al. (Eds.), Understanding Higher Education Internationalization, 107–110.

entire structure—built on trust, a commitment to mutual understanding, and benefits for students and researchers—a commitment built informally over decades will collapse. There are signs that it is already in deep trouble.

EXAMPLES AND IMPLICATIONS

A serious and unsolved problem is the prevalence of unscrupulous agents and recruiters funneling unqualified students to universities worldwide. A recent example was featured in Britain's Daily Telegraph (June 26, 2012) of an agent in China caught on video, offering to write admissions essays and to present other questionable help in admission to prominent British universities. No one knows the extent of the problem, although consistent news reports indicate that it is widespread, particularly in countries that send large numbers of students abroad, including China and India. Without question, agents now receive millions of dollars in commissions paid by the universities and, in some egregious cases, money from the clients as well. In Nottingham University's case the percentage of students recruited through agents has increased from 19 percent of the intake in 2005 to 25 percent in 2011, with more than £1 million going to the agents.

Altered and fake documents have long been a problem in international admissions. Computer design and technology exacerbate it. Fraudulent documents have become a minor industry in some parts of the world, and many universities are reluctant to accept documents from institutions that have been tainted with incidents of counterfeit records. For example, a number of American universities no longer accept applications from some Russian students—because of widespread perceptions of fraud, document tampering, and other problems. Document fraud gained momentum due to commission-based agents who have an incentive to ensure that students are "packaged" with impressive credentials, as their commissions depend on successful student placement. Those responsible for checking the accuracy of transcripts, recommendations, and degree certificates face an increasingly difficult task. Students who submit valid documentation are placed at a disadvantage since they are subjected to extra scrutiny.

Examples of tampering with and falsifying results of the Graduate Record Examination and other commonly required international examinations used for admissions have resulted in the nullifying of scores, and even cancelling examinations in some countries and regions, as well as rethinking whether online testing is practical. This situation has made it more difficult for students to apply to foreign universities and has made the task of evaluating students for admission more difficult.

Several countries, including Russia and India, have announced that they will be using the Times Higher Education and Academic Ranking of World Universities (Shanghai rankings), as a way of determining the legitimacy of foreign universities for recognizing foreign degrees, determining eligibility for academic collaborations, and other aspects of international higher education relations. This is unfortunate, since many excellent academic institutions are not included in these rankings, which mostly measure research productivity. No doubt, Russia and India are concerned about the quality of foreign partners and find the rankings convenient.

Several "host" countries have tightened up rules and oversight of cross-border student flows in response to irregularities and corruption. The US Department of State announced in June 2012 that visa applicants from India would be subjected to additional scrutiny as a response to the "Tri-Valley scandal." Earlier both Australia and Britain changed rules and policy. Corruption is making internationalization more difficult for the entire higher education sector. It is perhaps significant that continental Europe seems to have been less affected by shady practices—perhaps in part because international higher education is less commercialized and profit driven.

The Internet has become the "Wild West" of academic misrepresentation and chicanery. It is easy to set up an impressive Web site and exaggerate the quality or lie about an institution. Some institutions claim accreditation that does not exist. There are even "accreditation mills" to accredit universities that pay a fee. A few include pictures of impressive campuses that are simply photoshopped from other universities.

WHAT CAN BE DONE?

With international higher education now big business and with commercial gain an ever-increasing motivation for international initiatives, the problems mentioned are likely to persist. However, a range of initiatives can ameliorate the situation. The higher education community can recommit to the traditional "public good" values of internationalization, although current funding challenges may make this difficult in some countries. The International Association of Universities' recent report, "Affirming Academic Values in Internationalization of Higher Education," is a good start. The essential values of the European Union's Bologna Initiatives are also consistent with the best values of internationalization. Nottingham University, mentioned earlier, provides transparency, concerning its use of agents. It supervises those it hires and, in general, adheres to best practice—as do some other universities in the United Kingdom and elsewhere.

Accreditation and quality assurance are essential for ensuring that basic quality is recognized. Agencies and the international higher education community must ensure that universities were carefully evaluated and that the results of assessment are easily available to the public and the international stakeholders.

Governmental, regional, and international agencies must coordinate their efforts and become involved in maintaining standards and protecting the image of the higher education sector. Contradictions abound. For example, the United States Department of State's Education USA seeks to protect the sector, while the Department of Commerce sees higher education just as an export commodity. Government agencies in the United Kingdom and Australia seem also to be mainly pursuing commercial interests.

Consciousness-raising about ethics and good practice in international higher education and awareness of emerging problems and continuing challenges deserve continuing attention. Prospective students and their families, institutional partners considering exchanges and research, and other stakeholders must be more sophisticated and vigilant concerning decision making. The Boston College Center for International Higher Education's Corruption Monitor is the only clearinghouse for information, relating directly to corrupt practices; additional sources of information and analysis will be helpful.

The first step in solving a major challenge to higher education internationalization is recognition of the problem itself. The higher education community itself is by no means united; and growing commercialization makes some people reluctant to act in ways that may threaten profits. There are individuals within the academic community who lobby aggressively to legitimize dubious practices. Yet, if nothing is done, the higher education sector worldwide will suffer and the impressive strides taken toward internationalization will be threatened.

JANE KNIGHT

24. GLOBAL: ARE DOUBLE/MULTIPLE DEGREE PROGRAMS LEADING TO "DISCOUNT DEGREES"?

International Higher Education, Summer 2015, Number 81

The number and types of international double and multiple degree programs have skyrocketed in the last five years. According to the 2014 International Association of Universities report on internationalization there has been a 50 percent increase in double-degree programs in professional areas, 19 percent increase in Natural Sciences and 14 percent increase in Social Sciences during the last three years. These figures are indicative and do not capture the total growth, especially in Asia and Europe. But they clearly demonstrate the role of double/multiple degree programs in the current landscape of international higher education and their popularity with students and institutions alike.

DIFFERENCES AMONG THE DEGREES

A few words about what a double/multiple degree program actually means and involves is important, as there are multiple interpretations and hence mass confusion about the meaning of the term. An international double-degree (or multiple-degree) program involves two or more institutions—from different countries collaborating to design and deliver an academic program. Normally, a qualification from each of the collaborating institutions is provided. They differ from joint-degree programs or cotutelle arrangements. A joint-degree program offers one qualification jointly issued by two or more collaborating institutions, while a cotutelle arrangement involves partner universities working together on the development and delivery of a program; but only one degree is offered by the institution of registration. This discussion recognizes the contribution of all three approaches but focuses on the issues related to double/multiple degree programs only.

DOUBLE COUNTING OF ACADEMIC WORK FOR TWO OR MORE DEGREES?

As an internationalization strategy, double/multiple degree programs address the heartland of academia—the teaching/learning process and the production of new knowledge between and among countries. These programs are built on the principle of international academic collaboration and can bring important benefits to students,

G. Mihut et al. (Eds.), Understanding Higher Education Internationalization, 111–113.

professors, institutions, and national/regional education systems. The interest in double degrees is exploding but so is the concern about those programs, which double count the same credits for two or more degrees. A broad range of reactions to double-degree programs exists due to the diversity of program models; the involvement of new (bona fide and rogue) providers; the uncertainty related to quality assurance and recognition of qualifications; and finally, the ethics involved in deciding the required academic workload and/or acquired new competencies for granting of double/multiple degrees. For many academics and policymakers, double-degree programs are welcomed as a natural extension of exchange and mobility programs. For others, double/multiple-degree programs are perceived as a troublesome development, leading to double counting of academic work—thus, jeopardizing the integrity of a university qualification and moving toward the thin edge of academic fraud.

ATTRACTIVE TO STUDENTS

Students are attracted to double-degree programs for a variety of reasons. The opportunity to be part of a program that offers two or more degrees from universities, located in different countries, is seen to enhance their employability prospects and career path. Some students believe that a collaborative program is of higher quality because the expertise of two or more universities has shaped the academic program. Other students are not so interested in enhanced quality but are attracted to the opportunity to obtain two degrees "for the price of one." Students argue that the duration is shorter for a double-degree program, the workload is definitely less than for two single degrees, and there is less of a financial burden. This argument is not valid for all programs of this type, but there is an element of truth in these claims.

Even the traditional twinning arrangements, where an academic program and qualification from the parent/home institution is being offered in a different country through cooperation with a local host higher education institution, are now morphing into double-degree programs—one from the home institution and another from the host institution, even though the credits for only one academic program are completed. Not all double-degree programs involve student mobility, as it is more economical to move professors than students, and virtual classrooms are becoming more popular. Finally, the status factor cannot be ignored. There is a certain sense of elitism attached to having academic credentials from universities in different countries, even if the student never actually studied abroad.

BENEFITS AND CHALLENGES FOR INSTITUTIONS

For institutions, academic benefits in terms of curriculum innovation, exchanges of professors and researchers, and access to expertise and networks of the partner university make these programs especially attractive. Another important rationale is to increase an institution's reputation and ranking as an international university. This is accomplished by deliberately collaborating with partners of equal or greater status. Interestingly, some institutions prefer double-degree programs with higher-ranked partners, in order to avoid domestic accreditation procedures. For others, counting students from double-degree program cohorts can increase their graduation numbers and throughput rates.

While the benefits of double-degree programs are many and diverse, so are the challenges. Different regulatory systems, academic calendars, quality assurance and accreditation schemes, credit systems, tuition and scholarship programs, teaching approaches, entrance and examination requirements, language of instruction, thesis/dissertation supervision are a few of the issues that collaborating institutions need to address.

CRITICAL QUESTIONS

My analysis of double/multiple-degree programs, by several national higher education organizations, shows that there is no one model. Nor, should there be one standard model as local conditions vary enormously. However, important new questions are being raised as the number and types of double/multiple programs increase. For example, which is the best route for accreditation of double/multiple-degree programs—national, binational, regional, or international accreditation? Can one thesis/dissertation fulfill the requirements of two research-based graduate programs? Are international collaborative programs encouraging the overuse of English language and the standardization of curriculum? Will status building and credentialism motives eventually jeopardize the quality and academic objectives of these international collaborative degree programs? Are these programs sustainable without additional internal or external supplementary funding?

INTEGRITY AND LEGITIMACY OF QUALIFICATIONS ARE AT STAKE

A challenge facing the higher education community around the world is to develop a common understanding of what double/multiple programs actually mean, the academic requirements and qualifications offered, and how they differ from joint-degree programs. Joint-degree programs are very attractive alternatives but face legal and bureaucratic barriers, as it is impossible in many countries to offer a joint qualification with another institution. Most importantly, a rigorous debate on the vexing questions of accreditation, recognition, and "legitimacy" of the qualifications needs to take place to ensure that international double/multiple degree programs are respected and recognized by students, institutions, and employers around the world and that double/multiple-degree programs do not become known for offering "discount degrees."

CLAIRE MOREL

25. EUROPE: USING LESSONS FROM ERASMUS MUNDUS TO IMPROVE ERASMUS+ JOINT DEGREES

University World News, 24 January 2014, Issue 304

A recent synthesis report by seven independent experts presented the main results achieved through the first generation of 57 Erasmus Mundus joint master's programmes. Its recommendations are particularly timely since joint master's degrees will continue to be financed under Europe's new Erasmus+ programme that started in January 2014. The analysis shows that this type of international collaborative programme development brings important gains in internationalisation and quality, but that a number of areas still require improvement.

THE POSITIVES

One of the most positively evaluated aspects is the great attention that has been paid to the selection of excellent students through large worldwide promotion activities. The most successful joint programmes were those that collaborated closely at all developmental levels: in programme design, in the academic provision and in the training and mobility tracks. This joint approach worked best if collaboration was further extended to include employers too. It offered a high level of harmonisation in performance evaluation and joint supervision of students. Another positive development is the growing involvement of non-European Union universities in Erasmus Mundus consortia and the possibility to involve visiting scholars and professionals from outside Europe.

Graduate impact surveys have been carried out annually by the Erasmus Mundus alumni association since 2007. They show relatively low unemployment rates among Erasmus Mundus graduates and swift employment after graduation. Only 18% of now employed Erasmus Mundus graduates stayed unemployed for more than six months after graduation. On average, it took graduates who now have permanent posts less than four months to find a job. Erasmus Mundus graduates tend to work for international companies and organisations and the involvement of potential employers and guidance offered to students already during their professional internship or fieldwork research enhance employability prospects.

G. Mihut et al. (Eds.), Understanding Higher Education Internationalization, 115–117.

THE WEAKNESSES

Weaknesses were also identified by the experts who contributed to the report. They pointed to the need to develop more ambitious internship schemes or broader programmes through which additional competences and soft skills can be developed. These should be tailored to the needs of students and may include, for example, entrepreneurship, communication, publishing skills etc. Students reported that they could use additional training in areas such as negotiation and leadership skills.

More efforts would also be required to build common e-learning platforms to ensure regular contact between international students and universities, to facilitate their mobility track, and to develop more collaborative working patterns between university staff, students, and employers. One area that will receive special attention in Erasmus+ is the long-term financial sustainability of joint degrees. Too often, these rely on continued EU funding to operate. Generally, not enough has been done to achieve sustainability after EU support ended. Finally, Erasmus Mundus consortia are advised to more systematically implement tracer studies for tracking and measuring the employment status of their graduates.

WHY ERASMUS MUNDUS?

This was a review of the first joint programmes created under Erasmus Mundus and some of the criticism has already been successfully addressed by the second generation of Erasmus Mundus joint programmes between 2009 and 2013. This applies in particular to the development of placements and internships, the more systematic involvement of employers, and the creation of closer links with the alumni networks. The annual Erasmus Mundus graduate impact surveys reach conclusions that are quite similar to the current study.

Students choose Erasmus Mundus first of all to improve their knowledge and skills, particularly in highly specialised fields. They are interested in developing their intercultural competences in good part for the effect they expect this to have on their career prospects. The award of a joint degree also plays a role in their decision. Most students rate mobility highly. They see it as a way to become acquainted with various cultural environments. Surprisingly, language competences are regarded as being the least developed during the study period. Students also indicate that the broadened mind-set required for a joint international programme is helpful for learning to think outside the box.

They perceive Europe as an attractive destination for study and work, although many non-EU students find it difficult to obtain a work permit in Europe after having completed their studies. They find the European job market highly competitive. The most challenging issues, however, are of an administrative nature, with cumbersome and restrictive visa procedures standing out. The low visibility of Erasmus Mundus degrees among employers, in particular outside Europe, is another urgent issue to address.

Finally, students and graduates ask for a more thorough application of quality assurance measures to safeguard the high quality of all courses that make up Erasmus Mundus joint programmes. They report notable differences between these, referring to diverging grading systems, difficulties to obtain double degrees due to bureaucratic or financial issues and variations in the quality of teaching and teaching approaches. Erasmus Mundus has successfully promoted the recognition of joint degrees in laws across Europe and beyond. Yet, some students still find it difficult to have their diplomas recognised back home. But they also say that even if the degrees are not recognised by national authorities, employers value the competences gained during the studies, which is what matters in the end.

ERASMUS+

All of these challenges will be taken up by Erasmus+ after it incorporates Erasmus Mundus and other international academic cooperation programmes this month. To ensure that the selected joint master's programmes remain of high quality and to develop a strategy for their long-term sustainability, the funding system of joint degrees will be reviewed. Instead of receiving funding for five successive intakes (as was the case under Erasmus Mundus), selected university consortia will receive funding for an initial three intakes and will then be invited to undergo a thorough quality review. If they pass this review, they can receive additional support in the form of co-funding for up to three years to ensure future sustainability and quality assurance.

The first Erasmus+ call for projects that also covered joint master's degrees was launched in December 2013, with a deadline of 27 March 2014. Students from any country of the world are also encouraged to apply for a scholarship to enrol in one of the current 138 Erasmus Mundus master's programmes or one of the 42 joint doctorates.

CHRISSIE LONG

26. LATIN AMERICA: COSTA RICA REJECTS HIGH NUMBER OF MEDICAL GRADUATES FROM CUBA

University World News, 30 September 2012, Issue 241

Graduates of Cuba's Escuela Latinoamericana de Medicina, or ELAM, are "gravely deficient" in their preparation to practise medicine, the head of Costa Rica's most celebrated medical school told journalists last month. Of the 138 graduates who failed the medical licensing exams in Costa Rica, 59 were graduates of ELAM, said Ricardo Boza Cordero, director of the medical programme at the University of Costa Rica. According to Boza, the students were largely behind in fundamental areas including paediatrics and gynaecology-obstetrics, and failed to achieve passing scores in the 11 exams administered. "Taking into account that some who will practise as doctors in Costa Rica come from foreign universities, we have to make sure they understand the particulars of our national medicine," he told news sources. "We made the decision to institute a general exam that evaluates their knowledge of basic subject matters in the curriculum and clinical experience."

The fact that 43% of those who failed the licensing exam studied in Cuba comes as a surprise to those familiar with the health system there. Doctors from Cuba, a country that has long been known as an epicentre of medicine in Latin America, have been sent all over the world to aid in health missions in disaster zones. The country boasts one of the highest life expectancies in the hemisphere and excellent healthcare coverage rates, according to the World Health Organization (WHO). Venezuelan President Hugo Chavez sought medical care on the Caribbean island when he was diagnosed with cancer in June 2011.

LACK OF CONGRUENCE IN CURRICULUM?

But the issue may not be one of quality of education, but the lack of congruence in curriculum. While Costa Rica may be putting emphasis on some subject matters, Cuba could be preparing students for other areas of focus. The majority of the medical students who failed the test are graduates of ELAM, a university established in 1999 to provide medical care to the world's poor. The university accepts economically disadvantaged students from all over the world and, through a six-year, free programme run by the Cuban government, prepares them to practise medicine in their home country. Boza did admit that the ELAM and Costa Rican curricula were

G. Mihut et al. (Eds.), Understanding Higher Education Internationalization, 119–121.

not aligned in at least 80% of the subject matters. The students were tested on the 20% in which the curriculum diverged under a new examination system introduced this summer. Many of the students who took the exam have since protested, claiming they should have been grandfathered into the old testing methods—that is, they should not be disadvantaged by the new exam rule, because they were part of the rule that came before it.

ELAM GRADUATES FACE HURDLES ELSEWHERE

Costa Rica is not the only country in which ELAM graduates are facing hurdles in licensing exams. According to a 2010 WHO article, "Their degrees must be validated by sometimes reluctant medical societies and, even once they receive validation, there may be no jobs waiting for them in the public sector where they are most needed." According to André-Jacques Neusy, executive director of the Belgium-based non-profit Training for Health Network, who has studied innovative medical schools throughout the world and is familiar with ELAM, the Cuban medical school is well aware of the challenges of integrating graduates into the health systems of other countries. "ELAM has many graduates in many countries," he said, "and in many parts of the world, they are not accepted. Part of it is Cuba being Cuba," he added, referring to the political hurdles. "Another issue is that the receiving countries may not have the capacity to absorb additional doctors. There may not be enough jobs."

In Honduras, graduates from ELAM were excluded from a residency programme because the government simply did not have enough funds to extend to them. By contrast, in Uruguay last month, 90 graduates of ELAM were accepted into medical practice, news sources there reported. Referring to the situation in Costa Rica, Neusy said: "I find it hard to believe that the students were rejected on aptitude alone." Rachel True, who has been collaborating with ELAM through a US-based non-profit known as MEDICC, which focuses on enhancing health cooperation between the two countries, said the issue of accreditation is very possibly political. "With anything having to do with Cuba, there are politics involved," she said.

PREPARED TO PRACTISE IN UNDER SERVED AREAS

In True's experience, graduates are uniquely prepared to practise medicine in under-served areas. Because there is such a strong emphasis on community engagement and social accountability, the students who graduate from ELAM have a strong desire and a thorough training to improve health among impoverished populations. "ELAM does a better job than we do in the United States of preparing doctors to enter social service," True said. "Studies have shown that students enter medical school in the United States with a very high level of altruism. They want to do good. But that drops off significantly as they approach graduation because they have to find ways to repay their debt. "In the ELAM programme, students don't have debt."

True, who tracks the 200 students-graduates of ELAM who have returned to the US, said the students are very well prepared. "Many of them have entered residency and have been successful."

COSTA RICA SATURATED WITH DOCTORS

The students returning to Costa Rica faced the unfortunate situation of a health system saturated with doctors. The ELAM graduates are competing with doctors not only from the country's prestigious public schools, but also from a number of private universities that have surfaced in recent years. The country is also trying to position itself as a medical tourism destination for North Americans and Europeans looking for more affordable medical care. For that reason, quality control is of high importance, not only for the Costa Rican government but also for the country's medical schools. Boza brings that point home: "The University of Costa Rica needs to guarantee the preparation and high standards of all the professionals that come to the country with a degree in medicine and surgery obtained from a foreign university, with the goal of guaranteeing the welfare and health of all the inhabitants of the country as well as maintaining the high standards of quality in the medical sector." For the ELAM graduates who didn't pass the new examinations? The university is considering letting them take the exams retroactively.

SUVENDRINI KAKUCHI

27. JAPAN: CONSERVATISM, RED TAPE THWART INTERNATIONAL EDUCATION

University World News, 27 April 2013, Issue 269

It is bitterly ironic—Japan has the third largest economy in the world and is a leading exporter, but fails badly when it comes to international education. "Japanese university education needs to be urgently vitalised to survive against stiff global competition," said Dr. Akito Okada, who teaches comparative and international education at the prestigious Tokyo University of Foreign Studies. Universities "have stayed too long relatively unbothered by the global currents of education services seekers, due to the language barrier and traditional internal orientation of higher learning." Okada explained that a primary reason for slow change in Japanese tertiary education was resistance from conservative academics. He strongly advocates the development of a curriculum that prioritises students' needs in a globalised world.

RECOGNITION AND RED TAPE

The liberalisation of the Japanese higher education system, which is tightly regulated by the government, took a first legal step in 2004 under a regulation that allowed foreign universities to apply for Japanese university status. Under this law, named "Japanese Branches of Foreign Universities," campuses in Japan may offer courses and award degrees of a foreign university, and should be treated similarly to Japanese universities except for tax exemption. But research for the Asian Development Bank by Shintaro Hamanaka, under the theme of regional economic integration and released last December, revealed that critical issues remain; none of four foreign campuses in Japan have obtained formal university status. At the top of the list of Hamanaka's concerns is that the law recognises branches of foreign universities but not the establishment of foreign subsidiaries—a system, he said, that limits the scope of higher education services. He explained in his report that "the law implies the Japanese government acknowledges that the authorities responsible for a foreign university campus in Japan that do not rely on Japanese laws and regulation, are foreign authorities." One upshot is that while graduates of the Tokyo campus of Temple University, an accredited branch of Temple University in the United States, cannot apply for graduate studies at Japanese universities, students in the United States are qualified to do so.

G. Mihut et al. (Eds.), Understanding Higher Education Internationalization, 123–125.

Another issue for Hamanaka is the registration process for formal education services, which is subject to approval of the government that in turn relies on the recommendations of the University Council. He describes this system as highly regulated decision-making that is not transparent, given that the "demarcation between the two entities in exercising power is ambiguous." Another hindrance to the establishment of fully fledged foreign university campuses, he said, is the fact that official recognition involves the observance of inflexible regulations that do not necessarily conform to the standards of foreign institutions.

Professor Jeff Kingston of the Tokyo-based Temple University campus explained to University World News that the campus aimed to be recognised as different but equal to its Japanese counterparts. "Our curriculum has the reputation of being strong in Asia studies and able to develop students with critical thinking skills. Teaching is in English and follows American methodologies that are different to the traditional Japanese style, where students sit and listen to their professors and wait for instructions," he said.

Temple University's student body is around 1,100, roughly divided between Japanese and foreign nationals. The campus has not applied for formal recognition and is registered as a private entity, a status that does not allow faculty to apply for government research grants or tax exemption. Professor Takashi Inoguchi, an international relations expert and president of Niigata International University, is another leading advocate for change. He explained that registration in Japan requires foreign campuses to teach in Japanese and follow laborious and parochial rules and regulations that include heavy investment in infrastructure. Together, these can dampen the enthusiasm of most newcomers. "The advantage of gaining official recognition is tax waivers and jobs in Japan for the students. But the tedious process of maintaining standards that heavily focus on Japanese cultural traits, such as maintaining harmony, is not attractive to foreign universities. Ushering in internationalisation in higher education is a long way off," he said.

NEED FOR GLOBALLY MINDED YOUTH

The call to foster more globally minded youth in Japan is now widely supported by the Japanese business community, which is seeking such employees to meet overseas business expansion. In response, leading Japanese universities have begun to launch programmes aimed at achieving this purpose.

Private institutes such as the universities of Keio and Waseda, for example, have started English language graduate degrees, recruited more international faculty and plan to increase foreign student numbers—a process that Kingston pointed out poses stiff competition for foreign campuses setting up in Japan. Moreover, regional governments, faced with dwindling and ageing populations, are eager to woo foreign campuses to lure youth back to their areas. For example, Chatan Town in the Okinawa prefecture, which is the reluctant host to US military bases, is discussing the possibility of setting up a local campus with the University of Maryland. Still,

Akito Okada explained, the process is slow and Japan is faced with the very real threat of being left behind.

China and India are attracting top foreign universities such as Stanford, which opened the Stanford Centre at Peking University as a home base for visiting research faculty and students in China. There is a branch of Harvard Business School in Mumbai. Such names have yet to arrive in Japan. "Despite the stark reality facing Japan, another important fact that bogs the country [down] is that Japanese students, who have been reared in a narrow homogeneous society, would prefer to enrol in Japanese universities where they study in their language and do not confront the challenges of foreign cultures," he said.

PART 5

INTERNATIONALIZATION POLICIES AND STRATEGIES

INTRODUCTION

As internationalization is becoming an increasingly complex endeavor, and one imbued with heightened importance, national governments have taken steps to design strategies and policies aimed at steering its direction within their respective borders. This section includes articles that highlight some of relevant developments in this arena.

The first article in this section, written by Robin Matross Helms and Laura Rumbley, offers a comprehensive overview of national policies focused on internationalization as well as insights on their effectiveness. The article summarizes a recent study conducted by the American Council on Education and the Boston College Center for International Higher Education. The next article included in this section, written by Nanette Svenson, makes the case that the United Nations, as an agent for world diplomacy, should be included in discussions about international higher education. Svenson's piece also offers a summary of the current projects conducted by the UN connected to international higher education.

Internationalization policies increasingly take on a supra-national dimension. As featured here, Gilbert Nganga discusses the harmonization arrangement negotiated by Kenya, Uganda, and Rwanda. The harmonization policy includes provisions on transferable credits, tuition fees, and has paved the way towards developing a regional qualifications framework. Another frequent provision of internationalization policies (though at a national level) is the creation of government-sponsored scholarship schemes for international study. The next two articles offer more details about such programs. Aida Sagintayeva and Zakir Jumakulov explain the *Bolashak Scholarship* program, implemented by Kazakhstan's government. Marcelo Knobel offers a similar analysis with a focus on Brazil's *Science without Borders*, as well as a comparison with the US-based *100,000 strong Initiative*.

Together, the articles in this section highlight the increasing interest of national governments in using internationalization strategies to consolidate other national goals, but also varied and frequent attempts to regulate internationalization practices. It is noteworthy that international organizations and supranational arrangements— some of which are surveyed here—are becoming important voices in steering the direction of international education activities.

G. Mihut et al. (Eds.), Understanding Higher Education Internationalization, 129.
© *2017 Sense Publishers. All rights reserved.*

ROBIN MATROSS HELMS AND LAURA E. RUMBLEY

28. GLOBAL: NATIONAL POLICIES FOR INTERNATIONALIZATION—DO THEY WORK?

International Higher Education, Spring 2016, Number 85

In response to the demands and opportunities of an ever-globalizing world, governments in a wide range of countries are introducing policies and programs to promote higher education internationalization. These initiatives are underpinned by a variety of academic, economic, political, social, and cultural motivations; sometimes higher education internationalization is an explicit goal, while in other cases, the focus is more specifically on a discrete activity, or on broader national policy goals.

A recent study by the American Council on Education (ACE) and the Boston College Center for International Higher Education (CIHE) took a close look at the content of such policies—an overview, including a wide assortment of specific examples, is the basis for our recent report, *Internationalizing Higher Education Worldwide: National Policies and Programs*. Our analysis revealed five main categories of policies in place around the world, based on their primary focus:

Type 1: Student mobility. Policies designed to encourage and facilitate student mobility stand out as the most common focal point for policymaking related to internationalization of higher education. A broad array of nationally funded student mobility scholarship programs—from Saudi Arabia to Chile, Kazakhstan to Brazil, among many others—are the prime manifestations of this policy focus.

Type 2: Scholar mobility and research collaboration. Policy activity in this area is being undertaken by many countries around the world, as well as by key regions—notably Europe, where the European Union is investing heavily in this area under the Horizon 2020 initiative, and specifically through such mechanisms as the Marie Skłodowska-Curie actions. Common types of initiatives in this category include support for visiting scholars, programs, and grants to send faculty abroad, policies to repatriate faculty living in other countries, and project-based research grants.

Type 3: Cross-border education. Whether involving branch campuses and other kinds of physical "outposts," or virtual (or hybrid) forms—such as MOOCs—national policy and program activity in this realm include initiatives to foster partnerships for capacity building, create educational "hubs," encourage domestic institutions to

G. Mihut et al. (Eds.), Understanding Higher Education Internationalization, 131–134.

establish campuses and programs abroad, and more effectively regulate cross-border activity in practice.

Type 4: Internationalization at home (IaH). IaH is a nascent but rapidly emerging critical focal point for internationalization. Few policy documents currently address it overtly. The European Commission's 2013 strategy for internationalization, European Higher Education in the World, is a notable exception. But this is surely an important space to watch for future policy developments.

Type 5: "Comprehensive internationalization" policies. We see a small number of initiatives that present a rather sweeping set of rationales, action lines, focus areas, and/or geographic orientations, rather than being singularly focused on specific action lines. Again, the European Commission's policy vision for internationalization stands out, but so does Canada's 2014 "International Education Strategy" and Malaysia's 2011 "Internationalization Policy for Higher Education Malaysia," among others.

GAUGING EFFECTIVENESS

With national-level internationalization policies and programs proliferating in a variety of contexts and configurations, the question of effectiveness comes front and center. Do these policies positively impact the direction and progress of internationalization in their respective higher education systems? In the longer term, do they succeed in furthering the academic, economic, political, social, and/or cultural goals they set out to achieve?

As is often the case when it comes to education-related issues, determining the effectiveness of internationalization policies is challenging. Often, efforts to do so focus on easily measured, clearly quantified outputs. Did country A's policy achieve its goal of recruiting X number of new international students to the country's universities in the specified timeline? In addition to participant numbers, financial analyses—another easily quantified measure, and one that often appeals to policy-makers—may come into play as an evaluation tool.

When it comes to the more nebulous, longer-term outcomes and impact of such policies, studies by the British Council/DAAD and the HEFCE (the Higher Education Funding Council for England), the European Commission, and the International Association of Universities have made some inroads in delineating impacts of different policies, using various methodologies. Overall, though, specific data and clear answers about issues of impact are fairly scarce. In part, this is due to the newness of many of the internationalization policies now in place around the world—it is simply too soon to tell what their ultimate impact will be. In many other cases, evaluation of impact simply appears not be built into policy implementation structures.

Having examined a large number of such policies and the available data on effectiveness, however, it is clear that there are a number of key factors—both inherent to the policies themselves, as well as external factors impacting implementation—that affect policy effectiveness (positively or negatively).

Funding is of primary importance. Not surprisingly, policy effectiveness may be directly affected by issues such as the level at which policies are funded, the ways in which funding is distributed, and the degree to which funding is sustained over time.

How policies are implemented, and by whom, is also crucial. It is common knowledge that "one size fits all" is not a useful way to think about internationalization policy or practice. So, national policies may be implemented in a wide variety of ways—for example, involving many actors or just a few. The ways that policies are implemented can have a major effect on issues such as efficiency, and raise important questions about the capacity of policy implementers to advance their agendas and manage their work well.

Looking beyond individual policies themselves gives rise to the issue of policy interplay and alignment. For most countries, the national policy environment is complex and interlocking. Initiatives undertaken in one area can have a direct influence on efforts being undertaken in other policy spheres. Classic examples in relation to internationalization include the intersection between national objectives to attract international students and scholars, and visa and immigration policies that control access to the country. If policies are developed and implemented in isolation from one another, or directly at cross-purposes, policy effectiveness will suffer.

Finally, the level of convergence between policy objectives and institutional priorities impacts effectiveness of national-level initiatives. Internationalization of higher education is a phenomenon most directly experienced by higher education institutions themselves. For this reason, national policies for internationalization must be grounded in an understanding of institutional realities. National policies that fail to take into account institutional priorities, and vice versa, present major challenges for achieving successful outcomes.

INTERNATIONALIZING INTERNATIONALIZATION

Will individual countries' internationalization policies ultimately achieve their short- and long-term goals? Only time will tell. But, perhaps the more interesting question is what the overall impact of such policies will be on higher education worldwide. The growing number of countries that are committing—in very concrete, formal, and resource-intensive ways—to internationalizing their higher education systems suggests that the time is right to collectively take our efforts to the next level, and turn our attention to the "internationalization of internationalization." The impact of country-level policies will be maximized when we find the synergies among them—i.e., when our policies are mutually supportive and reinforcing.

This is not necessarily an easy task—it requires broad awareness of policies in place, and dialogue at the national policymaking and institutional levels. As we note at the end of the ACE-CIHE report, "ensuring that higher education around the world benefits from the best of what comprehensive, sustained, values-driven internationalization has to offer will take a great deal of creativity, substantial resources, and sheer hard work."

NANETTE SVENSON

29. GLOBAL: THE UNITED NATIONS, INTERNATIONAL HIGHER EDUCATION, AND KNOWLEDGE DIPLOMACY

International Higher Education, Winter 2016, Number 84

The term "knowledge diplomacy" has been used with increasing frequency in recent years to describe many things, including how international higher education (IHE) can become an instrument of soft power and a tool through which smaller nations may position themselves to negotiate beyond the parameters of their traditional power base. As the quintessential agent of world diplomacy, the United Nations (UN) should be included in these discussions as they relate to knowledge—even with regard to IHE, though this is not an area typically associated with the UN. Motivated by the furthering of social learning, center-periphery knowledge transfer, research generation and improved public relations, the UN has begun to engage in IHE programming. This article examines the nature of this activity and offers commentary on which aspects of it hold more potential for advancing the goals of the UN and its members.

UNIVERSITY DEGREE PROGRAMMING

Much of UN international higher education involvement revolves around university level training and degree granting. The UN has established a number of programs and schools through partnerships with other academic and professional organizations. Their purpose has been to bridge gaps between theory and practice in key areas of global governance and development, and to complement national academic institutions' programming.

The United Nations University (UNU) was established in 1972 as a global think tank and postgraduate teaching organization. Headquartered in Tokyo and endowed by the Japanese government, UNU has 16 partner institutes and programs in different countries, that concentrate on issues related to peace and security, human rights, governance, science and technology, and sustainable development. Most UNU work focuses on partner institution research, though in 2012 the university also began to grant Master's degrees. The University for Peace in Costa Rica, founded by the UN General Assembly in 1980, grants graduate degrees in disciplines related to peace and security and engages in non-degree programs and research, often collaborating

G. Mihut et al. (Eds.), Understanding Higher Education Internationalization, 135–137.

with international partners. The World Maritime University (WMU) is a postgraduate maritime institute in Sweden, founded in 1983 by the International Maritime Organization (IMO), another UN specialized agency. WMU emerged in response to a global shortage of qualified maritime experts, especially in developing nations, and provides various Master's degrees and professional certifications. The IMO also founded the International Maritime Law Institute (IMLI) in Malta in 1988 to train international maritime law specialists. IMLI offers graduate degrees, maritime diplomas and various short courses. Similarly, the International Labor Organization International Training Center established the Turin School of Development (TSD) in 2009 to introduce a series of postgraduate programs and courses on international labor legislation and development. TSD is the result of a partnership with the University of Turin, several other schools, and various UN agencies.

All these UN university programs have pursued local and international accreditation, attracted multinational faculty and students, and created new degree programs linked to UN knowledge and objectives. Collectively over the past three decades they claim thousands of graduates from countries all over the world and host a range of international conferences, research projects, and academic publications.

NON-DEGREE PROGRAMS

Beyond its university degree granting and research, the UN has pioneered other IHE initiatives that support shorter-term activities and facilitate partnerships between IHE institutions globally. Included in this type of endeavor are the UN Academic Impact (UNAI), Model UN (MUN), and UN internship programs, as well as UN sponsored faculty chairs and curriculum-building projects.

UNAI, launched in 2010, aims to link universities more closely with the UN, promote UN objectives, and create a global university network for peace and development. Nearly 1,000 schools worldwide have joined, agreeing to create new programs aligned with UN principles related to education, global citizenship, sustainable development, and conflict resolution. Examples of these include the Ukraine's national university pre-school for underprivileged children and Cornell University's recently launched International Architecture and Rural Development major. Almost as old as the UN itself, MUN is a UN-supported, externally managed educational simulation of UN experience and academic competition for university and high school students. MUN teaches UN principles and protocol, develops research and debate skills, and broadens participant knowledge on diplomacy, international law, and global politics. MUN conferences with thousands of participants are held annually throughout the world. UN internships, available through the UN Secretariat, specialized agencies and regional centers for graduate students with majors related to UN topics, are another component of UN IHE programming. Students offer unpaid labor in exchange for work experience and academic credit within a branch of the UN. UNAI, MUN, and the UN internship programs all seek to educate university students on UN activity, objectives, and careers, ideally fostering more socially responsible youth.

Other UN IHE non-degree programs include collaborative faculty exchange and curriculum development. The UNESCO university twinning and networking scheme, for instance, promotes a series of faculty chair positions and networking communities within universities around the world. This program involves 650 institutions in over 120 countries and drives higher education and research capacity building through sponsorship of exchange opportunities in areas related to UNESCO fieldwork—education, sciences, culture, and communication. Additionally, several other UN agencies with expertise, information, and educational experience in particular areas are beginning to partner with universities on projects that broaden curricula. Examples include the International Anti-Corruption Academy (IACA—a UN Office on Drugs and Crime-INTERPOL project that offers a broad professional training curriculum and executive graduate course in Anti-Corruption Studies) and the UN Food and Agriculture Organization's guides for food security, statistical analysis, and online curriculum development. These capacity development services have been widely accessed by developing country institutions.

KNOWLEDGE DIPLOMACY POTENTIAL

UN international higher education knowledge diplomacy activity spans a broad mix of programming and is still relatively new. Nevertheless, regarding its potential for advancing UN and member state ideals and goals, several observations can be made. The UN does not have higher education delivery in its mandate or experience base; therefore, any UN university program is dependent on host government endowments and external resources. This is expensive and sometimes unsustainable. Also, the UN's degrees are not yet prominently recognized and its university-oriented research is not its most widely disseminated and utilized product, which raises questions of cost-benefit justifiability. UN IHE endeavors yield most when tied to projects and issues immediately relevant to national economies, academic institutions, and professionals rather than to UN-generated agendas. Thus, the non-degree granting UN brokering of IHE professional and information exchange seems a more natural and cost effective fit. Countries on both sides of the equation have embraced UN provision of funding, networking, information, documentation, and publication for IHE exchange and there is significant room for expansion of these activities. That UN information, experience, and infrastructure can be beneficial to international higher education programs is certain; less clear is how the UN can best package and market these resources for optimal impact.

GILBERT NGANGA

30. AFRICA: KENYA, UGANDA, RWANDA STRIKE HE HARMONISATION FEE DEAL

University World News, 14 March 2014, Issue 311

Students from Kenya, Rwanda, and Uganda will in future pay local fees in any of the three East African Community, or EAC, states. A new deal has moved the countries closer to harmonised higher education, which has been elusive for the past five years due to difficulties in agreeing key parameters like fees and credit transfer. Previously, students studying in another EAC state were regarded as international students and charged in United States dollars. The deal was signed between the three countries under the auspices of the so-called "coalition of the willing," an economic partnership that has excluded the other two EAC countries of Burundi and Tanzania.

The coalition emerged early last year, as an initiative to fast-track the integration agenda that was seen to be stalling because of the relatively slow pace of Tanzania in adopting some of the principles. But it has been castigated as having the potential to break up the EAC—one of the most vibrant integration blocs in Africa. The "coalition of the willing" has mainly concentrated on major infrastructure projects connecting the three countries including a standard gauge railway, a joint tourist visa, a refinery, a pipeline and energy projects. The education deal was signed late last month after the coalition's latest meeting in Kampala, the capital of Uganda, on 20 February, and is a rare win in the drive towards harmonised education systems in the East African region. The three coalition countries have apparently resolved to drive the education harmonisation plan forward, as they have done with integration projects such as the joint tourist visa.

CREDIT TRANSFER

Higher education harmonisation is aimed, among other things, at establishing a fully-fledged credit transfer system that will allow students to move between universities in different countries without losing credits they have accumulated. This plan has, however, faced strong headwinds over the past four years due to growing nationalistic biases, with partner states unwilling to let go of educational sovereignty for the sake of a regional system. Major variations in the quality of learning, curricula and length of degrees exist in the region's higher education systems, highlighting the long

G. Mihut et al. (Eds.), Understanding Higher Education Internationalization, 139–141.

road the five countries still have to travel before they can achieve the envisioned integration.

With the exclusion of Tanzania and Burundi from the latest deal on higher education, the dream of achieving harmonisation for the entire bloc seems as far away as ever. The five countries have, however, already adopted a report that is key to implementing the harmonisation plan—a development that is giving the Inter-University Council for East Africa, or IUCEA, hope for a quick resolution of pending issues. "Discussions have been very difficult because the concept of harmonisation was not known. Most people across the partner states thought harmonisation meant that we must have the same education system across the entire bloc," said Professor Nkunya Mayunga, executive secretary of the IUCEA. "Nobody can accept that. Education is a constitutional issue in each country." While there had been achievements, such as agreeing on the broad framework for harmonisation, much work still needed to be done, said Mayunga. "As it is, you still cannot transfer credit from one university to another across borders. Universities and countries need to agree on the definition of a credit and what it means. Students can move across the region, but under bilateral arrangements between the governments." The IUCEA has set 2015 as the deadline for the region to have a working credit transfer system.

QUALIFICATIONS, SKILLS, ACCREDITATION

The council also hopes that by the end of this year, it will have developed a regional qualifications framework. While most courses are similar across countries in terms of names and content, in most cases, the qualifications and duration of study vary. For example, it takes five years for a student to finish an engineering degree in Kenya, against three years in Uganda. To pursue a medical degree at a Kenyan university takes five years, a year less than in Tanzania and Uganda.

At their recent meeting, Kenya, Uganda, and Rwanda also agreed to identify priority skills needed for joint projects and to develop strategies to address skills gaps through existing institutions of higher education. The leaders from the three countries—Uhuru Kenyatta of Kenya, Paul Kagame of Rwanda, and Yoweri Museveni of Uganda—agreed to allocate budgets for much-needed skills development at two institutions in Kenya and Uganda. "Partner states will acknowledge Carnegie Mellon University in Kigali as the regional training centre of excellence for ICT," said the presidents in a statement. The US-based Carnegie Mellon University launched its Rwandan campus mid-2012. It is the first top-ranked US research institution to offer graduate degrees in Africa with an in-country presence and resident faculty. EAC governments will also have to resolve a stalemate over whether to adopt a single university accreditation system in the bloc, rather than each country having its own system.

The plan was for the IUCEA to be transformed into a regional body with the core function of granting accreditation to universities in the five countries. But this has attracted opposition from all countries. The presidents also directed their ministers of education to address the issue of standardisation of student cards, which will be used as travel documents. The trio has agreed to stop the passport requirement, and to allow use of identity or student cards to cross borders.

SOUTH SUDAN

During the Kampala meeting, the heads of state noted the request by conflict-torn South Sudan for support in capacity building in the allocation of projects, particularly railways, and support for Sudanese students studying in the region. South Sudan has applied to be a member of the EAC bloc, but its bid is still under consideration by the five member states after it failed the preliminary test due to weak governance systems after years of political instability. The application is set to be considered later this year, a development that could further complicate the bid for a harmonised higher education system due to South Sudan's nascent university system, whose growth has been slowed by the decades of war.

AIDA SAGINTAYEVA AND ZAKIR JUMAKULOV

31. KAZAKHSTAN: KAZAKHSTAN'S BOLASHAK SCHOLARSHIP PROGRAM

International Higher Education, Winter 2015, Number 79

Emerging economies has increasingly realized the connection between human capital investment and economic prosperity. They are looking at more advanced countries for best practices to reform the tertiary education system at home. Among the approaches is sending students to study abroad on government-sponsored scholarships. This practice, which often entails a considerable financial investment by the home nation, is expected to accelerate the development of human capital.

Kazakhstan's Bolashak Scholarship is one example of a long-standing government-sponsored international scholarship program. In 1993, the Kazakhstan government launched Bolashak (Kazakh for "future") Scholarships to send students to attend colleges and universities abroad. About 100 students received the scholarships annually until 2005, when the number increased over time to average 800 per year. In an effort to maximize program effectiveness, program administrators have made various changes in the design over the past 20 years. Based on our review of program characteristics and outcomes, we identify five lessons for how this government-sponsored scholarship program has accomplished its goal for promoting human capital development.

SPECIFYING STRATEGIC PRIORITY AREAS

Wise investment of limited government funds for maximum return has always been a challenge in scholarship design. One approach is to match the educational priorities of the sending country with the academic programs available overseas. A recent examination of international scholarship programs shows that 45 percent of 183 government sponsored scholarship programs are in 196 countries with specific academic priority areas. Prior to 1997, when Bolashak had no guidelines on the areas of study, scholarship recipients were concentrated in humanities and social sciences, and the number of recipients in science and engineering remained extremely low.

The Kazakhstan government responded by creating a list of priority areas of study in 1997, giving weight to applicants in the majors identified as highly relevant to

G. Mihut et al. (Eds.), Understanding Higher Education Internationalization, 143–146.

the strategic development of the country. To further encourage applicants in science and engineering majors, the government also had lowered language requirements and offered applicants English-language courses. These alterations were designed to produce qualified specialists in line with the government's overall priorities for diversification and industrial development of the economy.

IDENTIFYING DESIRED INSTITUTIONS

A second lesson learned pertains to the types of institutions that students attend and the ways to recognize the asymmetric education provision between home and overseas institutions. Studying abroad allows students to enroll in programs that are not available or are of lower quality than in the home institutions. Funding bodies seek to support students enrolled in leading institutions abroad, in hope of providing greater access to high-quality higher education. In accordance with this rationale, the Bolashak program, as well as 85 percent of government-sponsored study-abroad programs offered worldwide, limit students' destination institutions.

The initial design of the Bolashak program did not restrict the choices of institutions by recipients, and thus it could not prevent them from studying at dubious institutions. The need for the Kazakhstan government to carefully appraise the quality of overseas institutions was exacerbated during the recent global financial crisis, when many institutions worldwide lowered their entrance requirements to recruit more fee-paying students. To better meet the aims of the program, the program's administration developed a list of recommended higher education institutions, compiled from the Times Higher Education Rankings and QS World University Rankings, to ensure that scholarship recipients would study at universities approved by the program. With these changes, the number of universities recommended for Bolashak students decreased from 630 in 2007 to the current number of 200.

ENSURING TRANSPARENCY

To be perceived as prestigious and available to top students, a program like Bolashak must ensure that the limited scholarships are awarded to recipients in accordance with its merit-based principles. A third lesson learned by the Kazakhstan government was the need for transparency. Between 1993 and 1997, there were no concrete rules governing the award of the Bolashak Scholarship. The lack of information and publicity, coupled with the limited number of awarded scholarships, generated a negative image of the program and triggered wide criticism, regarding the fairness of the selection process. The general public believed the program was tailored specifically for the offspring of the political elites. It was not until 1997, when the requirements for awarding scholarships were announced, that the Bolashak Scholarship gained acceptance by the public. Recent interviews with stakeholders show that transparency is in place.

RESTRUCTURING SUPPORT FOR THE LEVEL OF STUDY

Given the limited funds available, the level of study to support is a fourth lesson. In 2011, the eligible degree levels went through restructuring: scholarships to undergraduate students ended but scholarships for research and teaching staff were added. The latter initiative has already produced benefits related to the internationalization of curriculum, academic publishing, and joint research projects.

Several factors prompted this change. The age of undergraduate scholarship recipients (between 17 and 19) was perceived by policymakers as psychologically immature for studying abroad. In addition, employers provided conflicting feedback on preferred levels of study: some believed that undergraduates' longer stay in host countries would benefit their language skills, while others preferred more advanced skills of master's degree graduates. The total cost of supporting one undergraduate student significantly exceeded that of a postgraduate student. The opening of Nazarbayev University, an English-language university with international faculty offering high-quality fully funded undergraduate education in Kazakhstan, also contributed to the elimination of funding for undergraduate education.

REQUIRING THE RETURN OF SCHOLARSHIP RECIPIENTS

A fifth lesson pertains to incentivizing the scholarship recipients to return to their home country after they graduate. There has always been anxiety over losing government-sponsored scholarship recipients to their hosting countries, since the rationale to the scholarships is the recipients' future contributions to the home countries.

The Bolashak program addresses this concern by only awarding scholarships to individuals who can provide collateral immovable property equivalent in value to the scholarship or provide up to four guarantors who will assume financial liability for the government's investment, should the recipient not return to Kazakhstan. To fulfill their obligations, upon completion of their degrees, recipients are required to work in Kazakhstan in the field of their degree specialization for five years. After that, the contract is considered fully executed, and the Bolashak administration releases the collateral. As drastic as it may seem, this approach has succeeded to guarantee the return of the scholarship recipients. Only 1 percent of scholarship recipients has not returned to Kazakhstan since the Bolashak Scholarship program began.

CONCLUSION

The aim of the Kazakhstan government's Bolashak Scholarship is to invest in human capital development and ensure that this investment creates a long-lasting impact on the country's development. The program has gone through significant changes in the past two decades. The heart of the changes relates to the alignment of personal choice, industrial needs, and the country's strategic development.

MARCELO KNOBEL

32. BRAZIL: BRAZIL SEEKS ACADEMIC BOOST BY SENDING STUDENTS ABROAD

International Higher Education, Winter 2012, Number 66

Brazil has just launched a program to dramatically increase the number of Brazilian students abroad. Although it counts with public-financial resources, no one really knows if the ambitious quantitative goals can be reached.

SCIENCE WITHOUT BORDERS

Just a few days after the official visit of President Barack Obama to Brazil in March 2011, the Brazilian president Dilma Rousseff announced that it is a top priority of the government to send at least 75 thousand university students to spend a period in US higher education institutions. Today, it is estimated that there are around 8,800 Brazilians enrolled in American campuses, the 14th rank among such foreign groups. Although the statement was made with considerable fanfare, it was given without further details. Also, the speech mentioned this kind of program's importance for the hard sciences and technological programs, mainly engineering, in order to allow the country to have a more qualified workforce in these strategic areas.

Since this announcement, the Brazilian research agencies struggled to design the plan, now called Science without Borders, launched officially in July 2011. The program finally includes not only the United States, but also other countries. The Brazilian government claims that it will look for private sponsors to pay tuition and fees to partner universities. The plan includes undergraduate students (around 35% of the scholarships), PhD students (46% of the scholarships), and also fellowships for postdoctorate and senior researchers. The total budget for a period of four years is estimated to be around US$2 billion.

It is clear that the intentions of the Science without Borders program are significant; and clearly some international experience should become a fundamental part of higher education, especially for a country like Brazil, which has seen increasing engagement in the international arena. Providing students with the possibility of an international experience is considered to be an effective strategy—from a geopolitical perspective as well as the academic viewpoint.

G. Mihut et al. (Eds.), Understanding Higher Education Internationalization, 147–149.

HIGHER EDUCATION IN BRAZIL

Brazil has a population of 195 million inhabitants. Brazil has a quite diverse higher education system, with a relatively small number of public (federal, state, or municipal) research universities and a large number of private institutions—both philanthropic/confessional and for-profit. Approximately 6 million students have enrolled in undergraduate programs around the country, with 77 percent of those in private institutions. There are a number of consolidated research centers (both federal and state owned), which granted 12,000 PhDs and 41,000 master's degrees, in 2010. The consolidation of the graduate system during the 1970s and 1980s included a systematic effort to finance graduate and postdoctoral studies in other countries. A large part of the participants in those programs returned to Brazil and helped to qualify the higher education institutions and the budding graduate programs in the country, particularly in public universities. After this initial period, the federal policies changed to strengthen the different programs within the country, drastically reducing the number of fellowships to send students abroad. Such policies resulted in a decrease of the degree of international experience of faculty in research-intensive universities. Thus, the proposed initiative discussed here reveals the reversal of current federal policies toward the graduate education sector.

THE COMPARISON WITH THE US INITIATIVE TO CHINA

This program is certainly related to the so-called "100,000 strong Initiative," considered to be a key component of the Obama administration's foreign-policy agenda. Thus, there would be a coordinated effort designed to increase dramatically the number and diversify the composition of American students studying in China. Similar to the Brazilian case, this initiative is tempered by serious concerns about the achievability of such an ambitious target. However, contrary to the Brazilian case, the Obama administration is putting forward a challenge but no cash, claiming that financial support for the effort is required from private sources.

The main challenges in Brazil are of another nature, related to the number of qualified students able to undertake academic study in foreign universities. Considering the quality and leadership of the US higher education sector, for example, it is fair to suppose that any good student at a high-quality university would consider applying to a "bridge scholarship," given by the Brazilian government.

Nobody really understands how this "magic" number of 75 thousand students was set as a goal. In 2009, approximately 58 thousand PhD students and 104 thousand master students were enrolled in Brazilian universities in all fields of knowledge. Only 20 institutions granted more than 100 PhD titles in 2009. Considering these numbers, it is clear why undergraduate students and postdocs must also participate in the program. The challenge will be to verify whether there are enough qualified students, with minimum language requirements, capable and willing to travel abroad and study in top world universities.

PRIORITIES AND FUNDING

The program focuses mainly on health and life sciences and on the so-called STEM fields (science, technology, engineering, and mathematics), with an emphasis on engineering. It is well known that engineering and basic-science education (both in number and quality) are considered to be among the main constraints to the immediate and future development of the Brazilian society, and certainly a program centered in these fields is an urgent necessity. On the other hand, it would be interesting to extend the program to other fields of knowledge in the near future.

From the point of view of the partner countries, the program has already received some criticisms, mainly in the United Kingdom, where a recent £200 million cut of state funding for higher education was made by the government. It is expected that Brazilians would not attain places otherwise available to British and European Union students. Nonetheless, concerns were raised that the UK government's funding model for higher education is becoming increasingly reliant on attracting overseas nationals who, if born in the United Kingdom, might have struggled to become a regular student at a university there. Also, long-term partners such as Portugal were almost completely excluded, at least in this initial stage of the program, causing some negative reactions.

Finally, one of the most important criticisms regarding this program is its unilateral character. The program should be a real exchange program, with reciprocity from the counterpart university to support and stimulate their students to perform academic study in Brazil. This would be extremely beneficial to the Brazilian universities to boost their incipient internationalization process. Considering the total budget of the program, the issue of further planning and discussions in regard to priorities for spending public money in overseas universities becomes even more important.

The main stakeholders assume that a program like this needs further discussion and should be based on solid studies that constitute higher education policy, goals, and priorities, and taking into account the reality of the current Brazilian education scenario and the globalized higher education sector.

PART 6

INTERNATIONALIZATION THROUGH PARTNERSHIPS

INTRODUCTION

Internationalization is both supported by and, in turn, promotes the creation of partnerships between distinct actors in different parts of the world. This section offers key reflections on some of the tensions associated with partnerships and is a continuation of the previous section.

The first article in the section, written by Cornelius Hagenmeier, considers the importance of developing an appropriate framework to understand equality in partnerships between universities of different (perceived) status. Hagenmeier's piece distinguishes between the use of formal equality, or equality between similar partners, and substantive equality, where dissimilar actors receive customized treatments based on contextual factors. In the case of partnerships, substantive equity may be ensured by judging the meaningful contributions by different actors in their respective context. In a similar mode, Robin Middlehurst offers an analysis on the multiple international networks established world-wide among universities and also reflects on their sustainability.

When discussing partnerships in higher education, often north-south and developed-developing connections are emphasized. The following articles in this section offer insights into less discussed partnership patterns. Milton Obamba discusses China and Africa, placing university partnerships in the broader framework of international cooperation, and cautions against reestablishing patterns of dependency between the two actors. Hiep Pham describes a partnership between Vietnam and Russia aimed at building a technology university in Hanoi, while Ard Jongsma offers an overview of the increasing regional educational collaboration between Western Balkan governments. Finally, Joseph Stetar and Modi Li analyze the developments and slow progress made in implementing the bilateral agreement between the US and China aimed at enabling 100,000 from the US to study in China.

Collectively, the articles in this section reflect on the intrinsic power relations associated with international partnerships. They suggest an increasing diversity in types of partnerships and collaborations established around the world—a topic ripe for further study.

G. Mihut et al. (Eds.), Understanding Higher Education Internationalization, 153
© 2017 Sense Publishers. All rights reserved.

CORNELIUS HAGENMEIER

33. GLOBAL: ENSURING EQUALITY IN HIGHER EDUCATION PARTNERSHIPS INVOLVING UNEQUAL UNIVERSITIES IN DIVERGENT CONTEXTS

International Higher Education, Special Issue 2015, Number 83

A collaborative approach to internationalization through international partnerships is widely practiced and considered essential for higher education. However, the theoretical underpinnings of university partnerships have yet to be fully analysed and understood. The Nelson Mandela Bay Declaration on the Future of Internationalization (2014) proclaims that the future agenda for internationalization should concentrate on "gaining commitment on a global basis to equal and ethical higher education partnerships."

EQUALITY IN PARTNERSHIPS

While equality is commonly cited as a core principle underlying higher education partnerships, the doctrine is not yet clearly defined and the academic discourse on developing suitable concepts and strategies to achieve it is in its infancy. Inequalities are inherent to many higher education partnerships, and especially to those between universities of unequal strength. Inequalities are especially apparent when finance is provided by external donors, who may often be located in the context of the "stronger" university and who award funding exclusively to this partner because they share the same context.

FORMAL EQUALITY

Generally, recourse is made to a formal conception of equality in higher education partnerships, based on that aspect of Aristotelian understanding of equality which espouses that "things that are alike should be treated alike." This works well and achieves equitable results in instances where equality is to be accomplished between entities that are similar in their core characteristics, but has limitations with regard to realizing equality between entities with dissimilar features.

In higher education partnerships in which one partner makes a larger financial contribution than the other, pursuant to its superior economic strength, the stronger partner's influence on partnership decision-making processes is likely to be weightier.

G. Mihut et al. (Eds.), Understanding Higher Education Internationalization, 155–157.

This dynamic is at times used by universities to secure a competitive advantage, especially when the partners are universities that vary greatly in size, shape, research output, reputation, and economic strength. The absence of formal equality poses a threat to the success and sustainability of partnerships and can result in the dominance of one partner to the relationship over the other. The prevalent influence of the dominant, economically stronger partner on the decision-making processes in a partnership is often justified by reference to larger financial contributions.

SUBSTANTIVE EQUALITY

A consensus exists that higher education partnerships should be equal or at least equitable, but it remains to be determined how this can be achieved in a global landscape characterized by unequal resources and divergent strengths of universities and higher education systems. As demonstrated above, formal equality is problematic as a conceptual basis for equality in higher education partnerships. It is necessary to interrogate whether equality should not be defined differently, for example by using an understanding that emphasizes the second element of the Aristotelian conception of equality—namely that "things that are unalike should be treated unalike in proportion to their unlikeness." A substantive conception of equality based on this principle has been widely used in human rights, labor, and gender discourses. It provides for the unequal treatment of fundamentally different cases and may be used in the higher education context to avoid the inequitable tendencies alluded to above.

A substantive understanding of equality in partnerships could provide a suitable theoretical framework to achieve the equitable sharing of the benefits of joint endeavors and consequently lead to real equality in partnerships. Such an understanding would reflect the differences between the entities involved in the relationship and provide a framework which acknowledges that diversity can serve as the foundation for equitable governance structures for partnerships. It considers that the nature and quantity of contributions to partnerships should depend on the individual partner's respective strength, but that the relationship should remain reciprocal.

To create certainty and promote equity, it would be desirable to adopt a conception of equality that clearly defines the extent of contributions required by partners. A useful example for the application of the principle of substantive equality is the 2013 internationalization policy of the University of Venda in South Africa, which adopts a substantive understanding of equality and defines it to mean that "every partner to a relationship should make contributions which are equally meaningful taking the context of the partner into consideration."

CONCLUSION

To counter inequalities and even exploitative undercurrents, which characterize many contemporary higher education partnerships, it is necessary to develop a theoretically sound conception of equality in alliances between universities of divergent strength, which goes beyond formal equality and rather looks at substantive equality. Further research will be required to gain a deep understanding of the present paradigm, which could serve to appropriately conceptualize a model that can advance genuine equality in higher education partnerships. It appears, prima facie, that the adoption of a substantive understanding of equality may facilitate the development of an equitable paradigm, which would ensure that genuine equality can be achieved in mutually beneficial and reciprocal higher education partnerships.

ROBIN MIDDLEHURST

34. GLOBAL: PERSPECTIVES ON GLOBAL UNIVERSITY NETWORKS

International Higher Education, Summer 2015, Number 81

For centuries, higher education has been an internationally connected sector, as scholars have sought to exchange ideas and gain new knowledge. However, such connectivity appears to be reaching new heights, doubtless aided by the ability to connect physically and virtually, but not entirely explained by this. Kris Olds of the University of Wisconsin – Madison, discussing the "seemingly endless thicket of associations, networks, consortia and alliances," argues that we are witnessing a process of denationalization as institutions reframe the scope of their vision, structures, and strategies beyond the national scale. Contrastingly, an analysis of key moments in internationalization from the late 19th to early 21st centuries finds approaches to internationalization to "denationalize" the university usually do not succeed (or not for long). So why are global networks proliferating and institutional efforts to reach out beyond national borders doomed to failure?

Collaborative historical research across Europe, Asia, Australia, and North and South America, undertaken by scholars within the Worldwide University Network, identifies the development of international consortia and networks as a response to major historical-structural changes in higher education. Universities have joined forces to meet new expectations and solve problems "on an ever-widening scale." They have done this in the light of fluctuating enrollments and funding resources associated with economic booms and busts; new modes of transportation and communication facilitating mobility—among students, scholars, and knowledge itself; increasing demands for applied science, technical expertise, and commercial innovation; and ideological reconfigurations accompanying regime changes. These challenges still resonate as drivers for establishing global networks, but there are also new ones.

Competitive pressures are encouraging institutions and countries to seek competitive advantage through collaboration. The coveted goods of "global reputation" and "world-class status" lead toward rankings, positioning, branding, and reputation management. In the 21st century, when the power and influence of global media are ubiquitous, this driver may be stronger than in the past, supported and extended through new social and mobile technologies. Associating with others that are successful, well resourced, or powerful is assumed to bring added value, both

G. Mihut et al. (Eds.), Understanding Higher Education Internationalization, 159–161.

in substance and reflected glory. Being invited to join an exclusive network—such as the League of European Research Universities or Universitas 21—signals mutual recognition and a perceived hallmark of quality in the global research hierarchy. For other institutions in search of global partners, factors beyond the "scholarship of discovery" are important signifiers of differentiation and distinctiveness in a crowded marketplace of networks.

DIVERSITY OF GLOBAL NETWORKS

Global networks are not just proliferating among institutions; they also cross sectors to engage new partners and leverage partnership assets to achieve benefits for businesses, citizens, and universities. "Triple helix" innovation systems are one example where traditionally separated innovation sources have come together— product development in industry, policymaking in government, and creation and dissemination of knowledge in academia—to facilitate development of new organizational designs, new knowledge, products, and services. A new bridge between Denmark and Sweden helped create the Oresund University Network, opening new research areas and educational possibilities. However, the original network of 11 universities has shrunk to those institutions that have been able to gain most advantage from that network. New forms of cultural engagement between Birmingham (UK) and Chicago involve multiple linkages between museums, theaters, art galleries, and universities, utilizing long-standing "Sister-City" relationships. Businesses also take the lead in establishing networks: Santander Bank created Santander Global Universities Division to support higher education as "a means of contributing to the development and prosperity of society." There are now 1,000 university members in 17 countries and the bank has funded research, mobility, and scholarships. International associations have also facilitated global networks to pool resources, address pressing challenges, and contribute to the development of societies. The UNITWIN Networks and UNESCO Chairs—a program now involving 650 institutions in 24 countries—"serve as think tanks and bridge builders between academia, civil society, local communities, research, and policy-making."

MULTIPLE THEMES

Institutions coalesce and cooperate in global networks across multiple themes to exchange information and good practice, benchmark their activities, create new knowledge through research and joint-degree programs, facilitate mobility of staff and students, optimize resources and increase capacity, and promote and advocate services and values. Thematic networks include UNICA (a network of 46 universities in 35 capital cities of Europe), UArctic (a cooperative network of universities, colleges, research institutes, and other organizations from 10 countries concerned with education and research in and about the north), UASNet (a network of universities of applied science from 9 countries represented by their national rectors' conferences) and the Asian Association of Open Universities focusing on distance learning. Shared values also drive global networks. With 320 institutional members in 72 countries, the Talloires Network is committed to strengthening the civic roles and social responsibilities of higher education; the International Sustainable Campus Network with 67 member institutions across five continents is committed to sustainability in campus operations and research and teaching; the global Scholars at Risk Network of institutions, academic associations, and associated networks advocates to protect academic freedom, institutional autonomy, and related higher education values.

SUSTAINABILITY

Some of today's global networks are new: some have lasted for decades; others have restructured, like the Oresund Network, and some have disappeared, like Scottish Knowledge, an e-learning consortium across 11 universities. Past experience offers some clue to sustainability—suggesting that where strategies either ignore or downplay cultural, political, or intellectual differences, failure will ensue—especially when the pursuit of new international connections is perceived to weaken national ties. A further lesson is that all partners must gain benefits from the network if trust, effort, and flow of institutional resources are to be maintained. Managing relationships respectfully and productively across international boundaries is likely to be a core competence for sustaining global networks.

MILTON O. OBAMBA

35. GLOBAL: THE DRAGON'S DEAL: SINO-AFRICAN COOPERATION IN EDUCATION

International Higher Education, Summer 2013, Number 72

China and Africa have a long tradition of bilateral cooperation. The establishment of the Forum on China-Africa Cooperation (FOCAC) in 2000 has dramatically revolutionized Sino-African cooperation. It is an intergovernmental agency established jointly by China and African countries to provide a plan for strengthening bilateral cooperations between China and 50 African member countries. The emergence of FOCAC can be more accurately interpreted as part of the increasing institutionalization and intensification of Sino-African relations, at a time of deepening multilateral interactions, although critiques have intensified simultaneously. Since the establishment of FOCAC, trade volumes have significantly increased from US$10 billion in 2000 to US$160 billion in 2112. Similarly, the levels of China's official development assistance to Africa have also increased significantly, rapidly rising from US$5 billion in 2006 to US$20 billion in 2012. In short, China's cooperation with Africa runs deep and straddles a vast spectrum of strategic, economic, and sociopolitical spheres. To focus on the development, character, and scope of Sino-African cooperation in the field of education, the article is based on an analysis of policy documents produced by the Chinese government and FOCAC. The aim is to contribute to a more systematic characterization of China's bilateral education cooperation with Africa.

HUMAN CAPACITY AND ACADEMIC MOBILITY

The earliest form of educational cooperation between China and Africa consisted of relatively small-scale and diffuse patterns of exchanges involving the outbound mobility of African students and inbound movement of Chinese teachers during the 1950s and 1960s. This pattern provided small numbers of Chinese government scholarships to African students. In the 1970s, short-term training programs in China were established for African professionals in various fields. The First FOCAC Action Plan (2000) reaffirmed China's commitment to increase the number of government scholarships and inbound Chinese teachers to Africa. Significantly, the Action Plan also established the African Human Resource Development Fund, to provide a more coordinated mechanism for training African professionals. Over the last decade,

G. Mihut et al. (Eds.), Understanding Higher Education Internationalization, 163–165.

the volumes of Chinese scholarships and professional capacity opportunities have continued to increase. Scholarships, for instance, have grown from 2,000 in 2003 to 6,000 per year in 2012. This recent upsurge in Chinese initiatives in Africa has raised concerns regarding the transparency of criteria applied to training opportunities across all the 50 countries in Africa. Considering the vastness and diversity of the African continent, China's approach of an undirected continent-wide cooperation has triggered criticism around China's priorities and effective development cooperation of that scale.

CAPACITY BUILDING

Both within and outside the FOCAC framework, infrastructure development support has remained a significant agenda within China's engagement with Africa, for many decades. The third FOCAC summit contained Beijing's pledge to build 100 rural schools in Africa, while the fourth summit provided the construction of 50 China-Africa friendship schools and providing research equipment to African researchers returning from China. Some of the flagship Chinese educational infrastructure projects in Africa include the Ethio-China Polytechnic in Addis Ababa and the University of Science and Technology in Malawi. China's spectacular infrastructure projects have been criticized as a way for permitting corruption and political patronage by the ruling African elite rather than as initiatives to deliver sustainable development for the populations. However, China's role in infrastructure funding is vital for Africa, since traditional Western donors no longer support such initiatives and African governments also face severe financial constraints.

ACADEMIC PARTNERSHIPS

Although mutual academic mobility has been a significant feature of Sino-African educational cooperation since the 1950s, there has been little opportunity for direct interinstitutional engagement. This is because Sino-African engagement is predominantly engineered through intergovernmental bureaucracies, without scope for the participation of nonstate stakeholders. Interinstitutional cooperation is therefore a relatively recent and groundbreaking development. The 2006 Beijing Action Plan provided the first attempt to create institutional-level collaboration through the establishment of Confucius Institutes, although these are also largely organized at the intergovernmental level—as part of China's global "soft power." The 20+20 cooperation program established 2009 is another significant initiative. This program entails the launch of structured one-to-one partnerships between 20 Chinese and 20 African tertiary education institutions, to promote capacity building and sustainable development.

SUSTAINABLE DEVELOPMENT COOPERATION

The Fourth and Fifth FOCAC Plans of Action issued in 2009 and 2012 both portray a radical shift in the character, scope, and discourse underlying the emerging trajectory of Sino-African engagement. These blueprints demonstrate the emergence of a distinctive and dominant discourse of knowledge, science and technology, and its linkages to sustainable development and poverty reduction in Africa. Under this remit, China pledged to provide 100 postdoctoral fellowships for Africans and conduct 100 joint-research demonstrations. Significantly, the guides established three serious programs that are particularly critical to the emerging Sino-African development paradigm. These include China-Africa Technology Partnership Program, China-Africa Research and Exchange Program, and the China-Africa Think Tank Forum. All these flagship cooperation programs are generally focused on joint research and providing a range of initiatives to strengthen the capacity of African countries for science and technology development, policymaking, management, and technology transfer. A new technical cooperation focuses on areas that are critically connected to people's livelihoods—including health-care, environment, agriculture, renewable energy, and water development.

This trajectory denotes a Chinese shift toward poverty reduction and sustainable development, as opposed to the traditional preoccupation with grand infrastructure funding. The Think Tanks Forum represents a new focus on providing the scientific backbone and gravitas, required to strengthen the knowledge-base and robustness of Sino-African cooperation in a complex world. However, China's growing dominance in Sino-Africa cooperation is widely questioned for reproducing new patterns of dependency.

CONCLUSION

Chinese assistance for education development in Africa has evolved over many decades and is currently quite diverse and institutionalized in its scope and architecture. More recently, there is a distinct and unprecedented shift toward strengthening science and technology capacity and learning how knowledge can be more directly applied to improve people's livelihoods in Africa. This obligation suggests that Chinese development assistance may be a good force in achieving the Millennium Development Goals in Africa. However, these potential gains can be severely threatened or eroded if China reproduces the same patterns of dependency associated with the contemporary North-South cooperation. The spheres of Sino-African development cooperation should be expanded to incorporate nonstate actors from both sides—in order to create sufficient capacity and synergies for implementing Sino-African development engagement.

HIEP PHAM

36. ASIA: PARTNERSHIP WITH RUSSIA FOR NEW, WORLD-CLASS UNIVERSITY

University World News, 4 May 2013, Issue 270

Vietnam is to invest some US$150 million to create a state-of-the-art university of technology in Hanoi. Russia is to be the academic sponsor, the Ministry of Education and Training announced. This is the latest in a series of partnerships forged with foreign governments and aimed at creating world-class universities. The project will have two steps. In the first phase, from now until 2016, a Russian training institute will be established as a unit of the 47-year-old Le Quy Don Technical University. From 2016, the institution's name will be changed to the Vietnamese Russian University of Technology. Russian involvement in the project includes providing textbooks and curricula, granting degrees, sending professors to Vietnam to deliver courses in Russian, and hosting Vietnamese students and faculty on internships and fellowships at top Russian universities. The official agreement is expected to be signed next month in Moscow, during a visit to Russia by Vietnam's Prime Minister Nguyen Tan Dung.

AMBITIOUS PROJECT

The new institution is part of an ambitious project launched in 2006, aimed at establishing excellent universities delivering education of international standards with support and sponsorship from the world's leading higher education countries. Within this framework, the Vietnamese German University was established in 2008 in Ho Chi Minh City, and the University of Science and Technology in Hanoi was created in 2009 in a partnership with the French government. Two other projects are also being negotiated, one in partnership with the Japanese government and the other with the United States. According to experts, the new Vietnamese Russian University of Technology should be well prepared to confront the challenges faced by its two antecedent institutions.

In a recent article the local Thanh Nien—The Youth—reported that the Vietnamese German University had had difficulties recruiting sufficient numbers of students. Currently it has only 527 students, some 250 of them graduate students, within eight majors. These numbers are far short of the university's target of reaching 5,000 students in 29 majors by 2020. Besides the shortage of students there is a

G. Mihut et al. (Eds.), Understanding Higher Education Internationalization, 167–169.

more serious dilemma: according to official data, the passing enrolment scores at the German university are much lower than those at Vietnam's leading universities. A similar problem has also occurred at the University of Science and Technology in Hanoi, where the student population is only around 400. For Professor Jurgen Mallon, president of the Vietnamese German University, the preference of Vietnamese students for economic-related fields is one reason for the institution's current difficulties.

Xenocentric behaviour among students and parents is another reason. "The best students in technology fields will choose study abroad with scholarships" instead of studying locally, Mallon told Thanh Nien in an interview. A recent report issued by the National Assembly's committee for culture, education, youth, and children also identified obstacles to achieving "excellent" universities, including lack of facilities, unsustainable financial subsidisation and—especially—a shortage of full-time, highly qualified academic staff. Both the Vietnamese German University and the University of Science and Technology in Hanoi mainly use part-time lecturers, some from local institutions and others from their foreign university partners.

ACTION TO TACKLE PROBLEMS

To overcome this challenge, the University of Science and Technology is planning to send around 400 PhD students in the sciences to study in France in the coming 10 years, with the expectation of recruiting them back to become tenured lecturers in the future. However, according to Professor Pierre Darriulat, a retired French astrophysicist who has spent more than a decade teaching physics in Hanoi, the plan to send young PhD students to France "has nothing to gain if there is no follow-up to make a good use of their skills and talents at home." If not, Darriulat told University World News, this would "only lead to a catastrophic brain drain."

Darriulat, who is a member of the University of Science and Technology international scientific board, believes that the top priority for foreign-partnered and Vietnamese universities with world-class aspirations should be to make proper use of young Vietnamese postdocs present in Vietnam as well as those in the diaspora, giving the younger generation a chance to play an active part in the renaissance of higher education. To make that happen, Darriulat suggested that universities should create a habilitation degree, in order to select university teachers of sufficient level. Institutions should also establish centres of excellence, support them, and secure reasonable wage levels, working conditions, autonomy, and academic freedom.

Granting an appropriate degree of autonomy—especially in terms of funding, human resources, governance, and curriculum development—to aspiring world-class universities has also been recommended by Roger Chao Jr, a PhD candidate at City University of Hong Kong, whose dissertation compares regionalisation and internationalisation processes in higher education in East Asian countries. "If Vietnam's government still wants to leapfrog its universities to world-class level, autonomy is prerequisite," Chao concluded.

ARD JONGSMA

37. EUROPE: WESTERN BALKAN NATIONS COLLABORATE ON HIGHER EDUCATION

University World News, 19 January 2013, Issue 255

Education authorities in the western Balkan countries are gearing up for the second regional ministerial meeting in May. The ministers set the agenda in March 2012, prioritising higher education. The folks on the academic workshop floor followed up with a massive event hosted by the European Commission in Dubrovnik in November 2012. They have now sent a ball the size of a sphere in the Brussels Atomium back to their ministers. It contains a hotchpotch of red hot issues, including graduate employability, evaluation mechanisms for institutions and administrations, transparency, assessment, brain drain, brain recruitment, the efficient use of resources, recognition, structured dialogue with society and industry, the development of doctoral studies, and managing resources and reforms.

The meetings are taking place in the framework of the EU-led Western Balkans Platform on Education and Training, which was launched on 7 March last year and also convened the first ministerial meeting with most of the next countries in line for accession to the European Union. The platform's aim is to assist the western Balkans with reform efforts in the area of education and training, and to increase regional cooperation. The countries involved are Albania, Bosnia and Herzegovina, Croatia, Macedonia, Kosovo, Montenegro, and Serbia. It is chaired by Director General of Education and Culture Jan Truszczynski.

PRIORITIES

Interestingly, the platform was not pre-destined to become a higher education action group. "At the March 2012 meeting, the European Commission asked the ministers to prioritise one section from the huge hat with education and training topics," said Helene Skikos, the European Commission policy officer who coordinates the meetings from the Education and Culture offices at Madou in Brussels. "They chose higher education and teacher training, but the commission said that they could only pick one." They chose higher education. Good for us higher education journalists, but a shame nonetheless. Teacher training in the region is a dead interesting field that could do with a bit of spring-cleaning.

G. Mihut et al. (Eds.), Understanding Higher Education Internationalization, 171–173.

It is odd by international standards, partly because the teaching profession is peculiarly politicised in countries such as Macedonia, but also because the monopoly of universities in teacher training has hampered (and continues to hamper) a great deal of development in a number of former Yugoslav countries. Now that the ministers have chosen higher education as their priority reform area, what can the European Commission do beyond what it has already done for 20 years, together with a host of other donors: supporting higher education reform in the region?

DIFFERENT

"There are several actors in the region," said Skikos. "We are different because the others can do light things but there is usually very little follow-up because of funds. Beyond education support projects, we have the prospect of enlargement and technical assistance programmes so there is good funding. "The countries themselves often choose to earmark this for large-scale investments in things such as infrastructure, but Serbia has requested money for education now, and so has Albania." This is interesting too, and we will follow up.

Serbia is the country in the region where reforms have been initiated at the grassroots level. It seems to be having success, with some tremendously creative universities such as Novi Sad driving local innovation with a zest that the government has wisely begun converting into interesting progress. With that it is beginning to compare quite favourably to countries that are considered more advanced, such as Croatia, which has been legislating left, right, and centre and building institutions as if they were real estate—but has faced persistent problems implementing all this legislation and empowering all these new institutions.

REGIONAL COOPERATION

One of the objectives of the platform is regional cooperation, and the European Commission will return to the ministers with double sets of recommendations. "On the four sub-themes of the last conference we will try to work regionally," said Skikos. "These were managing resources and reforms, research in higher education, qualifications and competences, and linking higher education with the world of work." "But we also had national workshops in the conference. If the countries want assistance on a national issue, they can request support through Taiex, the technical assistance and information exchange instrument managed by the Directorate General for [EU] Enlargement."

And what about the poor teachers? "We are working on that too, but we need information first," said Skikos, "so we have launched a study based on a model that was used in the Eastern Partnership countries [the non-candidate countries east of the European Union except Russia] and in winter 2013 we will have a large meeting on this topic." Expect an update on the Western Balkans Platform on Education and Training from University World News in May, after the next ministerial meeting.

JOSEPH STETAR AND MODI LI

38. GLOBAL: IS AMERICA'S 100,000 STRONG CHINA INITIATIVE ANAEMIC?

University World News, 21 November 2014, Issue 344

It has been five years since President Barack Obama announced a bold 2009 bilateral initiative with China to enhance cooperation and understanding. The project had a goal of having 100,000 students study in China between 2010 and 2014. The Chinese government joined in by pledging to support more than 20,000 scholarships for United States students for study in China. For the US, the stakes were high as the programme sought, in the words of former US Secretary of State Hillary Clinton, "to prepare the next generation of American experts on China who will be charged with managing the growing political, economic, and cultural ties between the United States and China." In a March 2014 Peking University address, Michelle Obama echoed a similar theme by highlighting the value of studying abroad. She stressed the value of social and cultural integration, pointing out that American students can play a vital role in fostering American foreign policy and the projection of their nation's soft power. In October, the American Councils for International Education announced that it was partnering with the 100,000 Strong Foundation in recognition that it is "vitally important for Americans to develop the linguistic and cultural competencies essential for engaging Chinese citizens across the professions and areas of mutual interest."

Given the potential impact of the 100,000 Strong Initiative, it is important to ask if it is maximising its potential. For Chinese universities, the possibility of having 100,000 Americans studying in their universities provides a unique opportunity to influence the development of future American leaders while further internationalising their campuses—an increasingly important metric in the drive to have several Chinese universities enter the most elite class of universities worldwide.

AMERICAN STUDENTS ON PERIPHERY OF CHINESE HE

In its 2013 report the Institute of International Education indicated that 26,686 US students studied in China in 2011. However, more than 20,000 of those students were engaged in shorter-term study abroad credit programmes or study tours where the opportunities for integration into a Chinese university are limited. Only 2,184, less than 10%, were enrolled in undergraduate or graduate degrees in Chinese

G. Mihut et al. (Eds.), Understanding Higher Education Internationalization, 175–177.

universities and many of those were in programmes where English, not Chinese, was the medium of instruction. In such programmes, sustained interaction with Chinese students is limited, while social integration with other American and English-speaking students is maximised.

April 2014 data provided by the Peking University, or PKU, Office of International Affairs provides a snapshot of the type of studies American students are undertaking in China. Of the 1,619 international students enrolled in PKU undergraduate degree programmes taught in Chinese, 56 are Americans. Of the 630 international students enrolled in graduate degree programmes where the medium of instruction is Chinese, only 37 are US citizens. Another 93 American citizens are enrolled in PKU degree programmes taught in English in such disciplines as management, government, and international studies. Still another 78 Americans are enrolled in formal but non-degree "Chinese as a Second Language" programmes. Hundreds, perhaps thousands, of American students are given lectures by PKU and American professors as part of short-term—for example, two weeks to a semester—programmes offered each year by American universities which, for the perceived status conferred, often refer to PKU as their base.

INTEGRATION OF AMERICAN STUDENTS

While the United States seeks to increase the number of Americans studying in China, concerns are being voiced by US academics regarding the integration of Chinese students into the fabric of American higher education and a stereotype is beginning to emerge. Increasingly, Chinese students are characterised as living together, eating Chinese food, speaking Chinese most of the day, studying together, watching Chinese television, and socialising almost exclusively with other Chinese and having few, if any, American friends.

Articles such as "Chinese students try to explain to American students why they don't party" and "Many foreign students are friendless in the US," illustrate the disconnect Chinese students experience with their American counterparts. It is a disconnect that could well engender more xenophobic behaviour by American students, if not for immigration laws that severely constrain opportunities for employment in the US by international students both while studying and after graduation.

VALID CONCERNS ABOUT THE INTEGRATION OF CHINESE
STUDENTS RAISES COROLLARY QUESTIONS

Are the experiences of US students in China similar to those of Chinese studying in the US? Are the approximately 20,000 short-term American students studying in China integrating themselves into the centre of Chinese universities and student cultures or are they observing from the periphery? An increasingly common characterisation of American students who come to China for short-term study is often expressed by their Chinese counterparts along the lines of "the Americans live almost exclusively with other Westerners, speak English all day, listen to a few lectures delivered in English by Chinese professors, visit the Great Wall, go clubbing, purchase a PKU sweatshirt and proudly proclaim they studied at PKU." The intra-group bonding experiences may be strong, but how are Americans integrating more fully into the fabric of Chinese higher education and culture? Should they even try? Does it really matter?

HOW TO STRENGTHEN THE 100,000 STRONG INITIATIVE?

That American students can gain from studying in China is not disputed; the question is how can the benefits of the 100,000 Strong Initiative be maximised? With Peking, Tsinghua, and other elite universities being fertile breeding grounds for future Chinese leaders it is hard to characterise an effort which results in only 93 American students enrolled in Chinese-medium degree programmes at PKU as being successful. More needs to be done to prepare and support American students who can score sufficiently on the HSK—the Chinese equivalent of TOEFL or Test of English as a Foreign Language—to gain admission and succeed in Chinese-medium degree programmes.

US government programmes, such as the Boren and Pickering fellowships, need to reconsider their requirement that holders must be matriculated at an accredited institution of higher education located within the United States. Would not the goals of the 100,000 Strong Initiative be better served if American students enrolled in degree programmes at Chinese universities were eligible for the fellowships?

If the 100,000 Strong Initiative is to achieve its lofty goals, it needs to encourage American students to move more fully towards the centre of Chinese higher education. And moving towards the centre means, in part, more students enrolled in Chinese-medium degree programmes. The elite Chinese universities are rapidly improving and we need to prepare a new generation of American students who can meet their Chinese counterparts at the centre of Chinese higher education and Chinese culture. The need for these two great countries to forge a better understanding bound with a Gordian knot of economic, political, educational, and cultural understandings can best be fostered by universities in both countries.

PART 7

INTERNATIONAL STUDENTS: RECRUITMENT, ACCESS, AND STUDENT CHOICE

INTRODUCTION

Students remain key actors in all aspects connected to internationalization. This section and the next discuss the relation between students and internationalization from two divergent perspectives: recruitment and access on one hand, and the experience of student mobility on the other hand.

The section begins with an article written by Karen MacGregor highlighting some of the possible directions for student mobility in the coming years. The predictions included in the article are drawn from a study published by the British Council, providing important statistics for issues around student recruitment and access to international education opportunities. The next article in this section, written by Rahul Choudaha, argues for the creation of research-driven strategies to attract international students to a more diverse set of campuses within the US. While traditionally, international students have sought out western institutions as their base of study, new destinations such as East Asia are emerging as major players in the mobility realm. Ryan Allen describes some of the strategies countries in the region pursue to attract international students.

Chinese students still comprise a large fraction of internationally mobile students overall. The next two articles further discuss the realities these students face. Patrick Boehler describes the practice of Chinese students seeking university opportunities abroad traveling to Hong Kong to undergo the Scholastic Assessment Test (SAT). The article provides further analysis on how this practice interacts with the gaokao, China's own standardized examination. Peter Bodycott and Ada Lai discuss the intricate role of Chinese parents in decisions about student study abroad.

Hiep Pham's piece offers an overview of the challenges faced by Vietnam in attracting international students, as well as some of the policies the country designed to counter these challenges. The article offers analysis relevant for other countries that are not situated at the center of the academic world. Focusing on Sweden, a context with different obstacles, Nic Mitchell addresses the shift in 2011 from a tuition free policy to a fee-based system for international students. Mitchell analyzes the fall in the number of international students after the enactment of this policy, as well as some attempts of the country to re-imagine itself as an attractive destination for international students. The last two articles in this section focus on India. Wesley Teller and Don Martin offer an overview on mobility trends associated with Indian students who study in the US. Their article lists some of the challenges these students face. Veena Bhalla and Krishnapratap Powar, in contrast, report on trends associated with the growing population of international students in India.

G. Mihut et al. (Eds.), Understanding Higher Education Internationalization, 181–182.

The articles in this section highlight a broad array of trends relevant to international student recruitment, including the importance of reputation, access and cost issues, as well as educational quality. National governments and universities have much to gain from attracting international students, and as such, attentiveness to student needs is crucial.

KAREN MACGREGOR

39. GLOBAL: GLOBAL POSTGRADUATE STUDENT MOBILITY TRENDS TO 2024

University World News, 10 October 2014, Issue 338

India will have by far the most tertiary students in the world in 2024—48 million against 37 million in China—but China will still be the largest source of mobile postgraduate students, sending 338,000 abroad, according to a just-published study by the British Council. Nigeria will have the world's strongest growth in outbound postgraduate mobility, at 8.3% a year. While China continues to dominate the mobile student market in absolute numbers, in 2024 India is expected to account for 54% of growth in inbound postgraduate students to the United States. In the United Kingdom, China is anticipated to account for 44% of growth in inbound postgraduates. "Nigeria, Saudi Arabia, Indonesia, and Pakistan will become key postgraduate markets by 2024, next to India and China," says the study authored by Zainab Malik, director of research for Education Intelligence in the British Council.

The report, *Postgraduate Student Mobility Trends to 2024,* was launched last Monday at an Education Intelligence research forum on the eve of the 28th Australian International Education Conference in Brisbane. It is based on research undertaken by the British Council and Oxford Economics from June to September 2014, examines trends in postgraduate mobility between key origin and destination markets, and forecasts student flows from 2012 to 2024. "Overall, India is expected to be the fastest growing source of international postgraduate students over the next decade, while China will continue to dominate in terms of absolute numbers, despite demographic trends," says the British Council in a release on the report. But other countries have other major sources for international postgraduates: "France is forecast to send the highest number of postgraduates to Canada while Indonesia will be the second largest supplier of postgraduate students to Japan in 2024 with the highest annual growth expected from Saudi Arabian students travelling to Japan at a rate of 12.4%.

DRIVERS OF CHANGE

The report notes that the "massification" of higher education and growth in undergraduate students is "helping propel a wave of students seeking additional qualifications beyond the first degree." The trend towards attaining even more

G. Mihut et al. (Eds.), Understanding Higher Education Internationalization, 183–186.

advanced qualifications is being fuelled not only by people eager for better job opportunities but also by governments striving to create more highly competent workforces. Also, universities need to attract talented postgraduate students, among other reasons because of the growing importance of research in determining funding and international ranking. "The talent pool is increasingly seen as an international one in which ranked universities across the world are competing for the best students." In most of eight leading countries studied recently for a Higher Education Funding Council for England report, "around a third of all higher education awards are postgraduate, ranging from a low of 24.7% in Spain to a high of 37.1% in Scotland. "The percentage of postgraduate research to total postgraduate awards was much more varied, ranging from 8.6% in Australia to 31.4% in Germany."

THE MODEL

The report builds on the forecasts of two previous British Council studies, *The Shape of Things to Come: Higher education global trends and emerging opportunities to 2020,* and *The Future of the World's Mobile Students to 2024.* Based on experience gained, a model was constructed to forecast international postgraduate mobility flows, based on demographic, education and economic data, and historic trends. Economic and demographic data provide a solid foundation for analysis, the report says. "However, with the natural unpredictability of human interaction, no mathematical formula can account for all circumstances and possibilities; other considerations come into play that will affect a population's capacity to fund overseas education.

The study forecasts bilateral postgraduate student flows to 2024 between six destination markets and 23 origin markets, based on analysis of markets of interest, potential fastest-growing origin and destination markets over the next decade, and data availability. The six destination markets are Australia, Canada, Germany, Japan, the United Kingdom, and the United States. The 23 "origin" markets are: Canada, China, France, Germany, Greece, India, Indonesia, Iran, Italy, Malaysia, Mexico, Nigeria, Pakistan, Poland, Republic of Korea, Russia, Saudi Arabia, Spain, Taiwan, Thailand, Turkey, United States, and Vietnam.

KEY FINDINGS

The report outlines a number of key forecasts. One is that demographic trends will have a major impact on future postgraduate mobility trends. Not only is China's tertiary-aged population set to decline substantially, but this is also the case for Taiwan, Korea, and Vietnam. "By contrast, the tertiary-aged population in Nigeria, India and Indonesia are expected to boom, which will have a positive effect on tertiary enrolment levels within these countries," the report points out.

Economies in the surveyed countries will remain strong, especially in Asia, and tertiary enrolment rates are also forecast to grow in nearly all of the 23 origin countries. "Given their strong projected demographics combined with strong tertiary enrolment rate growth, India and Indonesia are expected to have amongst the largest growth in tertiary enrolments to 2024," says the report. In the next decade, India will overtake China as the country with the highest number of tertiary students—more than 119 million. China will have the second largest population at 79 million, with demographic decline cutting 30 million from its 2012 tertiary-aged population. India will have the highest number of tertiary enrolments in 2024, at 48 million, followed by China (37 million), the United States (22 million), and Indonesia (11 million).

India and China will fuel growth in outbound postgraduates: "In aggregate, total outbound postgraduates are forecast to rise by 335,000 to 2024 within the 23 origin markets, with India and China accounting for 36% and 33% of the total growth respectively." Despite its declining young population, strong enrolment growth and high outbound mobility means that China will remain the largest source of international postgraduate students in 2024, with total outbound postgraduates numbering 338,000 compared to India's 209,000. India will have higher growth in postgraduate mobility than China, however: "The strongest annual average growth in outbound postgraduate mobility from 2012 to 2024 will occur in Nigeria (+8.3%), followed by India (+7.5%), Indonesia (+7.2%), Pakistan (+6.4%), and Saudi Arabia (+5.2%)," says the report. India's growth in mobile postgraduates will be driven by rapidly expanding tertiary enrolment, economic growth and expanding household incomes. "For destination markets, this is likely to be the real opportunity for inbound student growth over the next decade," says the report.

Student flows to the UK from India and Pakistan have dropped significantly in recent years, and with the two countries among the fastest growing sources of outbound postgraduate students, the UK is anticipated to lose market share of these students over the next decade. "Students from Pakistan are forecast to travel to Australia and Germany in greater numbers over the next decade and Indian students will choose the US as well as Australia as a preferred postgraduate study destination."

America will continue to be the world's most popular student destination, with an increase of 154,000 students expected, followed by the UK with growth of 83,000. The US will host 407,000 postgraduates, followed by the UK with 241,000, Germany with 113,000 inbound postgraduates and Australia with 112,000. Australia and Canada are predicted to have the highest annual average growth in inbound postgraduate mobility, at 4.1% each, with America at 4%. "In relative terms, the UK is expected to be the second-slowest growing destination, with annual average growth of 3.5% from 2012 to 2024, down from 4.1% from 2007 to 2012, only ahead of Japan." For the latter, growth will be only 1.6%.

CONCLUSION

Report author Zainab Malik commented that while the researchers realised China and India would dominate international postgraduate mobility, the high level of destination countries' dependence on the two was surprising. "Considering the numerous factors that can affect international student mobility, diversifying postgraduate recruitment strategies may not only help lessen that dependence but also broaden and deepen global skills and knowledge exchange." Countries should keep an eye on parts of the world showing strong growth in international mobility—Pakistan, Saudi Arabia, Nigeria, and Indonesia.

RAHUL CHOUDAHA

40. GLOBAL: INTERNATIONAL STUDENT ENROLLMENT: EVIDENCE-DRIVEN STRATEGIES

International Higher Education, Winter 2015, Number 79

Interest in recruiting international students is growing among many institutions, for reasons ranging from reputational to financial. However, strategies translating intent into action are often devoid of research and insights. This lack of thorough examination before designing strategies often results in inefficient, expensive, and unsustainable enrollment strategies. Consider the case of the United States, which is the world's leading destination for international students. However, these students are concentrated in a small number of institutions; only 200 out of nearly 4,500 American postsecondary institutions enroll approximately 70 percent of all international students. This concentration of students shows that most of the institutions outside these 200 would face significant difficulties in attracting international students. The situation is further accentuated by the issues of resource constraints, location disadvantages, and rankings. While these challenges are difficult, they are not insurmountable. Often, institutions underestimate the importance of research in facilitating the understanding of international student decision-making processes in informing their strategies. The key is to know more about international students throughout their enrollment—who they are, how they choose institution, and how are their experiences.

Every year, there are numerous updates from various sources on how the number of international students is changing; however, little is discussed about the specific drivers of change, or about how student needs, experiences, and profiles are shifting. Most importantly, there has been little focus on how these changes apply at the campus level. Some institutions make the mistake of extrapolating national or regional trends, which may or may not apply in the context of their campuses. In other cases, school allows anecdotal evidence and stereotypical views on international students' needs and behavior to drive the strategies. Finally, the strategy sometimes boils down to "outsourcing" to a third-party commission-based recruiter. All of these approaches to strategy formulation are not only likely to be misaligned with the institutional strengths, resources, and capacities, but they also may result in enrollment of an international student body lacking in the diversity and academic quality to which the institution aspires.

G. Mihut et al. (Eds.), Understanding Higher Education Internationalization, 187–189.

RESEARCH TO BRIDGE THE GAP

Institutions can better inform their strategies if each one intentionally assesses needs, behaviors, and profiles of international students in its unique context. While there is national data on student enrollment available, there has been little research available on applying it to campus contexts. For example, the number of undergraduate international students in the United States increased between 2008/2009 and 2012/2013, bringing issues, challenges, and complexities for enrollment management professionals. However, the research has not kept pace with this. A search of the keyword "international" in the Journal of College Student Retention: Research, Theory and Practice, which has been in publication for the last 15 years, yields only four articles.

A recent research *report—Bridging the Gap: Recruitment and Retention to Improve Student Experiences*—produced by World Educational Services and released by NAFSA, aimed at addressing this need. It investigated an increasingly important yet complex issue for practitioners in an evidence-driven manner (nafsa.org/retentionresearch). The report also illustrated the gap between students and institutions. For example, according to the report, international education professionals reported academic difficulties and inadequate English-language skills as the third and fourth most important reasons why international students may leave institutions, but they were not among the top five for students.

Likewise, an upcoming report from *World Education Services, Bridge the Digital Divide: Segmenting and Recruiting International Millennial Students,* shows a similar disconnect. Based on the segmentation framework of different types of international students, the report analyzes nearly 5,000 17-to-36-year-old international Millennial students' penchant for technology and the psychographic characteristics that fundamentally influence their information-seeking behavior. It shows that universities may be underutilizing technology and some of their other most important assets in recruiting international students. For example, more than two-fifths of the respondents (42%) stated that either one of the university network (community members)—including faculty, admission officers, current students, and alumni—had the largest influence on their application decisions. In contrast, only 11 percent of the respondents indicated that "educational consultants" had an impact. Another challenge is due to the limited national data on international students. The available data is not only outdated but also suffers from definitional issues, making it difficult to project forecasts for new source countries in the next three to five years. This is especially detrimental, as it takes several years of developing and building relationships to recruit international students from new source countries.

In my previous article in IHE, *Preparing for Emerging Markets,* I argued that instead of intentionally looking into key source countries to engage within the next several years, institutions are responding to short-term student demand, and are missing the opportunity to cultivate the best-fit opportunities (http://bit.ly/EmergingRecruit).

CONCLUSION

Expanding international student populations on university campuses while maintaining the goals of cost, quality, and diversity is a complex optimization problem. It requires assessment of institutional goals, priorities, and capacities; investigation of student needs, profiles, and experiences; and, finally, mapping institutional and individual needs through a comprehensive strategy.

In a post-recession environment, an increasing number of higher education institutions are interested in attracting the next wave of international students. However, institutions must recognize the complexity and volatility of international student decision-making processes, and should invest in developing evidence-driven enrollment strategies. The quick-fix international student enrollment strategies are neither informed nor sustainable. In sum, it is important to "zoom-out" to look into big picture megatrends, but then to "zoom-in" as well, to see the applicability and relevance of these trends at the institutional level.

RYAN M. ALLEN

41. ASIA: FAR EAST AIMS HIGH FOR INTERNATIONAL STUDENT NUMBERS

University World News, 23 March 2013, Issue 264

International education used to be dominated by Western countries. While the US and the UK are still the leaders in foreign student intake, East Asia is quickly becoming a major player in this sector. China, South Korea, Taiwan, and Japan have made huge investments in international education, with the aim of attracting more students from around the world. China has caught up developmentally in higher education internationalisation compared to its East Asian neighbours, and even surpassed them in many ways. This is connected to the government's long-term effort to modernise the education system.

As China has rapidly grown in economic importance, countries and institutions have looked for ways to engage educationally with its massive market. This is evident in the rise of joint Chinese-international satellite campuses. For South Korea, the key to re-branding as a trendy educational spot has stemmed from Hallyu or the "Korean Wave." The "Korean Wave" encompasses Korean music—k-pop—drama, and film. Many in the West may have only recently learned about the Korean Wave via the YouTube sensation Psy, but fans around the world have taken notice for years now, and especially in South East Asian countries. The Korean government and education institutions have looked to capitalise on this popularity, establishing Hallyu-centred programmes targeted at international students, such as the Catholic University of Korea's Hallyu Knowledge Centre.

In the case of Japan, the island nation's international cultural popularity grew decades before the Korean Wave. But while this positively affected international student intake and language learning, there has recently been a sense of growing insularity that could result in a drop in international students. Taiwan too has recently been pushing internationalisation of its higher education. Yet its people are still hesitant to open up to an inundation of mainland Chinese students and this has negatively affected its intake, since Chinese students have been fuelling the international student sector worldwide in recent decades.

BIG AMBITIONS

China, Japan, Korea, and Taiwan have all used an increasing international student intake as a way to counter an ever-dropping birth rate and to better internationalise

G. Mihut et al. (Eds.), Understanding Higher Education Internationalization, 191–192.

higher education systems. The following chart shows the numbers that China and its neighbours aspire to in terms of international student numbers. It also includes world totals of international students. Each country examined has set a goal of doubling (at least) its international student intake by 2020. While these goals are lofty, they reflect a growing trend in international student mobility.

In 2011, around 3.3 million students studied outside their home nation, according to a University World News report. This number is estimated to more than double by 2025, up to eight million students, if current trends continue, according to the report's author, Geoff Maslen. This bodes well for China's and its East Asian neighbours' bold aspirations and goals. While it is unclear how realistic these goals are, all four nations are investing heavily in this sector. And the result could affect the growth of international student numbers in the Western market, which could prove unsustainable in part due to competition from East Asia.

LANGUAGE

One important factor for the Western lead is English. Right now, English is the de facto language of academia and international education. This is a factor in East Asian tactics for recruiting international students. China, Japan, Korea, and Taiwan have all expanded or created all-English curricula in order to make their higher educational systems more desirable or even accessible to international students. The four nations understand that using English is crucial for their immediate recruitment goals. Yet this tactic is not sustainable and is less than ideal for these non-English-speaking societies. This explains why the countries have invested heavily in language teaching. China is making the biggest investment in this category, with its Confucius Institutes. These government-sponsored language (and culture to a lesser degree) institutes were founded in 2004 and have proliferated around the world. In less than a decade, more than 300 of the institutes have been established, with an ultimate goal of 1,000 being set up by 2020.

CONCLUSIONS

China is now leading East Asia in sheer numbers of international students due to its amazingly rapid growth since the mid-90s, but the other East Asian countries all seem to be using similar tactics to pursue their goals. Each country has lofty goals, is using English language programmes, and is heavily investing in local language teaching. The region's international education standing will only grow in the coming years.

PATRICK BOEHLER

42. CHINA: THOUSANDS TO HEAD TO HONG KONG FOR US EXAMINATIONS

University World News, 9 March 2013, Issue 262

In early May, thousands of teenagers will queue up at Hong Kong's prime concert venue, the Asia-World Expo, which hosts major Western pop acts such as Lady Gaga, Oasis, and Coldplay. Almost all of them will have travelled from mainland China—not to catch a glimpse of a music idol, but to take their best shot at entering an American college. Last year an estimated 40,000 mainland Chinese students travelled to Hong Kong to take the Scholastic Assessment Test, or SAT, a standardised college admissions examination run by the US College Board. Because the exam is not offered in China, students have to travel to Hong Kong, which as a semi-autonomous region of China has its own economic and political system, or even further to Singapore. This year's SAT exam is scheduled for 4 May in Hong Kong. Organising these trips, often well in advance, has become a lucrative business.

China's largest private education company, New Oriental Education—which has almost 18,000 teachers in 50 cities across China—is the largest operator of "SAT exam groups," organising trips to Hong Kong and to Singapore. It charges each student US$800-US$1,300 for a three- to five-day journey to either city. Students take the trip three times on average before they achieve their desired SAT score, said Pang Ran, a teacher from New Oriental's VIP service in Beijing. Parents will have already spent US$4,800–US$8,000 in teaching fees before sending their children for the exam, she said. A year of "VIP classes" with private tutors from New Oriental can cost up to US$23,000. That compares to an average annual income of US$6,500 in Shanghai and a national average income of US$4,300 among urban employees, according to figures released in January by the National Bureau of Statistics. "Many middle-class families in particular consider sending their children abroad for education a very good investment," Joshua Ka Ho Mok, a professor at the Hong Kong Institute of Education, told University World News.

FAST EXPANSION

The study tours are expanding fast. New Oriental organised its first SAT exam trip to Hong Kong for a dozen students from Shanghai in 2003. The company, listed on the New York Stock Exchange since 2006, now sends thousands of students from

G. Mihut et al. (Eds.), Understanding Higher Education Internationalization, 193–195.

all over China to the former British colony every year. While student numbers are stagnating in China's own saturated hubs of Beijing and Shanghai, the company said it expected its revenue to grow by over 40% in China's second- and third-tier cities, according to a stock exchange filing in January. In the quarter that ended on 28 February, its revenue will have grown by a third compared to the previous year. "We took nearly 500 students to Hong Kong in January, 100 more than last year," said Liu Jindi from the China Shan Shui Travel Agency, which organises some of the tours for New Oriental. The agency helps students with visa applications and picks them up in Hong Kong. "Only 40 students went to Singapore, which has a nicer test environment" but is more expensive. Other students travel to Taiwan and even Thailand, according to New Oriental's microblog.

The US College Board does not publish SAT participation data for China, but said in an emailed statement that "participation in the SAT and SAT Subject Tests is increasing significantly among students reporting an address in mainland China but who take the SAT elsewhere." One in four foreign students in the United States is from China, according to the annual Open Doors survey published by the Institute of International Education, making China the country's largest source of foreign students. Some 194,000 Chinese students studied at US universities in the 2011–2012 academic year, an increase of 23.1% from the previous year.

OPTING OUT OF THE GAOKAO

Those venturing abroad are still a tiny, privileged fraction of the 27.6 million students enrolled in undergraduate degree programmes across China, according to the latest figures by China's Ministry of Education. The number of high school students taking China's national university entrance exam, the gaokao, has been decreasing since it peaked at 10.5 million in 2008. Last year, 9.2 million high school graduates took the exam, 180,000 fewer than in 2011. Most students opting out of the gaokao are either going abroad or choosing a branch of a foreign university in China, said Mok, adding that the Chinese government is encouraging students to stray away from China's traditional tertiary education path. "The government thinks that the local universities will take a lot of time to expand."

Complex local regulation also makes it harder for the children of China's migrant population to take the gaokao outside their parents' province of origin. Urban students can get into the country's best universities with scores lower than rural gaokao exam takers, because of the current admission preference for local students. The gaokao system is "a hard bone to chew," Minister of Education Yuan Guiren said at an education policy planning session in Beijing on 9 January, putting the exam's reform at the centre of his fourth year in office while also providing more incentives for students to study abroad.

The Hong Kong Examinations and Assessment Authority was not available to comment on whether mainland students strain its resources, but said in an emailed statement that it strives to cope with "the recent increase in mainland students for

SAT in Hong Kong," adding that it had no "plan at all to restrict non-local students." For Mok, more mainland students coming to Hong Kong could help it become an education hub. "If more come to Hong Kong, educational services could become another pillar of our economic drive."

PETER BODYCOTT AND ADA LAI

43. CHINA: THE ROLE OF CHINESE PARENTS IN DECISIONS ABOUT OVERSEAS STUDY

University World News, 5 August 2012, Issue 233

With the People's Republic of China's growth in economic prosperity and political influence, the number of students from China choosing to study overseas continues to increase. Of the 3.3 million internationally mobile students, China is the largest source country. In the 2009–2010 academic year, there were more than 127,628 students from China studying in the United States alone. The motivations for Chinese students seeking education abroad include a belief that it will open opportunities for increased wealth and migration.

Hong Kong, with its geographical proximity, high quality of competitively priced education, and shared Confucian cultural heritage, is an attractive option for students from mainland China. Like other Asian governments, Hong Kong is proactively pursuing international and Chinese students through a range of policy and educational initiatives. In 2009–2010 there were 9,320 non-local students pursuing full-time higher education degrees in Hong Kong, an increase of 200% from 2003–2004; and of these, most were students from China. Both the Hong Kong and the Chinese government see these students as a means of brain gain and future socio-political and economic stability and survival.

NEED TO UNDERSTAND PARENT AND STUDENT DECISIONS

To understand the international and cross-border movement of students from China, researchers, marketers, and recruiters have focused on the perspectives of these students. However, in traditional Confucian societies such as China, major decisions related to education and future employment are very much a family, if not a solely parental, affair. Yet we know little about how contemporary families in China make such decisions.

We studied Chinese higher education student perspectives at the level of personal and parent involvement in the decision to study across the border in Hong Kong. Our findings identified two main types of students: those who initiated the idea of studying in Hong Kong, and those whose parents initiated the idea. In the process of initiation and making decisions, Confucian cultural roles of child and parent were largely followed. The findings also suggest that although the factors that motivate

G. Mihut et al. (Eds.), Understanding Higher Education Internationalization, 197–201.

students and parents to pursue trans-local or cross-border study may be different, all pay homage to Confucian ideals and in so doing ensure greater security for the family and family members.

The students were motivated by the employment and study opportunities offered by cross-border education, the personal experience of visiting the country, the influence of family and friends, and stories by peers who had returned to give school talks. The influencing factors that "pushed" them to seek cross-border study are consistent with previous studies. The students viewed mainland Chinese higher education as limited educationally and felt that a degree from Hong Kong or from overseas generally would lead to enhanced language proficiency and the development of networks that would help secure higher paid employment in either China or Hong Kong. The exclusive nature of cross-border education increases the student's perceived educative and social status over students who elect to study for a local degree in mainland China. Added to this are perceptions that a local (Chinese) degree may not be as well recognised internationally as a degree obtained from a non-local institution.

Parents, on the other hand, considered the competition for university places, future employment prospects, and the longer-term prospects of immigration as the main motivating factors. The desire for the child to emigrate is consistent with Chinese parent decision-making when it comes to the choice of cross-border study.

STUDENTS HAVE A SAY, BUT PARENTS DECIDE

No matter who initiated the discussion about cross-border or trans-local study, there was evidence that students did feel they had a say in the decision-making process. This finding is consistent with another study that found that mainland Chinese parents listened more and involved their adolescent children more in family decisions. However, for the majority of students in this study (65%), the eventual decision on choice of country, programme and/or university was made by the parents. What the research does not provide is information about the actual family communication processes that occurred during such discussions; that is, the roles played and resources used by individual family members.

Such information is important to an understanding of the influence of culture and cultural change in Chinese family processes brought on by political and social change and increased economic prosperity. What the study demonstrates is the crucial role parents play in the decision to undertake cross-border higher education study. This role is shaped in part by their financial status, their personal education, and their Confucian culture. Those parents who were more supportive or open to their child's choices more often came from the wealthier city provinces and/or had personal experience of international study themselves. Although some parents initiated or took subtle control of the decision-making process, others overtly shaped and manipulated the aspirations of their child according to gender stereotypes and the longer-term needs and values of the family.

Such practices are consistent with Confucian traditions and the values associated with filial piety. Ninety-eight percent of students expressed dissatisfaction with aspects of the decision-making process and/or with the outcome. However, all either obligingly or somewhat reluctantly accepted the decision. For a small number of participants (15%), the parents were perceived by their child to totally ignore their preferences. This behaviour is consistent with Confucian roles and expectations of the child—respect for family authority and unquestioning obedience to parents.

From a Western perspective, many of the tactics used are consistent with an authoritarian approach to parenting in which parents make decisions and tell their children what to do. However, discussions with students revealed that they believed their parents were acting in their (adolescent child's) interests and their behaviour was consistent with being supportive and responsive to their needs. This is consistent with the tradition of authoritative parenting—parenting that provides rules and guidance with concern for the child but without being overbearing.

Our findings indicate that despite exerting considerable psychological and literal control over aspects of trans-local study decision-making, there was evidence that the cultural traditions were softening, with adolescent children having somewhat greater involvement in the decision-making process though not controlling much of it.

CHOOSING HONG KONG

The choice of Hong Kong as a trans-local study destination was like all decisions to undertake cross-border study; that is, a literal investment in the family's survival and future. In many ways it provided a safe alternative. Its shared Confucian Chinese heritage was seen as an advantage as were the British colonialists' influences on government infrastructure, including higher education. It provided a metaphoric bridge to the wider, more prosperous Western world and an escape from the rigidity and closed competitive exam-driven education system in China. The more open financial, education, and immigration systems combined with cost-effective, high-quality higher education and related opportunity were viewed as advantages over study in more distant study locales.

Changes in Hong Kong government immigration legislation are consistent with the factors that influence parent decision-making. The period of full-time study counts as time accrued toward achieving the seven-year mandatory period to achieve permanent residency. In addition, mainland Chinese students are permitted to remain in Hong Kong following graduation, to seek employment. An examination of mainland Chinese decision-making about cross-border or trans-local study in Hong Kong provides a unique insight into the influence of Confucianism and the family.

On the one hand, we see the adolescent child, often in contradiction to his or her own desires, adhering to the cultural values, expectations and choices of his or her parents. On the other hand, we see how parents use their culturally derived status and power to manipulate decisions in order to achieve what they believe is the very best education for their child and in so doing ensure their own and their family's longer-term status and security.

SOME CHALLENGES

We found that in Hong Kong, many students from China banded together in groups with other such students, with many of them sharing similar feelings of frustration with family decision-making and the translocation experience. The students reported that although these groups, often established by host institutions, acted as support, they also fuelled a level of resentment and an ongoing antagonism toward parents.

The perceived level of participation in family decision-making was found to have ongoing effects on student well-being and their approach and attitude toward their studies. With the support of mainland Chinese group and society members, a kind of subversive non-communicative planning had begun for future work and study. On the surface, the students continued to live their lives in a practical manner, to complete assignments diligently and to maintain a relatively positive attitude.

However, they admitted to suffering high levels of anxiety brought on by ongoing parental pressure, control over decisions and finances, and the fact that they were studying in a locale, a university or programme not of their choosing. The organisation and functioning of these ethnic enclaves and support groups that readily appear on university campuses is an area worthy of future study. For some students in this study, 15% (14), there was the added stress that the future security of their families hinged on their achieving certain specific outcomes and that the cost of funding their cross-border study was an ongoing issue for the family. The pressure to succeed in the shortest amount of time possible was a major concern for this group. This stress led to frequent bouts of sickness and depression. Differences in academic systems, while a reason stated for pursing trans-local study in Hong Kong, also resulted in challenges for students from China.

Language barriers were noted as a barrier to social inclusion. Hong Kong's higher education system is largely conducted in English, and the language of the street is a mix of English and Cantonese dialect as compared to Mandarin on the mainland. The students also experienced issues related to interacting with professors, levels of cultural difference, discrimination, and challenges of personal adjustment. These findings highlight the need for universities in Hong Kong, as elsewhere, to consider the effects of socio-cultural adjustment and acculturation associated with study across borders.

Although not the focus of our study, a myriad of emotions were reported by students, including feelings of isolation and even hostility to peers and family. These feelings were compounded by related decisions made in the home and were fuelled by involvement in organised groups and societies on campuses.

The expectations of parents, as indicated, are intense and can lead to some students imagining a lack of control of their own destiny, emotional distress and, at times, an inability to cope. Future studies need to examine the establishment, role and outcomes of organised ethnic societies on university campuses. In recognition of the cultural and social needs and goals of Chinese and all international students and their acculturation processes, there needs to be a closer study of the policies, strategies and services provided to support their inclusion, involvement and integration. Failure to do so will lead to ongoing confinement and isolation from the wider university community.

THE MAIN FINDING

The study's main finding, however, concerns the role of the family in mainland China in decision-making about study outside their home country. When combined, the family decision-making experience and cultural heritage as reflected in the decision-making process were found to inflict significant social and emotional impacts on students and their coping ability while studying trans-locally in Hong Kong. Such an impact is viewed as having the potential to affect the ongoing success or otherwise of the student's acculturation into the host culture. As such, universities that recruit and play host to increasing numbers of Chinese and international culturally diverse students need to develop comprehensive international student strategies.

The findings also indicate that traditional Confucian familial values are being somewhat relaxed, with adolescent children having a greater say in the decisions related to cross-border study. There is then a need to further understand the level of parental influence, and the levels of student (child) involvement, and to monitor the changing roles and influence of traditional familial values and ongoing influences throughout cross-border studies. Such culturally derived understandings should inform the development of host institution programme and support mechanisms that are more relevant to the student's unique experiences and problems, and stimulate campus community engagement in and enhancement of intercultural understanding and respect for the international student's cultural traditions.

HIEP PHAM

44. VIETNAM: STRUGGLING TO ATTRACT INTERNATIONAL STUDENTS

University World News, 18 December 2011, Issue 202

Vietnam is changing university enrolment requirements to make it easier for foreign students to study at its universities. The new rules are part of a strategic plan to internationalise universities, produced earlier this year, which also includes more courses delivered in English and inviting foreign scholars to Vietnam to conduct research. However, some academics doubt that the plan to attract more foreign students by issuing top-down government decrees, can be successful. In particular, without more courses taught in English attracting more international students will be an uphill struggle. "The success of the internationalisation in higher education plan does not depend only on the government's top-down aspirations, but also on suitable and dynamic bottom-up policies of institutions," said Dr. Hoang Nam Nhat, head of international relations at the University of Technology and Engineering, which is part of Vietnam National University in Hanoi.

Vietnam's Ministry of Education and Training issued a new decree in March that would allow university rectors to decide on their own criteria for enrolling international students from the admissions season that began in July. Previously, foreign students were required under Vietnamese law to take university entrance examinations in Vietnamese, making it difficult if not almost impossible for non-Vietnamese-speaking foreign students to apply.

In an interview in the official Tien Phong newspaper in February, before the regulation's formal release, Vice-minister of Education Bui Van Ga said: "International student enrolment is one of the criteria to rank [Vietnamese] universities. Attracting foreign students is also a way for Vietnam to promote Vietnam's education to the world." Ga was credited with a successful internationalisation plan at Danang University during his tenure as university president from 2005-10. Some 500 international students are now accepted annually at Danang, mostly from neighbouring China and Laos.

INTERNATIONAL STUDENTS STUDY VIETNAMESE

Although there is no official data on the figures, Vietnam National University (VNU), the Foreign Trade University, the National University of Economics, Hue University

G. Mihut et al. (Eds.), Understanding Higher Education Internationalization, 203–205.

and other leading institutions also enrol undergraduate and graduate international students every year. Most are from the Asia Pacific region including China, Japan, Korea, Australia, Laos, Cambodia, and Thailand, while a few come from the United States and Europe. "Most of them [international students] study Vietnamese studies, Vietnamese literature or South East Asian studies, which makes Vietnam the best destination [for them]," said Nhat of VNU. "In other disciplines such as science, engineering, economics, finance or law, it would be a big achievement if we could grant admission to one or two international students."

Leading institutions such as VNU-Hanoi and VNU-Ho Chi Minh, which have a tradition of hosting international students, run preparatory courses in Vietnamese for foreign students. However, "it's widely recognised that if they [universities] do not have programmes taught in English, they do have a challenge to enrol international students," Nhat said. Pham Truong Hoang, director of the international cooperation department at the National Economics University in Hanoi, told University World News that he would like the university to admit more foreign students. It currently has more than 50,000 students, about 500 from foreign countries, mainly Laos, Cambodia, China, and Mongolia. The university offers classes in English but does not have any full-time students from Europe or North America, although some come for month-long classes. According to Hoang, Vietnamese students would benefit from having full-time native English speakers on campus. "They will have more chances to speak in English, and it's a good opportunity for knowledge exchange," he said.

PROGRAMME TO ENROL MORE FOREIGN STUDENTS

The education and training ministry has been implementing the so-called Advanced Programme launched in 2008 with a budget of up to US$40 million for the first three years with the aim being to enrol around 3,000 foreign students by 2015. The programme will set up around 30 undergraduate courses in English, delivered by visiting professors from high-ranking universities and Vietnamese lecturers with PhDs from foreign institutions. Now in its third year, the programme has not been formally evaluated. However, observers suggest only 1% to 2% of the target enrolment has so far been achieved.

VNU-Hanoi, the country's largest institution, has been carrying out a similar project since 2008, setting up six undergraduate, three master's, and a PhD programme taught in English and duplicating the curricula of high-ranking partner institutions such as Tufts and Brown universities in the US, the National University of Singapore and the University of New South Wales in Australia. VNU-Hanoi has set a goal of full-time international students accounting for 3% of total admissions by 2015. But only one foreign student, from Korea, is enrolled in a course other than Vietnamese studies. He is studying on a bachelor of business administration course, an area in which Vietnam does not have an advantage over other countries. My Thu, a senior administrator in charge of academic affairs at VNU-Hanoi said:

"The case like the Korean freshman who enrolled in a course that is not sought-after [in Vietnam] is quite rare."

INTERNATIONAL NETWORKS TO ATTRACT STUDENTS

To attract more international students VNU-Hanoi has tried to take full advantage of membership of networks such as the Asian Universities Network (AUN) and BESETOHA, the forum of four major universities in East Asia including Beijing University, Seoul National University, Tokyo University, and Vietnam National University. "We have reached agreements with other member institutions about credit transfer in the BESETOHA forum and AUN," My Thu said. The university's leaders expect to receive more exchange students in the coming years and this programme will pave the way for the university to attract more full-time students in future. However, with 15 years of experience of lecturing at European universities, VNU's Hoang Nam Nhat is not upbeat about the likelihood of success in reaching the 3% goal. "Internationalisation is a global-level competition, and the most flexible player will be the winner. Bureaucracy still seems to remain the main obstacle for our higher education system," Nhat said.

NIC MITCHELL

45. SWEDEN: IS SWEDEN RECOVERING FROM THE INTERNATIONAL STUDENT CRASH?

University World News, 14 September 2013, Issue 287

Swedish universities are looking to build on the first signs of recovery in the international student market, following the collapse in overseas applications when "full-cost" tuition fees were introduced for non-European students in 2011. But they face a massive uphill task. Many feel more should be done to sweeten the attractiveness of Sweden's higher education, with improved scholarships, greater flexibility in the application process and liberalisation of the post-study work environment. The number of international applicants fell dramatically, from 132,000 in 2010 to 15,000 in 2011, as University World News reported two years ago. This was after students from outside the European Union and European Economic Area—EU-EEA—were told to find around €10,000 (US$13,300) a year to study for a bachelor or master's degree at a Swedish university—or apply for one of the very limited scholarships that the government introduced to try to soften the blow. At a stroke, for thousands of Indian, Pakistani, African, and Chinese students, the cost of fees for studying in Sweden became almost the same as going to a British or American university.

The result was a fall of 79% in newly enrolled non-EU students for the start of the 2011-12 academic year—a drop from 7,600 to just 1,600, according to the Higher Education in Sweden—2013 status report, published by the Swedish Higher Education Authority. Numbers did recover in 2012, but only by a meagre 7% and meant that just 1,700 "free-mover" students from outside the EU-EEA started degrees in Sweden last autumn.

HUGE IMPACT ON MASTER'S DEGREES

This has had a huge impact on Sweden's rapidly expanding two-year international master's degrees, which the country's universities had spent a decade developing in line with the Bologna system. With teaching in English, they hoped to satisfy growing local and global demand and were helping to make Swedish universities important international players. Universities were able to expand their postgraduate provision, particularly in economically important areas of science and engineering, by attracting considerable numbers of Pakistani, Chinese, and Indian students prior

G. Mihut et al. (Eds.), Understanding Higher Education Internationalization, 207–210.

to 2011. A large number were graduates from British universities, enticed by the Swedish offer of high quality, well-resourced postgraduate education and free tuition. Suddenly, the flow of suitably qualified overseas recruits was turned off.

And so institutions like Linköping (LiU) in south-east Sweden, Lund, and KTH Royal Institute of Technology in Stockholm have been forced to beef up their limited marketing resources and compete in the increasingly competitive global higher education market having lost one of their trump cards: free education. A spokesperson at KTH said: "We've boosted our public relations and marketing activities and are prioritising our strategic marketing efforts in regions like China, India, South East Asia, and Brazil."

Thankfully for Swedish universities, PhD students from outside Europe can still study for free. And, of course, Swedish and other EU-EEA students can still study for free at all levels. Sweden's fees for students from outside Europe followed a similar move by Denmark in 2006, when non-EU-EEA student numbers fell from 1,528 in 2005 to 995 in 2006—a 33% decline. Danish universities saw a brief recovery in 2008-09 but then numbers fell back again.

FOCUS ON QUALITY

So a fall in foreign student enrolments was fully expected in the wake of introducing tuition fees. Speaking to the Stockholm-based news outlet, The Local, in May last year, a spokesperson for the Swedish National Agency for Higher Education said: "In some ways, that was the point; not the reduction in itself, but as Education Minister Jan Björklund has explained, the fees are meant to focus on quality as the main attraction of studying in Sweden, rather than it being free."

State Secretary from the Swedish Ministry of Education and Research Peter Honeth went further in a University World News article in May this year, in which he was quoted saying: "It's satisfactory that so many fewer applied, this was exactly the effect we wanted. A large proportion of the applicants that had strained the system is now gone." And so they have. In their place has come a much smaller overall number of applications, but a higher percentage of eligible applicants in terms of English-language proficiency and relevant qualifications at bachelor level—and, slowly but surely, a willingness to pay.

MOVING IN THE RIGHT DIRECTION

Andreas Sandberg, from the Swedish Council for Higher Education, says the latest applications data shows signs of recovery. "In 2012 we had a 24% increase in the number of applicants compared to 2011, with an increase of about 20% when it came to applicants who had to pay. "In 2013, things continued to move in the right direction despite the total number of applicants remaining static. The key figure is the number of applicants that we could process and assess. Here, we saw an increase of 14% in international applicants—with fee-payers up 10%. "So compared to 2011, the increase is 30%—with paying applicants up by 27%. I think this shows that our communications have improved over the years and the applicants now understand the Swedish system better."

Another important change is in the way Swedish universities promote themselves abroad, with a new focus on attracting non-fee paying students from other EU-EEA countries to make up for some of the shortfall from Asia and Africa. Exchange students and those coming through strategic partnerships are also growing in importance as Swedish universities hold on to the value of the multicultural student experience on campus and the global impact of education and research. Full-time students from other EU countries were a minority in the international learning community before Sweden's new fees policy. But their number has been rising steadily—from 1,400 "free-movers" enrolling in 2010 to 2,300 last autumn. In the same period, new non-EU-EEA students fell from 7,600 to just 1,700 enrolling last autumn.

Germany is the top European country in terms of students being offered places again this year, with 624 admitted students. Greece is next with 451 being admitted, followed by the UK with 429 students offered a place this year. Sandberg stressed that the figures only show the country from which the students have their bachelor degree and not their citizenship. For example, of the 429 admitted students from Great Britain in 2013, 395 were not required to pay because they were EU-EEA citizens, while 34 had to pay.

Among the fee-paying countries, India is the top country for overseas applicants, with 2,085 applying and 634 offered a place; overtaking China, which had 1,483 applicants with 516 offered a place at Swedish universities. Critics of the international tuition fees policy complain that while the policy was supposed to be a bold show of confidence in the quality of Swedish higher education, it was implemented in a rush. On top of that, the fees are among the most expensive in the world and they come with a non-refundable SEK900 (US$138) application fee.

SCHOLARSHIPS

Lund University's Vice-chancellor Per Eriksson said that despite more fee-paying students applying, and paying their fees this year, more needs to be done. "Well-functioning and extensive scholarships are incredibly important if we are to get fee-paying students to our university. "We therefore hope that the government will make further investment in expanding the scholarships system and that we can continue to receive scholarships through donations from businesses, organisations, and private individuals."

Lund enrolled 298 new fee-paying master's students this year and its International Director Richard Stenelo said: "This brings [us] back up to 50% of the pre-fees numbers." At the Swedish University of Agricultural Sciences, which was badly hit by the loss of students from Africa and Asia when fees came in, the head of communications, Tina Zethraeus, said: "The post-study work environment for overseas students also needs to be liberalised, and more needs to be done to overcome the reluctance of Swedish companies to hire foreigners."

Swedish academics are also worried. Political scientist Shirin Ahlbäck Öberg, vice dean of the faculty of social sciences at Uppsala University, said: "We definitely want more international students. To many of us it is strange that our politicians on the one hand emphasise internationalisation as a main objective in all sorts of contexts, and at the same time "de-internationalised" higher education. "Charging tuition from non-European students might have been legitimate if the government had invested funds in scholarships that non-European students could apply for to finance studies in Sweden. But this has not been the case. "Moreover, people worry that charging tuition for non-European students might lower the threshold to institute tuition for Swedish students."

FUNDING ISN'T EVERYTHING

But funding isn't everything, says Niklas Tranaeus, marketing manager for Study in Sweden at the Swedish Institute. "Scholarships, although very important, are only part of the story. There are other issues which help to explain the sharp decline in numbers and which have been highlighted by universities. "To mention a few: the slow and rather cumbersome application process, the importance of allowing students to stay and look for work after they have completed their studies and the inflexible system which regulates how universities can charge fees. "The government is looking into several of these issues and we think that improvements in these areas will have a significant impact on the numbers of students from countries outside the EU that Swedish universities will be able to recruit in coming years." One thing for sure is that many in Swedish universities are eagerly counting how many international students have arrived and how many are likely to stay the course.

WESLEY TELLER AND DON MARTIN

46. INDIA: MOBILITY TRENDS

International Higher Education, Winter 2014, Number 74

After years of declines, the latest trends in international student enrollment in the United States from India show signs of a dramatic turnaround. In April 2013, the Council of Graduate Schools announced that applications from India to US graduate programs increased 20 percent, compared to a mere 1 percent increase worldwide. Similarly, the Education Testing Service reported that the Graduate Record Examination test volume in India for 2012 grew by approximately 30 percent compared to the prior year, which indicates a strong interest in graduate studies abroad. Most importantly, the American Embassy in New Delhi also confirmed that early data on student visa approvals showed an increase of a staggering 50 percent from October 2012, through early 2013 compared to the same period last year. These indicators of renewed growth are even more significant in the context of substantial declines in new enrollments from India over the past four years.

MOBILITY TRENDS

From 2009 to 2012, US enrollments from India decreased 17 percent at a graduate level and 16 percent at an undergraduate level—a downward spiral that was significantly underreported for a variety of reasons. For example, the total number of students from India studying in the United States held steady during this period (down just 3%). At the same time, Indian student participation in post-graduation internships—known as optional practical training—surged 80 percent over the same period, compared to a 28 percent increase worldwide. Participation in that training, particularly among science, technology, engineering, and mathematics students who can work up to 29 months, offset the declines and gave a skewed picture of the reality of student mobility trends from India.

In terms of fields of study among mobile students, the popular search engine (GradSchools.com) confirmed that engineering management and construction management are among the top three, most-popular searches by visitors from India. The related issues outlined below are expected to drive future mobility and should therefore act as a foundation for developing a long term view for student recruitment.

G. Mihut et al. (Eds.), Understanding Higher Education Internationalization, 211–213.

CAREERS AND JOB PROSPECTS

An astounding 54 percent of India's 1.2 billion people are under the age of 25. India's "demographic dividend," coupled with a rising middle class, is expected to propel demand for education and training and play a major role in the country's future economic development. However, India's economy for the fiscal year that ended in March 2013 grew by a relatively weak five percent—the slowest in a decade. Students and their families believe a US degree offers a competitive advantage for better jobs in an increasingly globalized job market.

Career prospects and return on investment are crucial factors to highlight when recruiting in India. Optional practical training, internships, and career services often help to justify a family's once-in-a-lifetime investment. For example, according to the National Science Foundation, doctoral students are particularly attracted by career prospects in the United States. Graduates from China, countries that were part of the former Soviet Union, and India reported distinctly low rates of returning to their home countries (3.7%, 4.1%, and 5.2%, respectively) compared with those from other foreign countries. In fact, Indian nationals were number one in the world for obtaining specialized US work visas known as the H-1B, securing an impressive 59 percent of the global total. Unfortunately, few institutions in the United States make a compelling argument about career prospects when returning to India with a US degree. Surprisingly, few success stories involve young graduates returning to launch their careers.

Student recruitment efforts in India should begin with helping students understand their academic and career goals and how a particular institution in the United States fulfills those needs. Institutions such as Tri-Valley, which was investigated for visa fraud by Immigration and Customs Enforcement in 2011, should not be allowed to dominate the discourse about education to employment prospects. US institutions can help their students overcome these challenges, by ensuring applicants can explain to a consular officer why and how they chose a particular school. Applicants who are unable to do so or are singularly focused on their career interests in the United States are unlikely to be granted a student visa. These prospective students would have to reapply for a visa or consider their options elsewhere.

ACCESS TO QUALITY HIGHER EDUCATION

Given limited access to quality education in India, a growing number of students turn to the United States, United Kingdom, Australia, and low-cost options closer to home. Part of the challenge is that local quality institutions, such as the Indian Institutes of Technology and Indian Institutes of Management, are highly competitive and unable to meet local demand. Due to a struggling quality assurance system, second-tier institutions are of widely varying standards. The world-class status of universities and colleges in the United States helps to justify the high cost of tuition.

When considering study-abroad destinations, rankings and perceptions of academic quality are the most important elements that prospective students in India and their families are evaluating when considering study-abroad destinations. In terms of recruitment, it is critical that US institutions highlight academic rigor and not "frills" such as new sports facilities, dining halls, and elaborate dorms, which add to the cost of education and have less to do with the quality of the academic experience or future employment prospects.

NEW FINANCING STRATEGIES

High inflation and the increasing cost of US tuition are major barriers to study abroad, particularly at the undergraduate level. Renuka Raja Rao, Country Coordinator for EducationUSA in India adds that "As the number one destination for study abroad, the question most students in India ask is not why study in the US, but how." The falling value of the Indian rupee, which dropped 22 percent from January 2009 to July 2013, is linked to the decline in student mobility to the United States. These dramatic shifts in currency value negatively impact a middle-class family's ability to invest in overseas education, even with partial scholarships. US institutions should not mistake recruitment opportunities in India as a means to overcome budget shortfalls. New financing strategies, such as creative academic partnerships and blended distance programs, are needed to overcome increasing costs for study abroad.

In the short term, participation in student recruitment fairs in India and an active social media presence can be highly effective outreach channels. Commercial service providers and recruitment agencies report substantial increases in the number of their students applying to US universities, yet little data are available related to visa approvals and other quality-control measures. US consular officers warn students that consultants sometimes "sell to students fake financial packages," which can lead to applicants being found permanently ineligible for visas, because they provided false information during an interview.

According to a survey by World Education Services, 46 percent of students from India selected "tuition and living costs" and 38 percent selected "financial aid opportunities" among their top three information needs. In contrast, the question that more and more US admissions officers ask is how to recruit self-funded undergraduate students without traveling to India, a question that illustrates financial pressures in the United States, but does little to reassure Indian families that US institutions have a genuine academic interest in recruiting talented students. Institutions with a compelling recruitment strategy, including scholarships or assistantships for science, technology, engineering, and mathematics fields, will be well-positioned to effectively recruit the next generation of leaders.

VEENA BHALLA AND KRISHNAPRATAP B. POWAR

47. INDIA: INTERNATIONAL STUDENTS
IN INDIAN UNIVERSITIES

International Higher Education, Winter 2015, Number 79

In the new millennium, Indian higher education has shown noteworthy growth, with the number of universities increasing from 266 in 2000–2001 to 700 in 2013–2014 and the student strength going up from 8.4 million to about 20 million. At the same time, the international student population has increased globally from 2.1 million in 2001 to 4.3 million in 2013. The growth in the number of international students in India, from about 7,000 in 2000–2001 to a little over 20,000 in 2012–2013, is, in comparison, anemic, and not commensurate with either the growth of the Indian higher education system or with the global growth in international student mobility.

DATA FROM THE ASSOCIATION OF INDIAN UNIVERSITIES

The Association of Indian Universities has been collecting information on international students in India since 1994. However, there has always been a significant shortfall in returns. Hence, the association, in its periodic reviews, has placed emphasis on evaluating trends in terms of percentages and has downplayed the absolute numbers. For the latest survey on international students, covering the academic year of 2012–2013 requests for information were sent out in August 2013 and the responses received from 121 universities till the end of May, 2014, were evaluated.

During the academic year 2012–2013, in the 121 institutions covered by the survey, 20,176 international students were pursuing diploma, degree, and research programs. A liberal guesstimate is that the figure could rise by 10–15 percent when returns from all institutions having international students are received. The number is small, compared to the 200,000 Indian students presently studying abroad, and minuscule, compared to the total Indian student population of 20 million.

WHERE STUDENTS ARE COMING FROM

Traditionally, the source for international students in India has largely been the countries from Asia and Africa, and this continues to be the case. However, over the last two decades there has been considerable change in the relative contributions of these two regions. Compared to the mid- 1990s the share of Asia has increased, in 2012–2013, from about 45 percent to 73 percent, while that of Africa declined from 48 percent to about 24 percent. Significantly, South Asia and the Gulf Region continue to be the most important providers, but new areas have emerged in Central Asia and East Asia. There is very low representation from the Americas, Europe, and Australasia. It can be argued that, in the case of India, international student mobility is more an example of regionalization than of internationalization.

PUBLIC VS. PRIVATE UNIVERSITIES

In 2012–2013 seven Indian universities had more than 1,000 students with the largest number, 2,742, coming from Manipal University—a private institution. Out of these universities, three are self-financing (private) universities, and the other four are public, affiliating-type universities. Significantly, in the case of the latter group the international students are largely in the affiliated self-financing colleges and not on the central campus. In India, most undergraduate and some postbaccalaureate colleges are affiliated to a public university.

A comparison of data for some leading universities, for 2008–2009 and 2012–2013, suggests that internationalization has not been accepted as a priority area by most of the public universities. On the other hand, the private universities are enrolling increasing numbers of international students. One is led to the conclusion that the public universities in India, with assured sources of government revenue, are not convinced about the importance of internationalization through international student mobility. The self-financing universities, under private management, see international students as an important revenue-source and actively pursue them through advertisements and even make use of agents.

2012–2013 DATA

As a part of this study, data from 28 university-level institutions falling in three regions were evaluated. These are Western India extending on the West Coast from Pune to Bengaluru (9 institutions); the North East from Amritsar to Kolkata (10 institutions); and the South East running parallel to the Eastern Coast from Bhubaneswar to Coimbatore (9 institutions). These respectively have 9,578, 4,478, and 2,812 international students. They are predominantly from Asia (71.23%) and Africa (24.25%) with minor contributions from the Americas (3.29%), Europe (0.85%) and Australasia (0.41%).

The Western region includes three large public universities (Pune, Mysore, Bangalore), each with many affiliated colleges covering diverse disciplines; a public professional university (Visveswaraya); four private deemed universities (Manipal, Symbiosis, Bharati Vidyapeeth, and Dr. D. Y. Patil); and a public deemed university specializing in arts and social science (Deccan College Post Graduate and Research Institute). These nine institutions together have almost half (9,578) of the number of international students (20,176) in 121 institutions. Pune city, with five institutions, alone has 4,298 students, which is one-fifth of all international students in India. This makes Pune the International Students' Capital of India.

CONCLUSION

Analyses of the data relating to the nine institutions lead to three important conclusions. Contrary to popular perception, as many as 40 percent of the international students are female. About 80 percent of the students come for undergraduate studies, about 18 percent for postgraduate studies, and approximately 2 percent for doctoral programs or research. Clearly there is a need to promote postgraduate programs abroad.

The choice of disciplines of the students is varied. About 30 percent of the students are in the liberal arts (arts, social sciences, science, and commerce). The remaining 70 percent of students are enrolled in professional education programs. The breakdown is health care (35%), engineering & technology (23%), management (9%), and law (about 3%). Clearly, India is now recognized in the developing world as a provider of professional education. What is required is the vigorous promotion of international student mobility.

PART 8

THE EXPERIENCE OF STUDENT MOBILITY

INTRODUCTION

Student mobility, as one of the most tangible and frequent manifestations of internationalization, is varied and accompanied by challenges and obstacles. This section includes a selection of articles that offer different national perspectives on the realities of student mobility.

The first article in this section, written by Bernd Wächter, engages critically with the stated imperative in the European context to increase student mobility. While supporting this policy priority, the author raises issues around brain drain, power relations between countries, and forced mobility. Next, Zha Qiang analyzes push factors associated with the migration of Chinese students abroad, including the decreasing age at which students choose to study abroad, and the pressures to increase the quality of educational opportunities in China in order to retain more students.

Immigration policies and regulations represent a significant challenge faced by international students. The next article in the section is written by Anita Gopal and discusses the case of Canada, a country that is attempting to streamline its immigration processes in order to the meet the needs of international students. The article also compares the immigration policies developed by Canada with those of the US and the UK. Related to immigration policies, another challenge faced by international students is that of employment. Bob Kinnaird discusses the exploitative realities faced by international students as temporary workers in Australia. The next article, written by Brendan O'Malley, discusses elements of recruitment trends and offers an interesting perspective on how the experience of students is considered by educational providers.

While the articles selected here offer key insights about the experience of international students, important aspects are missing. Relevant issues such as the quality of education and the commercialization of international education—highly influential on the experience of students—are addressed in other sections included in this book.

BERND WÄCHTER

48. EUROPE: QUESTIONING THE STUDENT MOBILITY IMPERATIVE

University World News, 14 March 2014, Issue 311

I am not going to make myself popular with this article, which will deal with some myths in the debate about international student mobility. In order not to be misunderstood, I wish to state at the outset that I have been happily mobile almost all of my life and that I am a supporter of international academic mobility, even though a slightly sceptical one. I cannot stress enough that there is no such thing as student mobility pure and simple. There are different forms of mobility—I call them "mobilities"—which are driven by very different forces and intentions.

First, there is degree mobility, for an entire study programme. Second, there is credit mobility, for a half-year or a year, like for example, in the Erasmus programme. Degree mobility is mainly "vertical," from countries of a quantitatively or qualitatively lower level of provision into those with a higher level. Credit mobility is, in the main, "horizontal," happening between countries with a similar quality in higher education. Credit mobility is driven by a desire for a linguistically and culturally different experience—or, as the sociologist Ulrich Teichler once called it, "learning from contrast." Degree mobility is fuelled by the attempt to get a better education than one could get at home. An international dimension is an accidental by-product in degree mobility, not something actively sought.

Perhaps these few remarks suffice to make it clear why one cannot make sweeping generalisations about "mobility." But this is exactly what is happening in the mobility discourse all the time.

RISING NUMBERS?

The literature and debate on student mobility make one believe that mobility is constantly on the rise. Well, it is and it isn't. In 1975, there were 800,000 students of foreign nationality studying outside their country of citizenship. By 2011, this number had grown to 4.3 million. Staggering growth? In absolute terms, yes. In relative terms, hardly. For total enrolment around the world went up by about the same factor. So we are still dealing with a very small minority of international enrolment (2%) globally. Incoming degree mobility into European countries is a bit higher, around 4%, but this hides dramatic differences between single countries. If we

G. Mihut et al. (Eds.), Understanding Higher Education Internationalization, 223–226.

excluded a small number of big "importers"—among them the United Kingdom, Germany and France with large numbers—the European record would be decidedly worse.

We are devoting much attention to a not at all sizeable phenomenon. It appears that the late psychologist Paul Watzlawick's rule of human perception applies to international mobility as well: if all you have is a nail, the world appears to be made up of hammers exclusively. On credit mobility, we have far fewer and less reliable quantitative data than on degree mobility. We know the numbers in funding programmes such as Erasmus, or some of their national counterparts. Is that all, or are there a lot of "free movers" around the world? It is impossible to answer this question. We safely know, though, that the numbers in credit mobility are far below those in degree mobility. This is telling—or irritating—because the (continental) European discourse is mostly on credit mobility. Once again, we seem to direct our analytical efforts to a "minority issue."

In Europe in particular, increasing mobility is a key political concern. This applies to national governments, but equally to the European Union as a whole or to the wider European Higher Education Area (EHEA or "Bologna area"). In their last meeting in 2011, the ministers of education of the Bologna signatory countries announced the target of a 20% share of outbound (degree plus credit) mobility, to be reached by 2020. The European Union followed suit, with exactly the same target. Other countries, including Germany and Austria, have outbound mobility targets of 50%. Mobility is all the rage. In political talk at least.

To be fair, some countries are already near or above the target. The most striking example is Cyprus, the majority of whose citizens study outside of the country (degree mobility). But this is "forced mobility." Cyprus does not yet have enough higher education provision to accommodate its citizens. Germany, a more "normal" case, comes close to the 20% target, though nowhere near the national 50% benchmark.

THE MOBILITY IMPERATIVE

Why are European governments so in love with mobility, and setting such high (and often unattainable) targets? There are, of course, a number of benefits of mobility, which I will turn to in a moment. But I believe I have discovered another reason, in the form of an anthropological assumption held by Europe's mobility policy-makers. This assumption reads roughly like this. Students in higher education are, by their nature, inclined to study abroad. If they do not realise their mobility intention, there can be only two reasons. Either there are insuperable barriers in their way—among them lack of funds, uncertainties about recognition on return, linguistic deficits—or they suffer from a slight mental disorder, which we might label mobility resistance.

Mobility has become an "imperative," to the extent that a Swedish student of medicine at the Karolinska Institute, which awards the Nobel prize in medicine, must feel guilty about not spending a semester or year at a much more "pedestrian" institution outside of Sweden. Now there are, of course, some perfectly legitimate benefits to be expected from student mobility. Let us look into them one by one.

First, there is the possibility of gains in academic quality, particularly in degree mobility from developing to developed higher education systems. Fine. Except that the flow might diminish if the developing countries build enough (good) capacity one day. Second, language learning. No doubt this is true, but languages can be (and are being) learned through non-academic forms of mobility as well. The same goes for intercultural learning. Intercultural awareness can be acquired through study abroad, though there are also reports of spectacular forms of breakdown of intercultural communication as a result of an unhappy study abroad experience. More important, however is the fact that intense intercultural encounters can happen in non-academic settings as well. A friend's daughter had, in the course of only three years, relationships with a Pole, a Norwegian, and a Portuguese. These were very intense intercultural experiences, no doubt, compared to common academic study. You could make a case for public support of transnational dating agencies on these grounds. "Erasmus romance" could be a good name for the new funding programme I have in mind.

EMPLOYABILITY

What other good reasons do we have to support international student mobility? Enhanced employability for graduates, particularly on the international labour market. This is no doubt true, although studies on the professional impact of study abroad have recently noted "declining returns" of mobility and, five years after graduation, hardly any differences in salary levels. But this could be due to the fact that study abroad has become much more of a "normal option" today than 30 years ago, thus losing its exceptionality. It is also often pointed out that the influx of foreign (graduate) students will keep European "knowledge industries" afloat in the face of soon worsening demographics. This is correct, but assumes that the foreign students stay in the host country's academic or wider knowledge systems. Some European countries are now openly advertising their mobility policies as a contribution to "skilled migration." A few years ago, this was still a political taboo in most of Europe. No doubt we all need "brain gains." But there cannot be gainers without losers. The politically motivated renaming of "brain drain" as "brain circulation" is nothing but a linguistic tranquiliser. But then, you cannot have your cake and eat it.

To repeat: I am a supporter of international student mobility. But mobility has become a mantra, and its supporters often argue like a religious group. We are faced with a "mobility imperative." This is not without risks. In order not to wake up one day and find we have thrown out the baby with the bathwater, we need a far more rational discourse—a discourse that is underpinned by evidence, in the guise of empirical facts and data and studies into the various effects of the different "mobilities."

I am not talking of "policy-based evidence," but of impartial inquiries. As examples, and as a first reading, I am recommending the Academic Cooperation Association's recent studies *Mapping Mobility in European Higher Education* (2011), *European and National Policies for Academic Mobility* (2012) and *Mobility Windows* (2013).

ZHA QIANG

49. CHINA: THE STUDY-ABROAD FEVER AMONG CHINESE STUDENTS

International Higher Education, Fall 2011, Number 69

With respect to Chinese higher education, two phenomena have been widely discussed recently. One is that the age of the Chinese students who choose to study abroad is increasingly becoming younger. Most Chinese students went abroad to study in graduate programs in the 1980s, then in undergraduate programs from the late 1990s, and now a rising proportion in high schools. It is estimated that high school students now account for half or even more of the Chinese students who choose to study abroad. Understandably, these high school students make this choice so that their access and transition to Western universities will be easier and smoother. The other notable phenomenon is the heightening call for improving and assuring the quality of higher education in China, evident in the emphasis laid in such milestone policy document as the National Outline for Medium and Long Term Educational Reform and Development (2010–2020) (or 2020 Blueprint), and most recently a national working conference on higher education quality control and assurance, held March 22–23, 2012 in Beijing. A discussion of these two phenomena together may shed some light on why more Chinese students choose to study abroad, even though access to higher education in China has been hugely expanded in recent years.

THE DETERIORATION OF CHINESE HIGHER EDUCATION QUALITY AS A FACTOR IN STUDY ABROAD TRENDS

While the world has been stunned by China's efficiency in moving to mass higher education on a short timeline, why are Chinese students increasingly drawn to studying abroad? Now the access to universities and colleges in China is much broader than a decade ago. In 2011, among participants in the national higher education entrance examination or gaokao (mostly fresh high school leavers), some 78 percent on average across the country had the chance to go to a university or a college. Yet an increasing proportion of Chinese high school students now choose Western universities instead.

Overall, Chinese higher education enrolment grew at an annual rate of 17 percent between 1998 and 2010, while the volume of Chinese students studying abroad increased by over 25 percent annually in the same time span. The number of Chinese

G. Mihut et al. (Eds.), Understanding Higher Education Internationalization, 227–230.

students studying in the US increased by 80 percent from 1999 to 2009. In 2011 the number of Chinese students who went to study abroad hit a record of 339,700. This figure is expected to rise to 550,000 to 600,000 by 2014. This group is also getting younger in age. In last five years, the number of Chinese students attending private high schools in the US grew by over 100 times, from 65 in 2006 to 6,725 in 2011. If this tendency continues, it may threaten student supply in Chinese higher education in the long run, combined with China's demographic change (a projected reduction of 40 million in the 18–22 age group in the population over the next decade). Since 2008, the population of gaokao entrants shrank by 1.4 million, for which these two factors are cited as being directly responsible. As a more immediate consequence, Chinese students are now estimated to contribute over $15 billion a year to the economies in their host countries (with $4.6 billion going to the US alone), equivalent to almost one half of China's total higher education appropriations in 2008. The fact that more and more Chinese households are becoming well-off could be a factor behind the scene, yet this single factor wouldn't be sufficient to explain the reasons behind an ever growing study-abroad fever among Chinese students and parents. Indeed, there are few cases like China, where the domestic higher education supply and the study-abroad volume are growing dramatically side by side.

In the rapid massification process, Chinese higher education suffered a serious decline in quality. This might be another fundamental reason responsible for the rising study-abroad fever. Ever since the huge expansion of Chinese higher education enrolment started in 1999, concerns and criticism over deteriorating quality in teaching and learning have been heard. After 2005, the enrolment expansion was slowed down considerably, while attention and resource were gradually shifted to addressing issues and problems associating with quality and equity. This process was fuelled by the famous question raised by the influential veteran scientist, Qian Xuesen (or Hsue-Shen Tsien): why have Chinese universities failed to engender innovative minds? Thus, with respect to higher education, the 2020 Blueprint, officially unveiled in July 2010, placed a focus on aspects improving and assuring quality, aiming to nurture creativeness among Chinese students and create a batch of "world class universities." The working conference on higher education quality explicitly announced a policy of stabilizing enrolment in Chinese universities (with future increases targeted at vocational education programs, professional graduate programs as well as private institutions), while pressing for immediate actions to address the higher education quality issues.

CHINA IS POURING EFFORTS AND RESOURCES INTO ENSURING
THE HIGHER EDUCATION QUALITY

Just before this working conference, the Chinese government unveiled two more important policy documents signaling concrete efforts and more resources to be brought in for this endeavor. One is the Higher Education Strategic Plan (promulgated by the Ministry of Education, as an implementation plan for the relevant parts in the

2020 Blueprint relating to higher education), which ranks assuring higher education quality as the top priority, through implementing a number of large scale projects organized around such tasks as university teacher and curricular development, gifted student creativity education, innovative professional program development, graduate program transformation, and the furtherance of Projects 985 and 211 that aim to create a batch of universities and disciplinary areas on Chinese soil with global competitiveness.

The other policy document, namely Opinions on Implementing the Program of Upgrading Innovative Capacity of Higher Education Institutions (released jointly by the Ministry of Education and the Ministry of Finance), launched the Project 2011(coded perhaps after Chinese leader Hu Jintao's remark at Tsinghua University's centennial ceremony in Spring 2011) that pushes for integrative collaborations among Chinese universities, between universities and research institutes, between universities and industry, and between universities and regional development needs, for the sake of drawing on and advancing Chinese universities' innovative capacity, in light of "nation developmental priorities and world-class standards." In a typical Chinese way, the State has put aside some funds to facilitate and support such integrations.

WILL THESE EFFORTS WORK TO EASE THE STUDY-ABROAD FEVER?

These policies may serve, to a certain extent, to retain some Chinese students. Yet, these policies and programs are largely derived from a human capital vision, which sees higher education as the deliberate (and utilitarian in the sense of State instrumentalism) investment in exchange for global competitiveness (on the part of State) and social status (on the part of individuals). This vision envisages Chinese universities as the State's educational and research arm for national development, and articulates knowledge production and transmission closely with a national development agenda. With massification of the Chinese system, this articulation demonstrates a vertical differentiation.

Now on a steep hierarchical structure, the top echelon universities are handsomely supported by the State, in exchange for their knowledge and student output to secure China's continuing success in a knowledge-based economy, while a majority of low tier institutions are left to survive on market forces. This approach, in turn, intensifies the tensions and competitions existing in contemporary Chinese society, where a kind of social Darwinism that stresses struggling for existence and the survival of the fittest has taken over and tends to dominating social life. University credentials are crucial to individuals in terms of gaining a competitive edge, and the perpetuating meritocratic tradition certainly has a big role in it. If one fails to get access to an upper tier university, one may risk losing the competition at the starting point. Naturally, when financial conditions permit, one would turn to the opportunity of studying abroad as an alternative strategy, believing an international degree would help raise one's competitiveness.

More recently, Chinese students start to be drawn to universities in Hong Kong, where the number of mainland undergraduate students registered a 129-fold increase over the last decade, from 36 in 1997 to 4,638 in 2010. Arguably, universities in Hong Kong take advantage of their liberal learning environment and international faculty.

Essentially, higher education plays a role not only in building human capital, but also in broadening human capability. Unless Chinese higher education provides an environment in which students are enabled to develop their full potential, and lead productive and creative lives in accord with their own needs and interests, there will always be many who seek an escape from the ever growing tensions and competitions. It seems an increasing number of people are now on their way to such an escape. With the growing size of this group, brain drain remains an issue for China, despite its economic success. Since China opened its door to the world in 1978, close to 2.3 million Chinese students and scholars went to study abroad. As of the end of 2011, over 1.4 million remained abroad.

ANITA GOPAL

50. CANADA, US AND UK: CANADA'S IMMIGRATION POLICIES TO ATTRACT INTERNATIONAL STUDENTS

University World News, 4 April 2014, Issue 314

Universities around the world engage in an intense competition to compete in the knowledge economy due to globalization. This situation has served as a catalyst for Canada to engage in immigration strategies and initiatives designed to attract and recruit international students. As also an urgent need for highly skilled individuals, since there is a concern that once baby boomers retire, there will be severe labor shortages, which will have negative implications for Canada's growth and nation building. Attracting and retaining international students is a way to boost Canada's economy, while promoting a welcoming international landscape. According to Citizenship and Immigration Canada, the government's priority is to seek highly skilled individuals (e.g., India, China) who are likely to succeed in Canada and to promote its economic growth, long-term prosperity, and global competitiveness. International students, who pursue their studies in Canada, are an ideal population because they would have already been integrated into Canadian society.

Recognizing that international students are vital to Canada's growth, the Citizenship and Immigration Canada has set out to transform Canada's immigration system as one that is faster, more flexible, and tailored to students' needs—a major distinguishing factor from other countries. Therefore, new immigration policies and programs have been specifically created to make it easier for international students to study, work, and become permanent residents in Canada, especially for graduate students. For instance, international students are permitted to work on and off campus, without a work permit to a maximum of 20 hours per week. They can also apply for a Post-Graduation Work Permit, a three-year open work permit, which enables students to work for any Canadian employer in any industry. International graduate students can apply to the Provincial Nomination Program for permanent residence in Canada—during their master's or doctoral program or upon completion of their degree.

Canadian universities are also interested in gaining its "market share" of the best and brightest international students in science and technology and acquiring a competitive advantage over countries such as the United States and the United Kingdom, which are major destination countries for international students. Moreover, international students generate a substantial amount of revenue to

G. Mihut et al. (Eds.), Understanding Higher Education Internationalization, 231–233.

Canada. According to a report conducted by the Department of Foreign Affairs and International Trade, in 2010, international students in Canada spent in excess of Can$7.7 billion on tuition, accommodation and discretionary spending (up from Can$6.5 billion in 2008). More than Can$6.9 billion of this revenue was generated by the 218,200 long-term international students in Canada. The report also indicated that the revenue from international student spending in Canada is greater than the Canadian export value of unwrought aluminum (Can$6 billion), or helicopters, airplanes, and spacecraft (Can$6.9 billion).

IMMIGRATION POLICIES IN THE UNITED STATES

After the 9/11 attacks, the United States' traditional open-door policy for international students was curtailed. Immigration policies have become more stringent due to the government's tightening of the border and strict visa requirements. As outlined in the *2013 International Student Mobility Trends* report, the United States has been slow to revisit their immigration and visa policies. However, it still remains the top choice for international students to study due to its prestigious universities' degree programs.

Unlike Canada's multiple pathways to work and become permanent residents, international students enrolled in academic programs in the United States holding F-1 student visas can only gain work experience by applying for Optional Practical Training, a temporary employment program that is related to a student's major area of study. Students can apply to this program after completing one academic year of their studies and could receive up to a total of 12 months of practical training, either before and/or after completing their program. Students in fields such as science, technology, engineering, and mathematics are entitled to a 17-month extension. If students are eligible to change their student status (F-1 visa status), they must apply for an H-1B visa (a nonimmigrant temporary working visa), which allows the holder to work in the United States for up to six years. However, the student must first have a job offer and an employer who is willing to file a "petition" or request with the Immigration and Naturalization Services.

CHANGES IN THE UNITED KINGDOM

Recent government policies in the United Kingdom have imposed tighter international student visa restrictions—affecting entry requirements, services available to students during their studies, and work options available to students after completing their program. According to *The Funding Environment for Universities* report, reforms to student immigration to the United Kingdom and to student visa applications will come into effect in the 2013/2014 academic year. This includes tougher, English-language skills requirements and an increase in the amount of credibility check interviews in terms of students' immigration history, education background, and financial support. The government has also discontinued the Post Study Work scheme. These changes make it more challenging for international students from non-European countries to qualify for a work permit to stay in the United Kingdom after graduation. Such policies do not promote permanent residence, postgraduate or labor retention, and have mainly impacted overseas recruitment of students from India, Pakistan, and Saudi Arabia.

FUTURE DIRECTIONS

While Canada is focusing on competing with the United States and the United Kingdom for its share of international students through its flexible immigration policies and pathways, higher education institutions have yet to come up with a strategy to manage highly skilled migration. Canadian universities are being urged by federal policies to double international student enrollment from 240,000 in 2011 to 450,000 by the year 2022. If Canada will compete for its share of international students, organizational mechanisms must be implemented to prepare for this shift in recruitment. Concurrently, Canadian higher education institutions must develop competitive programs and degrees to meet the needs of the target student population and provide access to relevant institutional resources (e.g., faculty, research funding, student services, library resources, etc.). Otherwise, how productive are immigration policies, if inadequate resources are available at Canadian universities, to support international students? As of yet, there are no official national strategies in place to prepare for and manage these changes.

It is clear that Canada has primarily focused on its own national interest of attracting international students to remedy its skilled labor shortages. As a result, it has not paid much attention to the problem of brain drain and the overarching consequences of luring highly talented students from developing nations to developed Western nations. For instance, the United Nations Development Program points out that brain drain has caused approximately 100,000 of the best and brightest Indian professionals to move to North America each year, which is estimated to be a $2 billion loss for India. As Canada continues to siphon intellectual capital from developing regions, it has neglected to think about its moral responsibility to these nations or how it could be harming their economic growth and well-being. Meanwhile, it is unclear how developing nations will recover the loss of their human capital.

BOB KINNAIRD

51. AUSTRALIA: FOREIGN STUDENTS EXPLOITED AS TEMPORARY WORKERS

University World News, 23 October 2015, Issue 387

More than 380,000 foreign students are currently enrolled in Australian education institutions, some 260,000 in the nation's universities. But recent media exposés have again revealed widespread exploitation and wage abuse of these students and other workers holding temporary visas, often by employers from the same ethnic background.

When Australia's international education industry started in the mid-1980s under a Labor government, overseas students had no work rights. The target market was foreign students whose families were wealthy enough that their fee-paying sons and daughters did not need to work in Australia to survive. They were also in university study only, not low-rent private vocational education colleges. Over the past 30 years, the international education policies of successive governments have changed dramatically and they now increasingly target overseas students from families with far less wealth and resources, especially in the vocational education sector.

Many students and their families go into debt to fund their Australian study and the students hope for a long-term employer-sponsored 457 temporary skilled visa or permanent residence visa—"the ultimate prize," said one independent report to the government. Many of the students have to work for much of their time here just to survive or to send money back home, and they are prepared to work for A$6 (US$4.3) an hour or less when the minimum level allowable is A$17. Some students even pay their employer for a job in order to secure a 457 employer sponsorship or employer certification of "work experience" that is required to obtain some visas.

EXPANDED WORK RIGHTS

Over time, federal governments have expanded work rights for overseas students and foreign graduates to give Australian international education providers a marketing advantage over competitor countries such as Canada, the UK, and US. What is being sold here is not the quality of the education offering but the right to work in Australia and, potentially, to remain. Those on student visas are now allowed to undertake 40 hours of paid work a fortnight during term time and unrestricted hours the rest of the year, although many exceed the 40-hour limit.

G. Mihut et al. (Eds.), Understanding Higher Education Internationalization, 235–238.

The most important recent development is the post-study work visa (a 485 visa) introduced by the former Labor government that now gives overseas graduates from higher education degree courses in any field of study unrestricted work rights in Australia for two to four years, depending on the qualification level.

Colleges in the vocational education sector are lobbying hard for the same post-study work visa and it is probably just a matter of time before they succeed. At present overseas vocational education graduates can only obtain a more restricted 485 visa that is limited to courses in occupations on the government's skill shortages list, and then only for 18 months. The Immigration Department says it expects 70% of eligible overseas student graduates to take up the post-study work visa. They will number a massive 200,000 by 2017–18, regardless of the unemployment levels among Australian graduates whose numbers are also set to grow rapidly, a result of policy-driven increased enrolments in the last five years or so.

All overseas students and graduates on 485 post-study work visas compete in the labour market with no legal obligation on employers to give preference to young Australians or to undertake labour market testing. Many overseas student graduates on 485 post-study work visas will end up competing in the lower end of the job market, if the UK experience with a similar programme is any guide. That means even more pressure on young Australians with low skills looking for entry-level jobs.

NO IMPACT ASSESSMENT

Incredibly, none of these extensions of work rights to overseas students or graduates, including the post-study work visa, has ever been based on any serious assessment of the impact on Australian residents in the job market. One government-commissioned review recommended introducing the post-study work visa yet completely ignored its potential labour market impact on local graduates and non-graduates.

The current federal government's response to the revelations of widespread work exploitation and wage abuse scandals has so far been underwhelming. This is strange given that the Trade Minister Andrew Robb has said the two "super-growth" industries for Australia's economic and jobs future are international education and tourism. Yet both are implicated in the exploitation scandals and a prudent government would do much more to secure their long-term future.

Employment Minister Senator Michaelia Cash has declared that there is no need for government regulation of the labour hire industry, one of the central players in this sordid scene. Cash has said that industry self-regulation was her preferred way. Yet when she was Assistant Immigration Minister, Cash had earlier announced that three months' "volunteer" or unpaid work by students on working-holiday visas would no longer qualify them for a second-year visa. That long-overdue correction was a reaction to an earlier exposé of mainly Asian working holiday-makers being exploited in Australia's fruit and vegetable industry.

Alongside the foreign worker exploitation issue, two related topics need urgent attention. The first is the impact on Australian workers, especially young people, who bear the brunt of cut-throat job competition from the burgeoning temporary visa-holder workforce. Between June 2007 and 2014, the number of overseas students and working-holiday visa holders in Australia increased by 50%, from 324,800 to 490,960. Expressed as a proportion of the 15–24 year-old labour force (in June 2007 vs 2014, latest figures available), the stock of working holiday-makers and overseas students grew from 16% to 24% of the total youth labour force in Australia. Most of these temporary visa-holders are young people themselves and they are competing in the entry-level job market.

UNEMPLOYMENT

The impact on young Australians is clear from many indicators: declining youth labour force participation rates; rising unemployment and under-employment among the young; increasing unemployment rates among new graduates; and many others. Competition from the growing temporary visa workforce is not the only factor responsible: increased participation rates in higher education and some welfare disincentives to work also contribute.

Yet successive governments have failed to commission any serious study of the labour market impacts of the recent explosive growth in the temporary visa workforce, even though this is bound to have major impacts, especially in times of sluggish employment growth, even before considering the characteristics of the additional labour supply.

The second issue is the role of government international education and visa policies that are feeding the growth in Australia of a vast under-class of temporary visa holders desperate for work and ripe for exploitation. These policies need to change or the already large under-class of temporary visa workers will grow even larger, especially if international education and tourism do become Australia's "super-growth" industries.

The main policy driver for governments, as always, is to grow the international education sector and increase overseas student numbers and the revenue they provide. Governments like this because it takes pressure off their education budgets, while business likes it because it means a larger domestic market for their products and services, increased labour supply and downward pressure on wages.

The policy changes needed are clear but unlikely, given the institutional resistance and vested interests. First, Australia's international education policies should not be targeting relatively poor overseas students for onshore course delivery in Australia. Onshore provision should be targeted more to high-yield/high fee courses and well-funded students, not to overseas students so poor they have to work 40 hours or more a fortnight just to stay alive. If this segment is to be targeted, more emphasis should be given to providing courses offshore. Second, the post-study 485 work visa for overseas student graduates needs a complete rethink. The timing is bad

237

enough, coming into operation just as the Australian economy is facing several years of below-trend growth, with no visa mechanism for protecting Australian graduates and job seekers.

The number of 485 visas is not limited in any way and will be determined simply by graduate demand for them. At the very least, the visa should be restricted to graduates in occupations on the skills shortage list.

BRENDAN O'MALLEY

52. AUSTRALIA: SCHOOLS ARE THE NEW BATTLEGROUND FOR FOREIGN STUDENTS

University World News, 15 July 2015, Issue 376

School education should be used as a recruiting ground for foreign students to secure higher education enrolments, according to a Victoria government paper published last Tuesday (State Government of Victoria, 2015). Increasing the capacity of schools to deliver the Victorian Certificate of Education, or VCE, to more international students around the world would ensure more foreign students applied to study in Victoria's universities, the discussion paper for the Future Industries Fund said. "An investment in the development of the Northern Hemisphere timetable represents a significant opportunity for our schools in delivering the VCE offshore, but also as a pathway for well-prepared students who have completed the VCE offshore to enter our universities," the paper said. "Creating more opportunities for students around the world to engage with our world-class schooling system benefits not only the schools who are delivering these programmes, but also feeds directly into further pathways into our higher education institutions." Currently the VCE is being delivered by more than 30 partners around the globe to thousands of students.

GO YOUNGER

At the same time there is the potential to build on the more than 5,000 full-paying international students enrolling in Victorian schools with "high transition rates into onshore higher education programmes." "The "go younger" trend, particularly from international students from China, means that increasingly parents are seeking to send their children abroad to study from a younger age, to help them build their English language skills, build friendships and networks, and acclimatise so that they are a step ahead of the competition when they are entering university," the paper says. "Victoria needs to be prepared to respond to this trend." The paper advocates increasing the number of places within the school system, ensuring high levels of English language provision and exploring new models of student accommodation as part of a strategy to realise "significant growth" in the school sector of the international student market.

G. Mihut et al. (Eds.), Understanding Higher Education Internationalization, 239–242.

International education has been Victoria's largest services export industry for more than a decade. It contributed A\$4.7 billion (US\$3.5 billion) to the Victorian economy last year, supporting an estimated 30,000 full-time equivalent jobs, mostly in Melbourne. But there is a growing opportunity to capitalise on Victoria's pioneering efforts in delivering higher education offshore and via partnerships, the increasing demand for "offshore" and online English language learning, and the growth of delivery models for higher education, for instance by "blended" online and offshore learning.

The government expects growing global demand for education services will see more than seven million higher education students studying abroad by 2020, with demand for international online education also rising. But Minister for Training and Skills Steve Herbert warned that Victoria's position in international education could not be taken for granted. "International education is a highly dynamic market with fast changing consumer preferences," he said.

RIVALS EMERGING

The paper identified ambitious growth targets among countries competing with Australia for foreign talent and emerging rivals. Canada aims to double the number of international students to 450,000 by 2022; the UK seeks to increase the number it attracts by 90,000 over the next three years; and New Zealand aims to double the value of its education exports over 15 years to around A\$10 billion per year. At the same time Malaysia is trying to attract 200,000 students by 2020; Taiwan is seeking to lure 130,000, twice the current amount, by 2022; China aims to attract 500,000 by 2020, compared to 300,000 now; and Germany is hoping to attract 350,000 international students by 2020.

Currently Victoria's two biggest markets are China and India, which are the source, respectively, of 28.1% and 16.4% of its international students. The minister's warning was echoed by an umbrella group for the business, academic, and community sectors, which said that increasingly aggressive competition is opening up worldwide in the sector.

The Committee for Melbourne, an independent umbrella group for more than 130 business, academic and community organisations, launched a strategy paper, also on Tuesday, identifying priorities for improving Melbourne's "brand and value proposition as a destination for international students." Committee for Melbourne CEO Kate Roffey said the international education sector is a key "economic driver and cultural connector." However, she said, there were signs of competition hotting up worldwide. "While we have always competed with markets like the UK and New Zealand, some very strong moves by the US to significantly increase the number of international students studying onshore should have us sitting up and taking notice," she said.

While Melbourne could offer world-class international education institutions, living costs are relatively high, the jobs market is tight and the accommodation market is not providing enough affordable options, she said. "So we have work to do to retain and build on our hard-earned status as one of the world's top international student destinations," Roffey said.

Current Victorian Government commitments to international education include marketing activities such as posting eight Education Service Managers in key locations across the globe, investing A\$12 million in inbound trade missions, and hosting the international education awards. Its attempts to provide a high-quality student experience include the setting up of A\$4 million International Student Welfare Grants, a three-year trial of a public transport ticket scheme for international students, the creating of more employability and work experience opportunities, including internships, and improved efforts to engage with international student alumni.

The Committee of Melbourne's strategy paper, *Melbourne—A Prosperous Future: World-leading international student city,* suggests there is a need to improve connections between international students and job opportunities and to address shortcomings in English language proficiency outcomes. It advocates various ways of improving students' experiences of living in Melbourne. These include finding more suitable and less costly accommodation for international students; giving them the same concessions on access to public transport enjoyed by domestic students; working harder to encourage international students' engagement with the local community; promoting Melbourne's "record as a safe city;" and providing more easily understood and readily accessible information for international students online and face to face.

POTENTIAL GROWTH MARKETS

According to the government paper, Indonesia, the Philippines, and Latin America offer potential growth markets from which Victorian universities could attract more international students. Currently international students make up around a third of the student body in universities in the state and around one in two international students are postgraduate students, many of them attracted to Victoria's position as "the research capital of Australia—particularly in health and the life sciences—and home to major research infrastructure such as the Australian Synchrotron," the paper says. "Offshore" and online delivery is increasingly providing an attractive pathway for students to move on to study "onshore" in Victoria. As part of these activities, Victorian universities are also collaborating with foreign partners to develop new teaching and research activity, such as dual degrees and licensed curriculum delivery, that will enable Victorian education and research to "reach right across the globe," the paper said. "In the next decade, models of education delivery, teaching and learning will continue to be transformed. How well Victorian institutions fully embrace and embed offshore and online delivery will be key success factors for the sustainability of the sector."

REFERENCE

State Government of Victoria. (2015). *Victoria's future industries*. Retrieved from
    http://yoursay.business.vic.gov.au/futureindustries/application/files/5114/3676/6619/
    DEDJTR_InternationalEducation_Discussion_Paper.pdf

PART 9

INTERNATIONALIZATION, FACULTY, AND STAFF

INTRODUCTION

Faculty and staff represent key actors in internationalization activities. Indeed, they serve as drivers of such activities and, increasingly, actively partake in mobility related programs and policy developments. This section includes primarily articles that discuss the intricate relationship between internationalization and faculty, but also briefly discusses the importance of staff for successful internationalization.

The first article in this section, written by Gerard Postiglione and Philip Altbach, makes the case that internationalizing faculty is crucial to increasing the quality of internationalization. The authors point towards decreased research collaboration between US faculty and faculty elsewhere, as well as the limited geographical dissemination of their research. Douglas Proctor tries to understand the ways in which internationalization has changed the academic profession using data from the 1992 and 2007 editions of the Changing Academic Profession survey. Further, as faculty mobility is one of the significant ways in which internationalization is shifting the academic profession, Yukiko Shimmi discusses the experience of visiting scholars and their relation to brain circulation. Karen Smith examines the increasing phenomena of flying faculty—where faculty commute long distances to reach their teaching destinations. The next article in this section, written by Tomoaki Wada, highlights the importance of encouraging the mobility of young Japanese researchers. The article also includes relevant references to the link between international mobility and the productivity of academic staff.

University staff, too, are affected by and a key part of internationalization. Nic Mitchell discusses the increased importance of staff mobility to increase the quality of the support provided to international activities. In a related article, Uwe Brandenburg uses the German case to emphasize the importance of training staff to better respond to internationalization realities on campuses.

Academics are increasingly asked to provide good quality education to an increasingly diverse group of students. However, the internationalization of faculty is not limited to appropriate teaching strategies and pedagogies, but includes aspects such as professional development and the quality of research. Similarly, university staff should optimally improve multiple areas of their practice via internationalization processes. Section nine includes key articles that speak to these issues.

G. Mihut et al. (Eds.), Understanding Higher Education Internationalization, 245.

GERARD A. POSTIGLIONE AND PHILIP G. ALTBACH

53. GLOBAL: PROFESSORS: THE KEY TO INTERNATIONALIZATION

International Higher Education, Fall 2013, Number 73

Universities continue to position their professoriates for internationalization. As the heartbeat of the university, the professoriate clearly has a special role in helping drive knowledge economies. This is particularly true in developing countries with aspirations for a closer integration into the global system. However, internationalization is a double edges sword for many countries. A university can hardly become world class without it. Yet, it wildly skews the balance of brain power in the direction of those few countries with world-class universities. In order to get the best out of globalization, the professoriate in all countries would need to increase its profiles and attitudes geared toward internationalization. At present, the willingness of the academic profession everywhere to deepen their international engagement appears stalled.

It would seem obvious that those who teach at a university, the academic staff, are the key to any academic institution's internationalization strategy. After all, the professors are the people who teach the classes at a branch campus, create the curricula for franchised programs, engage in collaborative research with overseas colleagues, welcome international students into their classrooms, publish in international journals, and the like. Indeed, without the full, active, and enthusiastic participation of the academics, internationalization efforts are doomed to fail.

Without the participation of the faculty, internationalization efforts often become highly controversial. Examples include Yale and Duke universities in the United States, where major international initiatives planned by the university president quickly became contentious on campus. Many of the New York University's faculty members have questioned some of that institution's global plans. There are many additional examples of faculty members refusing to take international assignments for the university, being unsympathetic to international students in their classes, and in general not "buying in" to the international missions expressed by many universities. Thus, the challenge is to ensure that the professoriate is "on board."

However, data from the two major international surveys of the professoriate reveal a puzzling array of indicators with respect to internationalization.

G. Mihut et al. (Eds.), Understanding Higher Education Internationalization, 247–249.

WHAT THE DATA SHOW

The two important international studies of the attitudes and values of the professoriate, one undertaken in 1992 by the Carnegie Foundation for the Advancement of Teaching and another known as the Survey of the Changing Academic Profession in 2007, have surveyed 14 and 19 academic systems, respectively.

These studies included a number of questions about the international commitments and interests of the faculty. In the United States, academic life is already known to be far more insular than in other parts of the globe. Most American academics earned all their degrees in the United States, including their highest degree. Less than one-third collaborate with foreign partners on research, even though a good number of them are foreign-born academics working at American universities; and they are the ones most likely to constitute the international collaborators. Only 28 percent of American academics have published in an academic journal outside of the United States, and barely 10 percent have published in a language other than English.

Yet, unlike universities in Japan or Korea, American universities are open to foreign born and foreign trained faculty. In fact, in most countries, nearly all academics are citizens of the country, and the percent of noncitizens are in the single digits—even in the United States with 9 percent. The percentages are somewhat higher in a few other English-speaking countries such as the United Kingdom (19% noncitizens), Canada (12% noncitizens), and Australia (12% noncitizens). The only other exceptions are small European countries like The Netherlands and Norway, where border crossing reflects the new reality of the European Union. The Hong Kong system is extraordinarily unique with 43 percent of academics being noncitizens, something that undoubtedly contributes to its having the highest concentration of globally ranked universities in one city.

Besides noncitizenship, doctoral study location also drives internationalization. In eight countries surveyed in 2007, more than 10 percent (and as many as 72%) of academics earned their doctorates in a different country than the one in which they are employed. Only a few countries were in that category in the 1992 survey. Exceptions include Japan and the United States, where most academics earn doctorates domestically.

It should be no surprise that academics nearly everywhere say that they emphasize international aspects in their teaching and research. Large numbers include international content in their courses, but not nearly as many have engaged in study or teaching abroad. In a good many countries, less than 10 percent have taught abroad. Only in places like Hong Kong or Australia have large numbers of academics taught elsewhere. Thus, academic attitudes toward internationalization are not a hindrance to a country's efforts to internationalize its universities, but it is the actual engagement of faculty that matters more.

Academics in developed countries often resist their universities' efforts to establish international campuses, and the professoriate in research universities of some developing countries often faces obstacles to becoming internationally wired due to state control. Surprisingly, the percent of academics collaborating internationally in research has dropped in many countries since the 1992 survey. The reasons are surprising and worthy of concern. Junior academics are collaborating less than their older counterparts, and everywhere junior academics are unlikely to have taught abroad. The fact is that the most productive academics, in terms of referred publications, are those with the most international collaboration, including copublication of articles and publishing in a foreign country. Again, the United States is the exception with less of a gap in research productivity, between those who do and do not collaborate internationally.

The international survey reveals what is perhaps one of major hurdles for internationalizing the professoriate—the economic driver of the university system. Unlike state or professor driven systems, market economies have high proportions of academics who view their universities as bureaucratically onerous. Moreover, academics in market economies are more likely to view their universities as being managed by administrators who are less than competent. This naturally works against the professoriate having a high level of institutional affiliation. The result means they are less likely to support the vision of their university leadership's about how to internationalize—including overseas campuses.

On the more positive side, those who publish in a foreign country journal increased since 1992 in all countries surveyed, except Australia, Japan, and the United States. Those who have published in a foreign language increased more in countries such as Mexico and Brazil (presumably in English). The relevance of this research is that the academic profession globally seems to be less internationally minded than might be expected—with inevitable implications for internationalization.

DOUGLAS PROCTOR

54. GLOBAL: FACULTY AND INTERNATIONAL ENGAGEMENT: HAS INTERNATIONALIZATION CHANGED ACADEMIC WORK?

International Higher Education, Special Issue 2015, Number 83

Scholars, practitioners, and professional bodies in internationalization education might not agree on what internationalization is, but they all concur that the involvement of faculty is crucial to its success. Certainly at an institutional level, with the adoption of comprehensive strategies for internationalization, faculty are now actively encouraged to reconsider their work in a new light. However, it remains unclear to what extent the internationalization of higher education has influenced or transformed the work undertaken by academic staff.

CHANGES TO THE ACADEMIC PROFESSION

Internationalization is considered to be one of the most transformative contemporary influences on higher education, its institutions, and communities, including teaching and research faculty. With faculty lying at the heart of the generation, application, and dissemination of knowledge, it is therefore reasonable to expect that internationalization has influenced the patterns of faculty work in higher education.

Over the last quarter century, two major international surveys of the academic profession—the 1992 Carnegie study and the 2007 Changing Academic Profession (CAP) survey—have sought to collect data on the attitudes of faculty toward their work, including some of its international dimensions. By virtue of methodology, these two studies have focused on aspects of internationalization that can be readily measured, such as patterns of faculty mobility. Where feasible, longitudinal comparisons have been sought between the two studies, although the relative lack of focus on international dimensions in the earlier Carnegie study has not facilitated this task.

Looking at the 2007 CAP survey alone, the principal findings in relation to the internationalization of the academy are based on a number of proxy indicators. These include personal characteristics, such as country of birth, current citizenship, and the place of origin of the respondent's highest degree level qualification. While analysis of these proxy indicators has enabled conclusions to be drawn in relation to the mobility and migration of faculty, as well as looking for possible patterns of generational change, the indicators provide little insight into faculty opinions about internationalization or their rationales for participating in international activities— let alone the possible effects of internationalization on academic work.

With over half of the available variables relating to academic mobility and migration, the CAP survey did, however, show a marked bias toward the international mobility of faculty as a vector for internationalization. This presupposes that the internationalization of faculty can be described by their mobility, and likewise that the cross-border movement of faculty is a significant component of their internationalization.

FACULTY RESPONSES TO INTERNATIONALIZATION

Moving beyond the international mobility of faculty (which has been a generally accepted practice in academia for centuries), various empirical studies have sought to confirm key drivers and barriers to faculty engagement with internationalization. Principally conducted in North America, these studies have outlined a range of motivating and resistance factors for faculty and have shown that institutional and disciplinary contexts are key determinants in shaping academic behavior in this area.

While senior leadership has been distinguished as an influencing factor on the internationalization of faculty (for example, in providing clarity for faculty on the nature of their involvement), many of the direct motivating factors for faculty to engage with the international dimensions of academic work relate to personal or intrinsic characteristics, such as prior personal or professional experience in an international context. Faculty appear to be motivated by rationales for internationalization focused on the "greater good," rather than by economic factors. Current involvement with international activities also leads to a greater perception of the importance and benefit of those activities.

Nevertheless, a wide range of individual resistance factors and obstacles to faculty international engagement has also been identified. Many of these can be framed in terms of institutional support for the international engagement of faculty, with barriers including the nature of academic employment policies, incentives for staff involvement, workload and time management issues, limited funding, lack of support personnel, and the availability of relevant professional development. Other resistance factors derive from personal rather than institutional barriers, such as fear of the future, a hesitancy to collaborate internationally, or an unwillingness to question the dominant international paradigms of a particular discipline for fear of censorship by colleagues.

However, the most common barrier to the active engagement of faculty with internationalization derives from the variable understandings and multiple definitions of internationalization which are in use. This fluidity in the ways in which individuals understand and make sense of internationalization, both among faculty and between faculty and their institutions, has been found to be a significant impediment to the international engagement of faculty.

Interestingly, but perhaps unsurprisingly, earlier studies into faculty engagement with internationalization have focused almost uniquely on the internationalization of teaching and learning, rather than on the internationalization of research or other aspects of academic work. Although growing sophistication in the analysis of citation data is now able to provide a measure of the changing exposure of faculty to international research collaboration, little macro-analysis of these data is currently available. Similarly, it is unclear how faculty engagement with the international aspects of research is connected to the internationalization of teaching and learning, and whether either aspect of internationalization has actually served to change academic work.

INTERNATIONALIZATION AND ACADEMIC WORK

Although analysis of research citation data may highlight changing patterns of faculty work in terms of international collaboration, earlier studies into faculty engagement with internationalization do not always shed new light on the ways in which internationalization has changed or influenced academic work. Furthermore, analysis of survey data on the academic profession suggests that the internationalization of higher education may have been more rhetoric than reality, given limited changes to demographic patterns and faculty behaviors over the 15 years between 1992 and 2007.

What is clear, however, is that the international strategies of many institutions now envisage a holistic or comprehensive approach to internationalization across all areas of activity. These strategies assume the active involvement of faculty, although it remains to be seen whether faculty are motivated to adjust their work in response, and whether particular levers are likely to influence this next phase of faculty internationalization.

YUKIKO SHIMMI

55. GLOBAL: INTERNATIONAL VISITING SCHOLARS: BRAIN-CIRCULATION AND INTERNATIONALIZATION

International Higher Education, Fall 2014, Number 77

International visiting scholars are scientists and professors who attend universities in other countries to engage temporarily in research or teaching, while also maintaining their affiliation and position at their home universities and returning after their visiting period ends. They usually have doctoral degrees or are professionally trained. Unlike international students, visiting scholars come and leave at their own schedules. The length of their visits varies, ranging from several months to a few years. While some visit by themselves, others travel with their family members. Some are junior academics, while others are senior professors. Their previous international academic experiences also may vary. Despite the fact that there are large numbers of visiting scholars globally, they have received only limited attention.

The application procedures and the fees to become visiting scholars vary between institutions, departments, and even between academic programs. Some universities offer programs that provide events, seminars, and other support for international visiting scholars, while other universities provide close to no services. International visiting scholars often rely on one or more funding sources, including their home and host institutions, governmental or private grants, fellowships, or scholarships; they sometimes also use their own savings to supplement their income, while living abroad. Due to the variances in scholars' backgrounds and situations, the experiences of international visiting scholars can be quite different for several ones.

Though some countries or individual fellowship programs report the number of visiting scholars, most countries do not report any information on the number of visiting scholars. In fact, UNESCO and the Organization for Economic Cooperation and Development do not report data, regarding the number of international scholars in their annual reports. As for the trend of international visiting scholars in the United States, it is useful to understand the differences and trends of the three categories of J-1 exchange visitor visas in the United States: professors and research scholars are each allowed to stay for six months to five years, and short-term scholars are allowed to stay for less than six months. While this broader group of scholars on J-1 visas does not precisely match the characteristics of the group I—studied with academic

G. Mihut et al. (Eds.), *Understanding Higher Education Internationalization, 255–257.*

afflictions, this data provides a trend of the group of people who largely overlaps the population of international visiting scholars.

The Institute of International Education reported in 2011 that there were 1,369 professors, 26,370 researchers, and 18,106 short-term scholars on a J-1 visa in 2009 in the United States. Chinese visiting scholars were the largest group in all three categories, and this number has dramatically increased recently. India also moderately increased numbers of scholars during the same time period. On the other hand, most other leading countries in sending J-1 scholars—including South Korea, Japan, Germany, Italy, France, Brazil, and Spain—decreased numbers of research scholars, while increasing the number of short-term scholars. Though there are some differences by country of origin, a trend seems to be that the number of short-term visits is increasing in relation to that of long-term visits.

FLEXIBILITY: OPPORTUNITIES OR CHALLENGES?

Since international visiting scholars usually do not have specific obligations at their host universities, they are very flexible regarding their activities during the visits. They can enjoy the opportunities at the host universities by utilizing their physical presence to use library resources, audit courses, participate in seminars, and interact with scholars and students. While many of them use their time to engage in their individual research, some might participate in collaborative research projects with scholars at the host universities. They can also be involved in teaching activities at the host universities or work on institutional relations between the home and host universities.

While scholars can decide to a great extent what activities they want to engage in during their visits, the lack of structure might be challenging to some of them. Scholars must take initiative in actively seeking out opportunities at host universities; otherwise, they likely will underutilize the opportunities. They can easily feel isolated from the community of the host university, unless they consciously try to interact with other scholars. Although there is institutional support for international visiting scholars to promote interactions with other scholars and students at some universities, these arrangements often rely on individual scholars. Finding opportunities for interaction can be especially challenging for scholars who have not had previous international academic experiences or existing networks with scholars at host universities, as well as for those who are not comfortable using the native language of the host country. This issue can be especially relevant for scholars in humanities and social sciences who do not work in labs that allow scholars to see other members on a daily basis.

BRAIN CIRCULATION AND INTERNATIONALIZATION

The importance of studying and serving this population can be discussed from the perspective of brain-circulation and internationalization. International visiting scholars who temporarily visit host countries, and then return to their home countries are considered one form of short-term brain circulation. Unlike brain drain or brain gain, brain circulation emphasizes the potential benefits for both the sending and receiving countries as a consequence of the continuous and circular moves of scholars. Previous studies have discussed the benefits of short-term brain circulation, such as the development of international scholarly networks, knowledge transfer and exchange, and the addition of human capital through return mobility. In order to fully realize the potential benefits from the circular moves of the international visiting scholars, further studies and policy arrangements on the population are crucial.

From the perspective of the internationalization of higher education, international visiting scholars are relevant in some key approaches in internationalizing universities. As participants in the international scholarly exchanges at universities, they can potentially stimulate international connections of scholars at universities in other countries. They might also engage in international research collaborations during their visits. In addition, their international experiences create important learning opportunities to broaden their professional and personal perspectives. As faculty members, their international academic experiences could influence university education through their instruction and curriculum, which directly or indirectly affects the education of their students. At universities that host international visiting scholars, they can be resources for internationalization by effectively integrating themselves in the community.

Although brain circulation and internationalization highlight potential uses of international visiting scholars, current institutional and national initiatives have not paid much attention to international scholar exchange—as compared with international student exchange. Although there are some governmental initiatives for international visiting scholars, such as Fulbright visiting scholar programs or the China Scholarship Council, many international visiting scholars move individually with little relevance to the institutional and national policies on the internationalization of higher education. The development of a more coordinated system of scholarly exchange through international visiting scholars will be meaningful—not only for the individual scholars but also for the institutions to enhance the research and teaching capacities, as well as the overall internationalization of the universities.

KAREN SMITH

56. GLOBAL: FLYING FACULTY TEACHING—WHO BENEFITS?

University World News, 11 March 2012, Issue 212

Stepping off the plane into the humidity of the hustle and bustle of Hong Kong, Dr. Cameron (not his real name) described his first teaching trip overseas: "Skyscrapers all over the place, washing hanging out 50 floors up, lots of stalls, the smells, the sights, the dynamism, the whole thing. I mean it's an experience in its own right—simple as that." Encounters such as these, with different cultures, environments, and people, are central to many academics' experiences of teaching overseas. Such experiences can offer strong stimuli for personal and professional development and, as one of my interviewees described, provide "variety in an otherwise quite dull existence."

Internationally mobile students have for a long time benefited from university education outside of their home country; increasingly, internationally mobile programmes of study and institutions define the global higher education landscape. This transnational higher education, where learners are situated in a different country to where their programmes are awarded, brings benefits for both those who export education and those who import it. For the exporters (predominantly the United States, Australia, and the UK), the rewards are monetary through increased fee income and an international presence; for the importers (predominantly Asia and the Middle East), transnational education offers higher education to places where demand outstrips supply, providing widened access to both education and qualifications that have currency in a globalised workplace. The importer countries are seeking to benefit from the exporter countries' expertise.

Transnational education models of teaching can vary significantly and include: online provision, local (to student) tutor-led delivery, and flying faculty. Flying faculty from the exporter country "fly in" to teach their overseas students in short, intensive blocks of less than a month before they "fly out" to resume normal duties at home.

CHALLENGES FOR FLYING FACULTY

Flying faculty teaching can be immensely challenging. These teachers are often taken outside of their comfort zones and find themselves having to operate in

G. Mihut et al. (Eds.), Understanding Higher Education Internationalization, 259–261.

classrooms and environments that are culturally very different from what they are used to. These differences manifest themselves in competing understandings of the role of higher education lecturers, and students' lack of familiarity with particular approaches to learning and teaching, such as group discussions or debates.

The relationships between flying faculty and their students; between the students themselves; and between the flying faculty and the local tutors can also be problematic and hard to determine in such a short space of time. There can be the added issue of working with students who do not have English as their first language; academics have to adapt the style, tone, and content of their materials in order to facilitate communication. Things are made all the more difficult when working in the students' first language through an interpreter. These challenges are undoubtedly faced by academics working with internationally mobile students at home; in a transnational setting they are writ large as the academic is the international traveller and the expectation is on him or her to adapt more to the majority culture.

The physical impact on flying faculty should also not be underestimated. These academics literally leave their long-haul flight and teach for long hours, spilling into the evenings and weekends, before returning home to tackle the backlog of the day job that does not stop while they are away. Although flying faculty often do report staying in nice hotels, they find themselves far away from family and having to deal with different climates, food, languages, and cultural practices—all of which can be exhausting. For most flying faculty, a lack of pre-departure support or development means that they did not know what to expect until they were confronted with it.

THERE ARE MANY BENEFITS TOO

Such a description of the experiences of flying faculty perhaps suggest that there is nothing beneficial about teaching overseas for academic staff. Yet my own work and other literature in this area provide very convincing narratives about the personal and professional benefits of spending time teaching outside of the home environment.

These benefits include opportunities for international experiences and institutional exposure that can be career enhancing; an increasingly globalised view of their discipline, which is replete with international examples; a questioning of pedagogical preconceptions that shape the way teaching, learning, and assessment are designed and delivered; an expanded worldview with greater awareness of where the internationally mobile students come from; and an understanding of different cultures and value systems. Flying faculty are undoubtedly the beneficiaries of transnational education in terms of both professional and personal development. But they are also the benefactors; not as deliverers of the "best from the West," but as the outward-facing, empathetic, cosmopolitan academics who draw on their overseas experiences in their interactions with students, be they situated at home or abroad. Travel, as they say, is the best form of education.

TOMOAKI WADA

57. JAPAN: YOUNG RESEARCHERS NEED MORE INTERNATIONAL EXPERIENCE

University World News, 20 July 2013, Issue 281

Since 1995, Japan has implemented Science and Technology (S&T) Basic Plans every five years. The current, Fourth S&T Basic Plan emphasises the promotion of basic research and the development of science and technology professionals, thus reinforcing the importance of graduate school education. The National Institute of Science and Technology Policy, or NISTEP, conducted a series of follow-up studies on the Third S&T Basic Plan before drafting the fourth plan. For one of these, NISTEP conducted a survey on the diversity of career paths and the international mobility of recent doctoral graduates in Japan. The survey collected career path information for all doctoral graduates of Japanese universities from 2002–2006. Data were collected from 414 universities and about 75,000 graduates. This was the first comprehensive survey in Japan on doctoral graduates from all universities in the country.

SOME FINDINGS

With regard to general trends among doctoral graduates of Japanese universities, 81% are Japanese and 19% foreign students. Among Japanese students, 16% mainly work in private companies. The number of foreign students has been increasing in recent years; in particular, the number of Chinese students is growing rapidly. Among those who completed doctoral courses between 2002 and 2006, approximately half assumed an R&D-related position immediately after graduation. Among graduates in physical sciences, engineering, and agricultural sciences, the percentage of those taking up an R&D-related role was particularly high. In physical sciences and agricultural sciences, the percentage of those who became postdoctoral fellows was also high, at around 30% each.

TOO FEW PHDS GO OVERSEAS

As for their locations immediately after completing the doctoral courses, 73% of Japanese graduates remained in Japan, while just 2% moved overseas. North America and Europe were the main overseas destinations. We believe that this figure is too small compared to other Asian countries. Most Japanese graduates who

G. Mihut et al. (Eds.), Understanding Higher Education Internationalization, 263–265.

relocated overseas became postdoctoral fellows in the US or Europe. About half of the Japanese postdoctoral fellows in the US returned to Japan after five years.

We surveyed 1,200 senior experts to ascertain why young researchers did not study or work abroad. The reasons given related to their career prospects on returning to Japan: low financial returns; concern about a dearth of good academic positions for postdoctoral fellows; and a lack of guaranteed positions for working individuals. There are few posts available to young researchers or postdoctoral fellows in Japanese universities. Moreover, private companies prefer recruiting graduates with a master degree rather than those with a doctorate. One reason for this tendency is that Japanese doctors studying at graduate schools sometimes do not have a broad perspective on science and technology, being adept only in their specialist fields.

INCREASED FUNDING

The Japanese government has been increasing its competitive research funding for universities during the five-year period, aiming to double the 2001 level. Its efforts have been successful to some extent, but the increase in competitive funding has decreased the proportion of research time invested by individual professors and other teachers.

A recent survey analysing the working hours of approximately 400 university researchers shows that research time has decreased from 47% to 36% on average. Another survey shows that it is becoming more difficult for university researchers to set aside three to four hours of uninterrupted research time. Consequently, some senior researchers are reluctant to send young researchers to laboratories abroad, due to concerns that the younger researchers' absence will unduly increase and intensify the workloads in their laboratories. When analysing the international mobility of doctoral graduates from Japan, about 90% of those who stayed in Japan or moved to Korea and China were home-country natives, while the remaining 10% were foreign nationals, who were mainly Japanese, Chinese, and South Korean.

On the other hand, almost all of those who moved to South East Asian or South Asian countries were home-country natives, while not many Japanese, Chinese, and South Korean graduates moved to these countries. The top 10 overseas destinations are China, the US, South Korea, Indonesia, Thailand, Bangladesh, Vietnam, Germany, Canada, and the UK. Of those who moved to Western countries, around 70%-80% were Japanese, which contrasts sharply with those moving to Asian countries. On graduating from Japanese universities, 36% of the Chinese students, who accounted for 39% of international graduates, remained in Japan. This figure is higher than the average for all international graduates. This is because the Chinese students are highly rated for their language and other abilities. In recent times, intense efforts have been made by some companies to recruit Chinese graduates. Of those who returned to China, more than 60% secured either full- or part-time positions at Chinese universities.

HIGHER PRODUCTIVITY THROUGH STUDY ABROAD

Another survey was conducted, on around 9,400 researchers from research organisations and universities in Japan. It shows that about 9% of them have worked in foreign countries as full-time researchers. They were more actively involved in research exchanges at their institutions, and their productivity in terms of papers in the past three years was superior to that of researchers without overseas work experience.

With regard to papers written in English and those co-authored with international researchers, those with overseas work experience produced more than researchers without such experience. Moreover, the ratio of the top 10% most cited papers and the number of times cited per international paper are double those of domestic papers produced by only Japanese researchers. The results show that Japanese universities should promote research cooperation by utilising a network of doctoral graduates. Moreover, they show that producing co-authored international papers leads to increased ranking and citations. The counterparts of international co-authored papers in Japan have changed drastically in comparison with 10 years ago, when researchers from Western countries were the main counterparts. China, Korea, and other Asian-Pacific countries have become more important in terms of counterparts of research cooperation for Japanese researchers.

We believe that more Japanese researchers should go to work abroad in foreign research institutes, and that more Japanese students should go to study at foreign universities. The government is trying to increase the budget to support students and researchers studying or working in foreign countries.

NIC MITCHELL

58. EUROPE: MORE FOCUS NEEDED ON HIGHER EDUCATION STAFF MOBILITY

University World News, 31 October 2014, Issue 341

Staff mobility needs to be given the same kind of attention as is paid to student mobility if universities' internationalisation strategies are to succeed, says a new report from the European University Association and the Academic Cooperation Association. The report, *Connecting Mobility Policies and Practice: Observations and recommendations on national and institutional developments in Europe* (Colucci, Ferencz, Gaebel, & Wachter, 2014), is largely based on the results of the Mobility Policy-Practice Connect, or MPPC, project supported by the European Commission's lifelong learning programme. This saw workshops, focus groups and university visits take place in three European countries in cooperation with the Lithuanian University Rectors' Conference, or LURK, the Conference of French University Presidents, or CPU, and the Hungarian Rectors' Conference, or MRK.

"CROSS-INSTITUTIONAL BUY-IN"

Among the many conclusions is that while higher education mobility in Europe is a long-standing political priority—often expressed through Erasmus, the European Credit Transfer System, and the Bologna Process—more needs to be done to encourage "cross-institutional buy-in for mobility objectives beyond the international office." In particular, staff mobility needs to be given "a stronger focus within strategies, whether for internationalisation, research, or teaching." "But this sentiment is not always shared across institutions," says Michael Gaebel, director of the higher education policy unit of the European University Association, or EUA, and one of the authors of Connecting Mobility Policies and Practice. "There can be assumption that everyone believes mobility is a good thing, but while some faculties support it, others don't see the value," he told University World News.

LACK OF STRATEGIC DIRECTION

Citing earlier studies, such as the EUA's *Closing the Gap report of the Mapping University Mobility of Staff and Students*, or MAUNIMO project (2010–2012), Gaebel said mobility was often driven by the particular interests of faculties,

G. Mihut et al. (Eds.), Understanding Higher Education Internationalization, 267–269.

departments, individual staff and students, or the latest funding opportunities which can suddenly change, and there can be a lack of strategic direction at the institutional and national levels.

The new paper, which Gaebel co-authored with Elizabeth Colucci, Irina Ferencz, and Bernd Wächter, argues that while practically all universities in Europe have internationalisation strategies, these need to spell out the benefits of mobility more clearly. Data collection must be improved and case studies shared, both within countries and between countries, for quality assurance and other strategic purposes. "Effective institutional strategies for mobility and internationalisation require fit-for-purpose and well-articulated structures," says the paper. This means looking beyond Erasmus credit mobility and fee-paying students and including joint degrees, exchanges through partnerships and staff mobility.

DIFFERENT TYPES OF STAFF MOBILITY

"Institutions are starting to pay more attention to different types of staff mobility, given the potential link to strategic internationalisation, enhancement of research and teaching and general professional development," says the report. But it recognises that academic staff is a very "heterogeneous category," and that the situation and status of staff differs greatly between higher education systems in Europe. "Project participants felt that institutions should better assess the potential of academic staff mobility for diverse purposes, such as research, teaching, preparing joint study programmes, language training, and inter-university development cooperation projects. "These different types of staff mobility would need to be considered in conjunction with strategic goals and further incentivised and supported. "Staff should be encouraged to take a proactive role in mobility programmes and opportunities, both by taking advantage of existing partnerships and initiatives but also by pioneering new ones," says the report. "Institutions should also consider the duration of staff mobility, which can vary from a few days—conference attendance, for example—to shorter-term teaching assignments, to longer mobility periods, such as sabbaticals or mobility in the framework of joint projects."

In both the French and Lithuanian workshops for the mobility project, it was felt that longer-term staff mobility while clearly a challenge from the point of view of resources—could deepen the teaching and research experience abroad and yield a wider institutional impact, both for the host and the home institution.

DON'T FORGET ADMINISTRATIVE STAFF

Staff mobility should not be restricted to academics, according to the paper, which said: "So far, the personnel of international relations offices seem to be the only type of mobile administrative staff, and in very limited numbers, due mostly to a lack of demand from other administrative staff categories and linguistic limitations." But there are examples of institutions starting to provide professional development opportunities abroad for all kinds of staff, with examples in Lithuania, France, and Spain of international staff training weeks—both sending staff abroad and receiving staff from partner universities. Gaebel admitted it was often easier for academic staff to be mobile—it is part of the accepted culture. "Sometimes you have to overcome suspicion that going abroad for a conference or exchange is work, and not a holiday, especially if it involves administrative staff."

The paper also noted that international staff are increasingly perceived as a key factor for internationalisation and quoted a recent EUA project on the internationalisation of doctoral education—FRINDOC—which reaffirmed that the number of international staff is one indicator of how institutions perform internationality. "However, in most European countries higher education institutions predominantly recruit domestic staff, due to financial and regulatory restrictions, as well as cultural and language issues. A forthcoming EUA study clearly indicates a widespread preference for hiring domestic academics with international experience."

NEXT STEPS

As for the next steps, Gaebel hopes to see staff mobility given a much higher profile in the Bologna ministerial conference being held in the Armenian capital, Yerevan, in May 2015. He also wants the European Commission to create a repository, or living archive, where reports such as the *Connecting Mobility Policies and Practice* paper can be stored in an accessible manner for future policy-makers and researchers. "The European higher community has, over the past two decades, undertaken a vast amount of work through European Union projects, which could make for a rather rich resource for both reflecting on the past and developing ideas the future. "It is pity that that the memory of this sits just with a few individuals," he said.

REFERENCE

Colucci, E., Ferencz, I., Gaebel, M., & Wachter, B. (2014). *Connecting mobility policies and practice: Observations and recommendations on national and institutional developments in Europe.* Brussels: European University Association. Retrieved from http://www.eua.be/Libraries/publications-homepagelist/EUA_MPPC_Mobility_policies_ Web.pdf?sfvrsn=4

UWE BRANDENBURG

59. GERMANY: THE VALUE OF ADMINISTRATIVE STAFF FOR INTERNATIONALIZATION

International Higher Education, Spring 2016, Number 85

Studies on internationalization usually focus on students and at best academics. But when you think about it: Who is the international student's first contact at the host university? It is usually not the professor and most likely not even the international office staff, but rather core administrative and service staff such as the porter or the housekeeper in the dormitory. For outbound students, it is not necessarily a professor with whom the students deal when organizing their studies abroad, but rather an administrator. Nevertheless, most strategies and analyses ignore administrative staff as a crucially relevant component (administrative staff is defined here as staff that is predominantly not engaged in academic-scientific work.) This trend is slowly changing. A good example is the *Erasmus Impact Study*, which explicitly investigated the role of administrative staff in mobility and internationalization. Administrative staff also gets more focus at the political level: The Bologna Follow Up Working Group stressed in its report that in future mobility programs, special efforts will be needed for administrative staff. If we concede this point, measuring the effectiveness of internationalization activities for this target group becomes pivotal.

In a large-scale study called InHoPe, which started in 2014 and was funded by the German Federal Ministry of Education and Research, we tackle this question and aim at analyzing the level of internationality of nonacademic staff and its effects on internationalization activities in German Higher Education Institutions (HEIs). The goal is to develop recommendations for the effective management of internationalization, with a focus on staff recruitment, structures, and development.

Tentative findings from the first two rounds of data collection and analysis indicate that this group forms an important information resource for an HEI, as well as its cultural basis, not the least because of its usually much longer affiliation at the institution than academics. More than 40 percent of the respondents were employed for more than 20 years, and three out of four were permanently employed. The results also show that the day-to-day work of administrative staff at HEIs has become increasingly international over the last decade: one third has monthly contact with international academics or students. However, it looks as if most staff are still inadequately equipped for such experiences: only one third spent at least

G. Mihut et al. (Eds.), Understanding Higher Education Internationalization, 271–273.

three months at a time abroad. The work environment, therefore, seems to develop quicker than staff development and selection processes.

THE UNTAPPED POTENTIAL OF SENSITIZING ADMINISTRATIVE STAFF TO INTERNATIONALIZATION

Not only does the majority of administrators at HEIs have no prior international experience, they also do not have much opportunities to improve this deficit during employment. 89 percent never participated in staff exchange, 87 percent never benefited from intercultural trainings, and 60 percent never even took a language course while working at the university. It is wrong to assume that administrators are not interested in such activities: two thirds would be interested in participating in an intercultural training or in staff mobility, and four out of five would be willing to take a language course. There are of course reasons for not engaging in these activities, in particular lack of time and an unclear perception of their direct benefit on the work to be performed. Administrators also very often lack information on how to participate in internationalization activities, especially staff mobility and intercultural trainings. The study also shows that such activities are not futile, but quite on the contrary have substantial effects.

FIRST INSIGHTS ON THE EFFECTS OF INTERNATIONALIZATION ON ADMINISTRATIVE STAFF

We conceptually assumed that experiences made in the context of internationalization activities influence the internationality of nonacademic staff on three levels: personality traits, attitudes and competences, and work environment. Firstly, we expect changes in personality traits that are relevant for coping with typical international and intercultural experiences in the workplace. Secondly, we assume that participation in internationalization activities influences individual attitudes, with an impact on the level of internationalization in the HEI. Thirdly, we aim to reveal under which conditions effects in the first two dimensions (traits and attitudes) alter work-related practices of nonacademic staff.

Our model of three levels (personality traits, attitudes and competences, work environment) seems to work. We find intercorrelations between all three levels, and the data seems to confirm that personality, in the end, strongly defines all results on the other two levels.

INTERNATIONALIZATION OF ADMINISTRATIVE STAFF THROUGH RECRUITMENT AND STAFF DEVELOPMENT

From the data, we can infer that, in general, recruiting staff with prior international experience has a stronger impact on internationality than developing the capacities of staff through internationalization activities (such as mobility or intercultural trainings). Recruiting is more relevant when seeking to increase the level of internationality of higher rank positions, and of staff at the international offices, while staff development is especially effective for lower rank positions, and for higher rank staff not focused primarily on internationalization. Staff recruitment is nevertheless pivotal for setting a framework for internationalization in any HEI. You need to use the right criteria to find the right people. Further, internationalization activities can have a strong impact on mindsets, but they do not have the same effect on everybody. They seem especially advisable for those without previous experience and on lower responsibility levels. In essence, both measures are necessary and quite complementary.

WHAT CAN BE LEARNED FOR PRACTICAL IMPLEMENTATION?

We need to improve targeting instruments and procedures for recruitment of internationally oriented nonacademic staff. On the staff development side, firstly, far more people want to participate in internationalization activities but lack information on how to proceed: thus more information is crucial. Also, many respondents state that they lack time. Internationalization must not "come on top on everything else." It must be integrated in the staff development strategy and regular work life, e.g. by inserting mobility windows into the annual feedback meetings between executives and employees, or by including regular time slots for preparation to trainings and courses, as well as mobility activities in staff contracts. Internationalization activities for the administrative staff (e.g. language and intercultural courses, participation in mobility programs, staff weeks) must be closely integrated into a differentiated and systematic framework of staff development. HEIs should base their programs on information on the predispositions, prior knowledge, and experiences of their administrative staff. Activities such as mobility programs should explicitly target nonacademic staff as a particular group. We need to allow for, and support, bottom-up initiatives of staff related to skill development activities.

This needs more coherent HR structures, such as a systematic follow-up of internationalization activities for administrative staff in order to stimulate organizational learning in the HEI, and integrating different internationalization activities into structured programs. The SprInt program at Technische Universität Dresden is a good example, where a certificate consists of a language course, an intercultural course, and an optional mobility stay. When it comes to internationalization today, non-academic staff can be described as a crucial group, whose performance can significantly improve with the right measures of targeted recruitment and well–planned HR development activities.

PART 10

INTERNATIONALIZATION OF GOVERNANCE

INTRODUCTION

Internationalization has not only become an important agenda item for higher education governance bodies, but has also started to steer their direction, composition, and activity. This section includes works that highlight the increasing importance of internationalization of governance.

Philip Altbach, Georgiana Mihut, and Jamil Salmi start this section with an article focused on international advisory councils. Their piece summarizes a recent study conducted by the Boston College Center for International Higher Education in collaboration with the World Bank. John Hudzik continues this section with an article discussing the importance of institutional leadership in steering the implementation of successful internationalization strategies. The article also offers a comprehensive overview of some of the strategy tools available to leaders to create a culture of internationalization on campus. The next article, written by Hans de Wit, considers the increasing importance of senior international officers for international education and the professionalization trends in this domain.

Internationalization has also shifted the practice and conceptions of higher education governance at a national and supranational level. The next two articles in this section discuss the increased importance of regional cooperation to increase competitiveness as well as representation. Maxim Khomyakov comments on the importance of increasing collaboration between universities in BRICS countries, while Roger Chao advances the idea of creating an ASEAN university, using the model of the European University Institute. This proposed initiative suggests the increasing importance of creating spaces for higher learning as agents of soft-diplomacy, where internationalization imperatives are built into the very fabric of the institution and its governance. The last article in this section discusses the increasingly prevalent practice of international hiring searches for senior level university governance positions. Foreign-born faculty, Mary Beth Marklein suggests, are increasingly sought for university president positions. As such, on occasion, emerging university leaders are themselves products of internationalization.

Together, the articles in this section highlight the importance that governance structures have on internationalization and the means through which supranational imperatives steer the direction of universities to center around international cooperation and representation. Finally, authors also address the specific modes through which internationalization shifts the activity of governance bodies.

G. Mihut et al. (Eds.), Understanding Higher Education Internationalization, 277.
© *2017 Sense Publishers. All rights reserved.*

PHILIP G. ALTBACH, GEORGIANA MIHUT AND JAMIL SALMI

60. GLOBAL: INTERNATIONAL ADVISORY COUNCILS: A NEW ASPECT OF INTERNATIONALIZATION

International Higher Education, Fall 2016, Number 87

The latest accoutrement of world-class universities, or those aspiring to world-class status, is an international advisory council (IAC). Heidelberg University, in Germany, has one headed by a former Oxford vice chancellor; the Higher School of Economics committee, in Moscow, is chaired by a Nobel Prize–winning American economist; and several prominent Saudi Arabian universities have committees composed of top-ranking academics and a few business executives. The launch of national excellence initiatives in various parts of the world—China, France, Germany, the Russian Federation, Spain, and South Korea, to mention only a few—has often been associated with the creation of such advisory boards at the institutional level. Indeed, some countries have mandated that the universities benefiting from added funds appoint such councils.

We define international advisory councils as advisory bodies formed primarily or exclusively by international members, external to the institutions, serving the upper levels of the administration and governance.

Globalization has created an environment where international expertise and linkages have become de rigueur for universities aspiring to world-class status. The idea is that universities must pursue the highest standards of research and, in some cases, teaching, and that international experience and expertise are very helpful to achieve these goals. IACs are seen as a way of obtaining relevant global knowledge about how to best organize and build top research-intensive universities. An IAC shows that the university has a cosmopolitan outlook, that it receives advice from top university leaders and scholars from world-class institutions, and that it can "benchmark" itself with the best international practices. Some feel that they need an IAC because their peer universities have them. Most want to take advantage of the prestige of the IAC members, and hope that those members will be informal ambassadors for their universities internationally.

IACS: WHAT THEY ARE AND HOW THEY WORK

Research we recently conducted sheds light on international advisory councils. IACs can be seen as a contribution to the internationalization of academic

G. Mihut et al. (Eds.), Understanding Higher Education Internationalization, 279–282.

governance, although in no case do councils have actually decision-making roles. Our research found most IACs with a membership between six and fourteen members. In order of frequency, IAC members are current or former high-level administrators (usually presidents, rectors, or vice-chancellors), higher education researchers or scholars in areas relevant to the university appointing then, individuals with a policy background, or industry representatives. The IAC landscape seems to be heavily dominated by men, from Western countries, and in general affiliated to prestigious institutions. Both open and fixed terms are prevalent among IACs. Some IAC members have had some relationship with the university before they are appointed—through social networks, having spoken at the institution, or other contacts.

Members agree to join IACs out of a sense of service and a desire to be helpful. They are sometimes attracted by the specific institution and their relationship to it, the country in which the university is located, or a specific field of specialization that interests them. Relating to their participation, members identified several themes they found valuable: learning opportunities, academic service, the chance to influence policy, and the relationships with other members of the council and colleagues at the university—among others.

Most IACs meet once or twice a year, sometimes with additional virtual meetings. Meetings usually are from one to three days in length—although at least one council meets for a week and asks members to give lectures on campus. Some councils pay members an honorarium, but most seem not to, paying only all travel expenses of council members.

Meetings typically include the senior leadership group of the sponsoring university working with the IAC members. In some cases, additional faculty and sometimes students are invited to participate. Meetings are generally chaired by the university president, sometimes in collaboration with the IAC chair. Topics include reports on the progress of the university and questions about which the university leadership team would like to consult the IAC.

WHAT THEY DO

As perceived by both IAC members and university sponsors, the main function of IACs is to provide external advice on the design and implementation of the university's overall strategy. Sometimes, the IAC provides additional services, such as interpreting university initiatives to external constituencies or even to university faculty or others on campus. Everyone participating in our research project emphasized the key role of IACs in providing a global perspective and a sense of best practice from respected academic leaders and distinguished scholars. IAC members are much more than consultants—they are senior colleagues who have some inside knowledge of the university, and a commitment to its goals, values, and plans.

There was widespread agreement among the study participants that IACs are effective—if they are well organized, have clearly targeted agenda, and are taken seriously by the academic community—and if the university follows advice from the IAC.

RECOMMENDATIONS

Based on the findings of our research, we suggest that tertiary education institutions interested in establishing effective international advisory councils consider the following key questions in order to benefit fully from such an initiative:

- Do you value lessons from international experience to inform strategic decisions about the future of your university?
- What is your actual purpose in setting up an IAC? Have you defined the actual goals that you seek to achieve by establishing an IAC and working with its members?
- Does the composition of the proposed IAC reflect a healthy diversity in terms of voices and experience (gender, academic profile and disciplines, geographic distribution, balance between practitioners and researchers, etc.)?
- Do the IAC members have a clear notion of the specific inputs that are expected from them?
- What are the learning and decision-making objectives of each IAC meeting from the viewpoint of your institution? Is the meeting agenda sufficiently focused to achieve these objectives?
- Are you willing/able to objectively share the challenges that your institution faces and listen to constructive guidance with an open mind?
- Do you have a mechanism to ensure systematic follow-up after IAC deliberations and monitor the results of these actions on a regular basis?
- Do you have clear rules to replace IAC members and bring new ones on board in line with your evolving agenda?
- In what ways are you able to obtain useful contributions from IAC members, beyond their inputs during the regular meetings, when you seek additional advice on key decisions that your university needs to consider?
- Are you able to efficiently organize IAC meetings, providing sufficient advance notice to members, and help with logistics?

Finally, while IACs have so far been mainly limited to universities interested in strengthening their international profile and level of peer recognition, there is no reason why other types of tertiary education institutions could not benefit from IACs in their search for excellence in the areas that correspond to their specific mission and characteristics. Indeed, the institutions on which this article is based are all research-intensive universities—but other kinds of tertiary education institutions can draw the same benefits from the expertise and international perspectives of an IAC.

JOHN K. HUDZIK

61. GLOBAL: INTEGRATING INSTITUTIONAL POLICIES AND LEADERSHIP FOR 21ST CENTURY INTERNATIONALIZATION

International Higher Education, Special Issue 2015, Number 83

Higher education is challenged to respond to a wide set of motivations and purposes for internationalization. There is pressure to mainstream student, staff, and faculty access to international perspective, involving all institutional core missions, and making ubiquitous who is expected to contribute and to be involved. In consequence, the need for deliberate and systemic institutional policies and leadership to support a more pervasive internationalization becomes necessary.

Motivations behind internationalization now encompass diverse purposes and intended outcomes, including access to global sources of cutting edge knowledge and partnerships, building cross-cultural knowledge and skills, developing an informed citizenry and workforce for a global environment, enhancing the global standing of the higher education institution, and promoting peace and mutual understanding, to name some.

The outcome expectations for internationalization have expanded beyond teaching and learning to also strengthen cross-border scholarship, research, and problem-solving service missions. The contemporary stakeholders of internationalization are diverse, each with particular outcome preferences (e.g., faculty for scholarship, career opportunities, and reputation; students and families for learning, jobs, and access to global opportunities; institutional leaders for access to funding and improved institutional reputation and capacity building; governments for workforce development and connections to the global marketplace).

Governments can help higher education internationalize through policy and funding, but it is what happens within the higher education institution itself that is the decisive variable. As detailed in my 2015 publication, *Comprehensive Internationalization: Institutional Pathways to Success*, there is a strong case for success in institutional internationalization being dependent on the interplay of (a) effective change leadership, (b) a strong institutional culture for internationalization, (c) strategic inclusion, and (d) key administrative practices and policies. These four strategies need to be integrated and mutually reinforcing. None are sufficient on their own; all are necessary.

G. Mihut et al. (Eds.), Understanding Higher Education Internationalization, 283–286.

EXTEND THE LEADERSHIP TEAM

Leadership is needed from the top (presidents, vice-chancellors, provosts, deans); from the middle (directors and chairs); and from the base (influential faculty, staff, and students). Effective leadership for internationalization is neither solely top-down, nor solely bottom-up; rather, it is both. Top leadership sets institutional tone, reaffirms institutional values and coordinates overarching priorities, but the work and creativity of internationalization depends on the faculty, key staff, and academic and support units.

While the international office can play important facilitation and coordination roles, internationalization will not be robust without a diverse leadership team of people and offices from throughout the institution being fully involved. The international office, regardless of its particular form must effectively partner with leadership at all levels throughout the institution.

BUILD A SUPPORTING INSTITUTIONAL CULTURE

Institutional culture defines driving values and priorities in practice. Comprehensive and strategic internationalization is stymied if there is no widespread culture to support it. Building such a culture relies in part on an institution-wide dialog up, down and throughout to educate and mobilize attention to integrating international dimensions into all core missions—building understanding of what it means, why it is important, and how it strengthens an institution and its intellectual core in the 21st century. A widespread dialog builds an appreciation for all to play roles in the internationalization process.

ENGAGE IN STRATEGIC INCLUSION

Strategic inclusion incorporates internationalization into key institutional processes and decisions relating to missions and values, policy and budget planning, institutional branding and human resource management, and contributes to key moments of institutional change during leadership transitions, quality reviews, curricular revisions, and strategic planning. It is not that internationalization dominates decision making in these arenas, but rather that it becomes fully and consciously incorporated into them.

IMPLEMENT KEY POLICIES AND PRACTICES

Institutional case stories and the literature point to several actions that further strengthen the position and role of internationalization in higher education. Policies and practices of considerable importance include:

Define goals, success, and intended outcomes. A clear sense of intended goals and expected valued outcomes from internationalization provides the basis for directing people toward action and for defining success. Different stakeholders have particular priorities for defining success; and institutions also will differ on how they define it. The key is to identify the success motivators for the particular institution; even better are assessments that demonstrate actual outcomes along these lines.

Reward success. What is counted and rewarded is what counts and motivates action. Students look for what counts in their curricula and matriculation requirements and what will advance their learning and careers. Faculty want to advance their careers, strengthen their intellectual reputations, and improve access to funding and scholarly opportunities. Institutions want to build their rank, stature, reputations, and access to support. Will efforts of people and units to internationalize be rewarded in a way which is consonant with such objectives? If international effort is not even counted in curricula or in personnel actions, or at best only tolerated, the motivations are weak; if it is encouraged, supported and expected, motivations strengthen. Does the institution reward international engagement and activity by students and staff?

Integrate internationalization into existing missions and dual purpose funding. If internationalization is seen to add another mission to the traditional three (teaching, scholarship, and service), it will be marginalized. If internationalization becomes integral to strengthening existing missions, it becomes much more sustainable. There is not enough new money available at almost any institution to fund internationalization completely on its own. There are many examples of institutions successfully funding internationalization by dual purposing existing programs and expenditures to include an international dimension: for example, expanding existing faculty domestic expertise and research priorities to include cross-border work and partnerships; taking existing courses and curricula; and integrating international content and dimensions.

Challenge the status quo and encourage adaptive bureaucracy. Strategic and comprehensive internationalization is almost certain to require organizational change. Yet, in most organizations the status quo and comfort of the familiar is a powerful narcotic inhibiting change. However, internationalization forces change in curricula, research foci, and inclinations toward forging partnerships abroad. Partnerships with institutions in other countries and cultures will require adaptability and a willingness to recognize that "our way" is not the only way of doing things; administrative policies and procedures will change. A key enabler of change is building an institutional openness to examining policies, procedures, and rules that were designed for a different age and primarily for domestic stakeholders.

Recruit and develop human resources for internationalization. Internationalization is driven and delivered by faculty, staff, and students, who at a minimum are interested in and see the importance of international engagement. An important enabling condition therefore is whether the institution has and seeks to attract such individuals. Is there an institutional commitment to international engagement in its branding, in its messages to prospective students, and when advertising faculty vacancies? Furthermore, what commitment is the institution willing to make to further educate and develop its existing faculty and staff for international activity?

IN SUM

Institutions will vary substantially in the exact ways they approach more comprehensive and strategic internationalization. There is no best model per se; rather, there are several valid models. The "best" model for an institution is the one that fits its particular culture, capabilities, core values, and missions. Practice must be fashioned from within, but giving attention to the leadership and policy factors above in institutionally relevant terms helps to build success.

HANS DE WIT

62. GLOBAL: THE CHANGING ROLE OF LEADERSHIP IN INTERNATIONAL EDUCATION

University World News, 10 June 2012, Issue 225

Over the past year, several conferences, reports, documents and articles have addressed the changing role of internationalisation in higher education and the need to rethink the why, how, and what of it. One aspect has received little attention in this debate: how the change impacts the role of leaders in international education— referred to in the United States as senior international officers—both now and in the future. The recently published call for action by the International Association of Universities (IAU), *Affirming Academic Values in Internationalisation of Higher Education,* describes the changes in internationalisation clearly. It states among other things: "Internationalisation today is remarkably different from what it was in the first half of the 20th century, in the 1960s or 1980s (…) The resulting changes in goals, activities and actors have led to a re-examination of terminology, conceptual frameworks and previous understandings and, more importantly, to an increased but healthy questioning of internationalisation's values, purposes, goals, and means." These changes inevitably have an effect on management and leadership in international education, but are these well prepared for the impact?

TRAINING BY TRIAL AND ERROR

International education has thus far not been perceived as a profession for which you can prepare at the undergraduate or graduate level, not in the US nor Europe or elsewhere. It is also a subject that is multidisciplinary in nature and so is not based in one specific school or discipline. Of course, there are programmes called "international education" or "international education development" in the US, but they focus more on development education and do not, or only marginally, address internationalisation. The same is true for higher education management programmes in different parts of the world. In general, one can say that senior international officers (SIOs) receive their training primarily by trial and error, either emerging from positions in administrative international offices (commonly the case in Europe) or from academia (commonly the case in the US). One can question if the current broad and complex state of internationalisation can build

G. Mihut et al. (Eds.), Understanding Higher Education Internationalization, 287–289.

an adequate leadership if leaders are drawn from either of these backgrounds. As was discussed recently in Club 33, a gathering of SIOs from different countries, both in the US and Europe it appears increasingly difficult to find SIOs who fit the current requirements. Neither an administrative nor an academic record seems to be sufficient.

The IAU document states that "internationalisation (...) requires an active, concerted effort to ensure that institutional practices and programmes successfully balance academic, financial, prestige, and other goals." Where can one find people with a combination of these skills?

STRONG INTEREST IN STUDYING INTERNATIONALIZATION

There is certainly a strong interest among young academics and practitioners in the study of internationalisation of higher education. Professor Jeroen Huisman, director of the International Centre for Higher Education Management at the University of Bath, told me that most of his professional doctorate and PhD students these days want to do their thesis on an aspect of internationalisation. The management of international higher education master's programme at Edge Hill University in the UK has attracted students from different countries; there are other programmes in countries like Australia that are drawing students; and at the Centre for Higher Education Internationalisation, which I am developing in Milan, I have also noticed a strong interest from all over the world in PhD and master's studies in internationalisation.

The people taking part in these programmes are mostly students who combine an administrative job in an international office with part-time graduate study, as they want to move up to more senior positions. They realise that you need to have not only administrative but also academic qualifications to be a leader in international education, because mainstreaming of internationalisation implies a stronger focus on teaching, learning, and research, an intensive interaction with deans and faculty, and a broader and deeper understanding of internationalisation. It will take some time though before this new generation is experienced enough to take over. In the meantime, intensive training programmes are required to fill the gap. The pool of academics from which institutions can draw for supervising new master's and PhD programmes and training courses is limited, though.

Barbara Kehm and Ulrich Teichler from the University of Kassel published an article in the *Journal of Studies in International Education* in 2007 in which they noted that there are "only a few researchers who continuously engage with the issue and have made it their field of specialisation. There are even fewer centres or institutes that have internationalisation of higher education as a core theme of their research activities." This is still the case, although initiatives such as those described above provide some light at the end of the tunnel. Universities should stimulate and facilitate their junior administrative and academic staff to develop the skills and knowledge to direct the new internationalisation agenda. That investment will pay off in the future.

MAXIM KHOMYAKOV

63. GLOBAL: BRICS UNIVERSITY LEAGUE STARTS TO FORM, BUT NEEDS TRUE COLLABORATION

University World News, 29 November 2013, Issue 298

Internationalisation—together with massification, globalisation and, one should also add, innovation—is key for understanding contemporary academia. Science and scholarship, of course, were always international: one can recall Plato learning in India or the scholars of the early modern period somehow united across Europe in the international Republic of Letters. However, academia has never previously known the truly global circulation of minds (talent and resources) that we experience nowadays.

True enough, medieval scholars did travel a lot—but not as far as China or New Zealand. Even if the science was international, it was not really global. Internationalisation has several faces, one of which is the circulation of minds to which I referred above, while another relates to the sheer impossibility for individual scientists to do proper research on their own. Science requires more and more resources and has become more and more expensive. Thus, inevitably, some research projects are so expensive that they simply cannot be done in a single country. The Large Hadron Collider is the most obvious example here.

Being expensive, science must prove its usefulness to larger society. What seems to be an obsession with innovation is just the reaction of society to expensive and sometimes risky projects of fundamental science. In the absence of clear success criteria society cannot understand why it should pay the price for "hosting" contemporary science. Moreover, since massification of education inescapably leads to an inflation of its value, there must be clear criteria for distinguishing higher education of international quality from all other types of higher education. The result of both processes is, of course, the concept of the world-class university, as well as the highly contentious but really useful practice of international academic rankings.

In this loop of internationalisation, massification and innovation, in this process of distinguishing world-class universities from all others, in this global circulation of minds, all of which constitutes a global educational market—a phrase which would certainly have seemed insane to Humboldt—there are winners and losers. Obviously, all losers think that they deserve better; some of them, however, have enough human and material resources to try to capture a share of the market.

G. Mihut et al. (Eds.), Understanding Higher Education Internationalization, 291–293.

THE AMBITIOUS BRICS

The BRICS—Brazil, Russia, India, China, and South Africa—countries do lag behind the United States and some European countries in all major university rankings. But all of them think they can do much better. Consider Russia, for example. Secondary education in this country is traditionally strong and is followed by equally strong higher education, especially in the STEM disciplines of science, technology, engineering, and mathematics. The evidence is clear: it is enough just to point out the presence of Russian university graduates in major universities, research centres and large companies. But where is Russia on the rankings charts? Arguably the country could have done much better. BRICS countries are all different, but they all want better visibility and a bigger share of the global education market. Importantly, their booming economies provide them with the necessary resources. So one cannot but wonder why the universities in these countries do not collaborate on a larger scale?

Globalisation, massification, internationalisation, and innovation all enhance the value of networking. Networks really do play an important role in today's research and scholarship. Various foundations and programmes nowadays prefer to sponsor international consortia and not just research projects initiated within the framework of bilateral agreements. Education is also moving in this direction: various Erasmus Mundus and Tempus projects provide good evidence to substantiate this claim.

It is this need to be more visible internationally, to get a share of the international education market and, slightly less cynically, to be better integrated into global academia which seems to be responsible, partly at least, for the fact that many countries in emerging markets are developing various large university consortia and educational networks. My own Ural Federal University in Ekaterinburg is, for example, a member of almost a dozen networks and consortia, including the Shanghai Collaboration Organisation (SCO) university network, the Commonwealth of Independent States university network, the University of the Arctic—even if Ekaterinburg is not really part of the Arctic region—the Association of Sino-Russian Technical Universities etc.

LEAGUE TABLES

Arguably, BRICS are very different from the SCO, even if Russia and China are prominent members of both clubs, while India is an associate member of the SCO. Brazil and South Africa certainly add to the diversity, which is further deepened by the fact that the BRICS are not really an organisation—unlike the SCO—but just a club of countries that share a vague ambition to become something more.

These countries, however, do share certain concerns about the international visibility of their education systems and are quite committed to working together to jointly advance their interests. That is why about three months ago in Shanghai, several leading Russian and Chinese universities signed a document called the

Initiative Towards the Formation of a BRICS University League, in which they agreed to work together on holding a founding conference for this new university network.

Some representatives of Indian, Brazilian, and South African universities were present as well, but were not ready to sign the initiative at that stage. The university signatories, the majority of whom—interestingly—already knew each other quite well from their participation in the SCO university network, expressed concern about their current positions in academic rankings and their general visibility in global academia. The signatories think they will be able to enhance their performance through organising wide-scale collaboration between member universities. The importance of this new network was, surprisingly enough, recognised even before it was really conceived. Two of the main international university ranking agencies—Times Higher Education and QS—decided to create specific BRICS-related charts.

THE is going to announce the first results of its BRICS and Emerging Economies Ranking on 5 December in Istanbul, Turkey, while QS will present its BRICS Ranking less than a fortnight later—on 17 December in Moscow, Russia. The rankings, however, will be as artificial academically as the BRICS countries' club currently is mostly political, if not based on true collaboration between universities in these countries. The formation of a BRICS universities league provides us with some optimism. But these universities still have a very long way to go in global academia.

ROGER Y. CHAO JR.

64. ASEAN: THE NEED FOR AN ASEAN UNIVERSITY

University World News, 18 July 2014, Issue 329

With the ASEAN Community set to be established in December 2015, there is a need to revisit the failed 1992 ASEAN initiative to establish an ASEAN University. Its failure should not be attributed to lack of political will among ASEAN member states, but rather to an immature regionalisation process. Compared to 1992, the ASEAN region today has progressed dramatically towards ASEAN regionalism, creating a community with a population of over 600 million and a regional economy with a gross domestic product (at current prices) of US$2,318,156 million and with total trade of US$2,476,427 million based on 2012 figures.

The establishment of the ASEAN Free Trade Area in 1992, the expansion of ASEAN membership in 1997 and 1998 to include Lao PDR, Myanmar, and Cambodia, and various regionalisation initiatives—including the ASEAN Framework Agreement on Services and Mutual Recognition Agreement on key professions—provided the core policy framework for ASEAN regional integration. It has also encouraged collaboration between a demographically, politically, and socio-economically diverse group of nation states at a time of increased competition brought about by neo-liberal globalisation.

A BEACON UNIVERSITY FOR THE ASEAN

Although the ASEAN University initiative was shelved, it facilitated the establishment of one of the core organisations in ASEAN regionalisation of higher education, the ASEAN University Network, AUN. With AUN university membership representing two to four key universities from each ASEAN member state, the network has facilitated enhanced collaboration at institutional level and more recently at regional level with other key regional organisations dealing with higher education.

The ASEAN Credit Transfer System, Student Mobility Programmes, and Internal Quality Assurance have been initiated, established and implemented across AUN member universities. Although its mandate is not at the regional level, AUN member universities and the policies and programmes initiated within the AUN aim to promote good practices among all ASEAN universities. While there is a growing

G. Mihut et al. (Eds.), Understanding Higher Education Internationalization, 295–297.

number of ASEAN-related courses and a few programmes, there is a lack of ASEAN centeredness in any ASEAN university. This can be attributed to the highly competitive global higher education market and the competition within ASEAN universities for students, funding, and global recognition primarily in terms of global rankings.

No single ASEAN university or institution is focused on conducting research on ASEAN-related issues such as history, culture, society, and the challenges and opportunities brought about by the establishment of an ASEAN Community. Furthermore, there is no authoritative institution that serves as a repository of ASEAN-related knowledge or serves as a think-tank focused on the current and future challenges of the ASEAN and its member states.

EUROPEAN UNIVERSITY INSTITUTE

The original idea of an ASEAN University was based on the need to promote ASEAN-ness among its regional population as well as regional collaboration and integration. The ASEAN University that I envision, however, looks to the European University Institute, or EUI, located in Florence, Italy. The EUI is a graduate research institution funded by the 21 European Union member states, which not only serves as the historical archive for the European Union but is also engaged in research on various European issues and challenges usually focused on political science, social science, and the humanities.

The ASEAN University should have an institutionalised funding arrangement with ASEAN member states, institutional autonomy and full academic freedom. As such, it will be free to engage in graduate research on ASEAN-related topics especially focused on political science, social science, and the humanities. Such an ASEAN University will not only serve the original idea for the institution but also create new knowledge on ASEAN-related challenges, serve as an authority on ASEAN topics and enhance the promotion, conservation, and dissemination of the ASEAN region's rich cultural diversity.

The challenges of establishing an ASEAN University will centre on finding a sustainable institutional funding arrangement, a governance structure that enhances institutional autonomy and inculcating a culture of academic freedom given its focus on ASEAN-related topics. Lastly, its collaboration with existing research centres and institutions focused on ASEAN studies and the need to deliver ASEAN-related courses needs to be addressed.

The success of an ASEAN University will depend on the ASEAN region's commitment to establishing and sustaining institutional funding, and ensuring institutional autonomy and academic freedom, but in return the region will have a beacon university embodying ASEAN's core values while respecting the region's cultural, political, and socio-economic diversity. For these reasons, I call for ASEAN leaders to revisit the establishment of the ASEAN University in the hope that the region will truly have a beacon university in the near future and in time for the challenges the ASEAN Community faces in the coming years.

MARY BETH MARKLEIN

65. UNITED STATES: VALUE OF FOREIGN-BORN UNIVERSITY LEADERS IS RISING

University World News, 8 January 2016, Issue 395

In his inaugural speech as president of Westminster College in Fulton, Missouri, Benjamin Akande spoke of a world that is "rapidly shifting," a world that is "harsh and competitive" and a world that is "empowering and liberating." As he encouraged the campus community he now leads to move toward what he calls a "Yes World," his message was ultimately one of hope and possibility on a global scale. The appointment last year of Nigerian-born Akande underscores Westminster's embrace of its international heritage.

The campus takes pride in its role as host, 70 years ago—in 1946—to former British prime minister Winston Churchill. It is there that Churchill made his famous speech decrying the descent of the "Iron Curtain" across Europe with the creation of a Soviet Bloc of communist-controlled countries separated from the rest of the world, and the campus has since hosted former Soviet Union leader, president Mikhail Gorbachev, and former British prime minister Margaret Thatcher on its campus.

It describes its mission today as "educating and inspiring young leaders to change the world." Of the nearly 1,000 students at the liberal arts college, 14% come from abroad, representing more than 75 countries. Akande joins an ever-expanding and diversifying club of US university presidents who were born outside the 50 states. In New Jersey, Seton Hall University's president is from the Philippines; Stevens Institute of Technology's is from Iran. Two years ago, a native of the Republic of Trinidad and Tobago was named president of Howard University, a historically black college in Washington, DC. And within the past five years, natives of India have been tapped to lead a number of large US research universities, including the University of Massachusetts at Amherst, the University of California at San Diego, Carnegie Mellon University in Pittsburgh, the University of Texas at Arlington, and Lawrence Technological University near Detroit.

VALUABLE CREDENTIAL

While place of birth may not be a deciding factor when search committees look for a new president, a foreign-born status has become a valuable credential,

G. Mihut et al. (Eds.), Understanding Higher Education Internationalization, 299–301.

particularly as higher education becomes an increasingly global enterprise. In a statement last year announcing that Andrew Hamilton, a Brit from Oxford, would head New York University, the board praised his understanding of the school's "distinct global presence." When George Mason University in Fairfax, Virginia, hired Angel Cabrera, a Spaniard, in 2012, the chair of the search committee noted his "impressive global vision." "The cross-cultural experience of a foreign-born president gives them in most cases a head start in understanding why international education is so important," says Patti McGill Peterson, who oversees international initiatives for the American Council on Education, a non-profit group representing higher education.

It also reflects a natural evolution: As US universities look increasingly abroad to attract more undergraduate and graduate students, international students increasingly feed the pipeline that leads to top administrative and leadership positions in academia. With few exceptions, foreign-born presidents rose through the ranks of US higher education. Akande, for example, earned his bachelor degree at Wayland Baptist University in Plainview, Texas, and a doctorate in economics from the University of Oklahoma. Before joining Westminster last year, he served 15 years as dean of the business school at Webster University in St Louis, where his responsibilities included expanding and exploring international partnerships. "As we have diversified our institutions over the past generation or two, we are likely to see more and more [international students, faculty, and staff] ascend into leadership roles," says Lucy Apthorp Leske, a senior partner with the executive search firm Witt/Kieffer, where she specialises in higher education. She expects to see proportional growth rather than a dramatic opening of floodgates.

FAVOURED FIELDS

Leske also notes that presidential searches in recent years have favoured scholars in the science, technology, engineering, and mathematics fields, and that is where many foreign-born students have concentrated their studies. Recent data from autumn 2015 on enrolment from the US-based Council of Graduate Schools hint at how trends may be unfolding. Engineering remains the most popular field of study for international graduate students, the council said in a report released last month.

While most of the foreign graduate students entering US universities were pursuing master's or certificate-level degrees, 47% of South Korean students, and 44% of students from the Middle East and North Africa entered doctoral programmes. More than one third of international doctoral students (35%) were from China, followed by India (12%). Akande's vision for Westminster's global aspirations blends the practical application of the liberal arts with skills that he says "are in line with what the market wants." Already in the works is a public-private partnership with Oyo State in Nigeria, which funds and oversees the Ladoke Akintola University of Technology, a public university in Southwest Nigeria.

The partnership will facilitate exchanges of students and faculty, with a focus on information technology, cybersecurity, and the sciences, based on needs identified by his counterparts in Nigeria. Also, Westminster is poised this month to test drive a bachelor degree in leadership designed for working adults. The programme will be delivered to employees at a nearby corporate office, not yet announced, who may have earned some college credits but never completed their college degree. Eventually, Akande says, he intends to look for opportunities to deliver the programme, along with a liberal arts philosophy, around the world.

CREATIVE APPROACH

Akande, whose parents earned doctorates in the United States, says he wants to build on the creative approach to education that attracted him to the United States for college in the first place. "American higher education is not just in the classroom," he says. "That has informed my perspective on where higher education should go today." Asked why he took the job of college president, Akande says it is a way for him to give back. And his foreign-born status, he adds, allows him—and his foreign-born peers—to both appreciate what makes US higher education unique and to challenge the status quo. "We have lived in two worlds," he says. "We have lived in the world of America and of our respective native countries. We bring to this job a very diverse perspective, one that understands and appreciates the value of American higher education. But one that also says, 'We need to think differently'."

PART 11

INTERNATIONALIZATION OF RESEARCH

INTRODUCTION

The next three sections aim at illustrating the connections between internationalization and the key missions of universities—research, teaching, and the social or "third" mission. Section eleven includes articles that highlight the manner in which internationalization affects and shifts research activities.

The first article included in this section, written by Agnete Vabø, discusses the relationship between research, internationalization, and gender. The article, which draws on the study *Changing Academic Profession*, suggests that gender norms harm the prospects of female researchers to engage in international research collaborations, but that male researchers, too, are not immune to some of the associated challenges. Piyushi Kotecha offers an overview of the promotion of research collaboration on the African continent, noting the critical importance of this venture and inherent challenges. In a related article, Sharon Dell shows how research collaboration in Africa varies by field of study. The article also illustrates regional collaboration patterns, citing trends associated with collaboration between African nations and non-African nations.

Internationalization of research is often characterized by embedded power relations. The next article, written by Karen MacGregor, offers a comprehensive take on some of the tensions and problems associated with research mobility in Europe. MacGregor's perspective is based on the *Researchers' Report 2014*. Unsurprisingly, world regions with a relatively smaller research output struggle to create international research collaborations. This is the case of Central America, as described by Nanette Svenson. Svenson's piece presents some of the challenges faced by the region, as well as some of the more recent promising initiatives.

As research collaborations become more frequent, researchers have been interested in understanding what are the effects of international collaboration on research productivity. Marek Kwiek describes the results of the study *The Changing Academic Profession*, which highlights the positive impact that internationalization of research may have on research outcomes. Further, as research is a key component of university rankings, many universities and university systems have active policies aimed at recruiting successful international researchers. The next article in this section discusses the case of Saudi Arabia and its push towards attracting international researchers. Manail Anis Ahmed places his discussion of Saudi Arabia in the broader context of academic capitalism. The last article in the section, written by Yojana Sharma, summarizes the state of joint research collaboration in China, as joint research centers that follow the model of branch campuses are becoming more common in the country.

G. Mihut et al. (Eds.), Understanding Higher Education Internationalization, 305–306.

The articles in this section suggest a growing relevance of international research cooperation. This is partially connected to the increased importance of research to universities as well as the emerging opportunities that internationalization presents.

AGNETE VABØ

66. GLOBAL: GENDER AND INTERNATIONAL RESEARCH COOPERATION

International Higher Education, Fall 2012, Number 69

The internationalization of higher education and research is becoming increasingly essential, as higher education becomes an industry in which institutions and countries compete for the best brains, exchange students, and collaborate on research. International activity is also increasingly important for the enhancement of individuals' academic careers.

A survey conducted in 2008 within the framework of the international research project, the Changing Academic Profession study, reveals that a much lower share of American academics and United States–based female academics, in particular, reported research collaboration with international colleagues. Given the increasing influence of international collaboration and competition in science and, not at least, efforts of internationalization undertaken in other regions such as the European Research Area, this pattern is striking.

In the United States, only 28 percent of female academics and 37 percent of male academics (of all ranks) report research collaborations with international colleagues. In contrast, in the United Kingdom 69 percent of male and 53 percent of female academics report such collaboration; in Germany, the proportions are 52 percent for men and 43 percent for women academics. The highest levels of female participation are found in Australia, Canada, the Netherlands, Finland, Italy, Norway, Portugal, and the United Kingdom. In Latin America—Argentina, Brazil, and Mexico—less than 50 percent of both men and women report taking part in such collaborations.

GENDER AND INTERNATIONALIZATION

To a certain extent, these gender variations reflect well-established differences that exist between various fields of science, based on modes of international cooperation and publication. Science, technology, engineering, and mathematics disciplines are characterized by more international collaboration and publication than the soft or feminized subjects in the humanities and social sciences.

The Changing Academic Profession's data, nevertheless, suggest that some of these barriers are also related to marital status, spouses' employment, and parental

G. Mihut et al. (Eds.), Understanding Higher Education Internationalization, 307–309.

status. It is found that female academics with partners, who are employed full time and with children, are less likely to take part in international research collaboration than male academics (with or without children) and are also less likely to do so than single female academics without children. The long hours and extensive travel abroad often required by an international career may make it incompatible with the traditional divisions of labor between men and women and may help explain why women academics are more active in internationalization at home. The international career path seems to be a less legitimate option for many women. The Changing Academic Profession's data also reveal that more academic women are single, compared to men.

IMPORTING AND EXPORTING KNOWLEDGE

Academics have always been international in the sense of knowledge sharing—via publications, conference attendance, and through sojourns at academic milieus abroad. As is also revealed in the Changing Academic Profession study, academics are often involved in internationalization at home, in teaching foreign students and offering international study programs.

As a large nation with a well-developed academic system, containing many excellent research institutions, across most disciplines and research areas, the United States naturally serves a serious role as an importer of academics and students, rather than as an exporter. Given the range and number of prestigious institutions in North America, international activities are not viewed as being as critical as they often are in European countries, particularly smaller ones. Furthermore, mobility between North American institutions is part of the traditional career dynamic for American faculty. In contrast to many European countries, in the United States it is generally accepted that one should not apply for a first position at the same institution where one has earned a PhD.

BARRIERS TO INTERNATIONAL MOBILITY

The factors that contribute to the traditional gender roles found in countries also interact with some of the distinctive features of the academic career structures in various countries. Some academic systems are gender segregated, along education-oriented and research-oriented tracks—for example, in Mexico, which has a low proportion of women at the PhD level. In countries with competitive tenure-track systems, like in the United States, it may be particularly risky for women academics to go abroad rather than continue making a name for themselves at home.

The tenure-track system has been argued to hinder international mobility among US academic staff, in general. Academic careers are also characterized by the extensive use of temporary positions. This means that a great deal of importance rests on key stages of an academic career in America, to determine if one can make a name for oneself institutionally—as a researcher, lecturer or supervisor. Consequently, staying abroad is often risky, especially for women, as it could mean losing visibility or dropping out from the national competition for prestige and tenure.

One should not underestimate the extent to which such features limit the realizations of international collaboration and hinder possibilities to profit from such networks and cooperation. More internationalization could not only broaden the basis for collaborating, with excellent academic milieus in other countries and milieus with complementary expertise and data, but could also lead to further funding opportunities.

PIYUSHI KOTECHA

67. AFRICA: THE VALUE OF RESEARCH NETWORKS IN AFRICA

International Higher Education, Fall 2011, Number 65

Much of the discourse around higher education in the southern African region promotes the imperative of a knowledge economy. However, participation in today's globalized economy requires significant investment in capacity and systems needed to generate, use, and share knowledge. The past three years have witnessed unprecedented improvements in telecommunications infrastructure in the South African Development Community region, bringing the goal of a knowledge economy within closer reach of SADC's 15-member countries and their research and educational institutions. However, without concerted support for the creation of research and education networks that connect nation states with each other and the rest of the world, the full opportunities presented by recent technological developments are unlikely to be realized.

CONNECTIVITY: RECENT DEVELOPMENTS

At the end of 2007, only three of the 15 SADC countries—Angola, South Africa, and Mauritius—had access to a single international submarine cable known as SAT3/SAFE. The international bandwidth of most SADC countries was still below 100 megabits per second (Mbps), while landlocked countries—such as Malawi, Zambia, and Zimbabwe, and the island nation of Madagascar—had no external fiber connectivity at all. By 2010, however, the region had access to three submarine networks and now has the potential to benefit from lower connectivity costs. All countries, with the exception of the Democratic Republic of Congo, had high-capacity-fiber connections to their neighbors and onward, to the rest of the world. All countries had over 100 Mbps, with South Africa registering several gigabits of international fiber connectivity—a first in Africa. The future continues to look highly positive: by 2012 it is envisaged that all SADC countries will have fiber connectivity to at least two networks at competitive prices, and the region will be connected to Europe by at least six submarine cables.

-Broadly speaking, improved information and communications technologies mean that universities and researchers gain more ability to access global research

G. Mihut et al. (Eds.), Understanding Higher Education Internationalization, 311–314.

facilities, collaborate with experts in the continent and the world, conduct complex research and, essentially, build, store, and share their own knowledge bases. In the SADC region, in particular, this tendency gives countries the opportunity to participate in emerging regional research facilities—such as the Square Kilometre Array radio telescope—or take advantage of high performance computing facilities being established in South Africa.

However, without national research and education networks, which constitute the building blocks for an inclusive regional network, the full benefits of the telecommunications liberalization currently sweeping through Africa are unlikely to be realized.

NETWORKS: NATIONAL AND REGIONAL ASSETS

Studies in Europe support the idea that national research and education networks are a national asset for economic growth and prosperity (http://www.serenate.org/publications/d21-serenate.pdf). Not only are such practices a fundamental source of innovation, allowing researchers to pursue complex research; but they provide a fast and widespread technology transfer to society and industry—unlocking the potential of theoretical research to produce both social benefits and commercial applications. These networks are considered vital national assets that support research, innovation, and collaboration in all fields, with direct contributions to knowledge production and advancement in the areas of education, health, environment and climate, biotechnology, and science and technology.

At a regional level, not only do networks improve the academic and research project by linking academics and researchers across borders, but they can be a powerful economic tool. In Africa, in particular, where the costs of telecommunication remain relatively high, they have the potential, as argued by Duncan Martin in a 2010 Southern African Regional Universities Association's report, to play a role as "a nonprofit-seeking aggregator of [educational] institutions' buying power." He goes on to state that national research and education networks have "ever-widening opportunities" to deliver more bandwidth at lower costs, by becoming operators themselves and by developing their own infrastructure—where this makes economic sense.

In the context of relative scarcity in the region, pooling facilities and resources to achieve an efficient, high-speed, interconnected regional network with a conducive policy environment would give all countries the chance to reap benefits.

CHALLENGES FOR THE SADC REGION

All countries in Europe, North America, and (to a large extent) Asia, Latin America, and North Africa have established national research and education networks. Yet, the SADC region lags behind significantly, with only two functional national networks—in South Africa and Malawi—while most other SADC countries have networks in formation only. The challenges facing SADC countries are not insignificant: they range from limited national telecommunications facilities to poor-campus infrastructural facilities. There are also problems associated with a lack of coherent policies, strategies, and plans for research networking at all levels—as well as the absence of national regulatory frameworks in which to promote cross-border connectivity.

Lack of government investment is another challenge. Greater commitment from individual SADC-member states is needed to stimulate the operation of the networks in each country and enable relevant stakeholders to focus on the promotion of cross-border links through the regional network.

THE IMPORTANCE OF LEADERSHIP

Studies suggest that in the developed world, high-speed connectivity for academic and research purposes has, in the main, been the product of direct government intervention and support. The establishment, based on South African government funding, of the South African National Research Network—with Gigabit-speed connectivity for academic and research networking—shows what is possible when forward-thinking leadership intersects with innovation. Already, this network is linking major universities in South Africa's Gauteng province, thus accelerating cutting-edge research and development.

Other developments serve a potential impetus for the development of a regional network in Africa and the operationalization of nascent national research and education networks. These procedures include the establishment of the Ubuntunet Alliance, recognized by the European Union as a possible operator of a regional research and education network, comprising cross-border links between national research and education networks in eastern and southern Africa. The West and Central African Research and Education Network—a regional research network for west and central Africa—has also been formed.

Also encouraging is the recent interest by the European Union, through the AfricaConnect Project, in providing stimulus funds for African research and education networks operation. AfricaConnect is a poverty reduction program that aims to harness the potential of information and communications technologies for sustainable development of the region.

QUO VADIS?

Ideally, the development of regional networks should be part of a broader cross-border regional program for information and communications technology in higher education. Such an ambitious and wide-ranging project requires support and investment—not only from national governments but from the private sector, donor community, and the regional higher education sector itself. It is only in bringing together such role-players that the region is likely to take tangible steps toward realizing its ideal of full participation in the global knowledge economy.

SHARON DELL

68. AFRICA: INTERNATIONAL COLLABORATION IN AFRICAN RESEARCH—WHO WINS?

University World News, 7 February 2014, Issue 306

Africa's heavy dependency on international scientific collaboration may be stifling research individualism and affecting the continent's research evolution and priorities, according to recent research. A scientometric analysis, co-authored by University of Pretoria academic Professor Anastassios Pouris and Professor Yuh-Shan Ho of Asia University, shows that scientific papers produced by African academics in collaboration with international partners grew dramatically—by 66%—over a recent five-year period. Single author articles, by contrast, appear to be "on the verge of extinction" on the continent.

In their paper *Research emphasis and collaboration in Africa,* analysing co-authorship patterns in Africa and published online by Scientometrics (DOI 10.1007/s11192-013-1156-8), the researchers show how African research areas are dominated by medical and natural resources fields. Instead of collaborative research driven by foreign funding sources, Pouris and Ho suggest that Africa's science and development might be better served by the creation of regional research and innovation systems.

The study analysed a total of 111,877 articles published by authors in African countries in journals indexed by the Thomson Reuters Web of Science between 2007 and 2011. The researchers found that African countries generally exhibit substantially higher collaboration patterns than other countries in the world, with 29 countries publishing more than 90% of their articles in collaboration with others.

RESEARCH SKEWED BY FIELD

Most of the collaboration, according to the study, is with the United States, France, and the United Kingdom—three countries that are also the largest funders of research in biosciences, with emphasis on medicine and agricultural sciences, in Africa. Thus another anomaly highlighted by the study is the "over emphasis" in Africa on research in the medical and natural resources fields including biodiversity, water resources, entomology, and mining.

In relation to the scientific "size" or capacity of the continent, Pouris and Ho argue that these disciplines are over-emphasised and significantly exceed world averages for research in these areas. For example, the most emphasised research

G. Mihut et al. (Eds.), Understanding Higher Education Internationalization, 315–317.

fields in Africa are those of tropical medicine (12.5 times larger than expected from the scientific size of Africa), parasitology (6.5 times larger) and infectious diseases (4.6 times larger). Pouris and Ho ask whether such an emphasis best serves Africa's needs, particularly in light of Africa's under-emphasis on disciplines such as engineering, physics, chemistry, materials science, and instrumentation—all of which underpin modern technologies and economies and, unlike in Africa, have been prioritised by newly industrialised nations such as China.

IGNORING INTERNATIONAL EXAMPLES

"The obvious question is why Africa does not follow international examples?" write Pouris and Ho, who suggest that without the benefit of regional capacity, overemphasis on a particular discipline is unlikely to move research beyond subcritical levels. "The argument is that the small research community and activity on the continent will not be able to resolve current scientific challenges, such as the HIV-Aids pandemic. If the regional capacity is not able to provide a scientific or technological solution to a challenge, overemphasis on particular disciplines will not be fruitful," they argue. "Similarly, while internationally the effort is to develop high technology industries based on brain power, African countries ignore these trends. "Hence, the argument can be developed that it may be preferable to move away from expensive fields like medicine and focus on wealth-creating disciplines that may require less investment and may be easier to be diffused in the economy and society." Thus, Pouris and Ho conclude that Africa suffers from "subcritical research systems and collaboration dominance."

TOO MUCH COLLABORATION?

Although growth in collaborative research publications is a global phenomenon—rising in the rest of the world from 10% to 25% during the period 1990 to 2010—the levels of collaboration remain far lower than in Africa where the share of co-authored articles increased from 52% to 58% over the shorter period of 2007 to 2011. For example, South Africa, the highest producer of publications in Africa, had an international collaboration rate of 53%. By comparison, fellow BRICS countries generally reflected much lower rates of collaboration: 25% for Brazil, 20% for India, and 23% for China. The United States—the top international producer of publications—had a collaboration rate of 33%. Although higher collaboration rates were found in countries such as Germany (51%), Switzerland (67%) and Sweden (59%), individual African countries exhibit substantially higher collaboration patterns.

LITTLE REGIONAL COLLABORATION

While collaboration rates with the international academic community are high among African countries, between African countries it is dismally low. South Africa, for instance, undertook regional collaboration in respect of only 1,145 or 3.9% of its total five-year publication output. The percentage rises to 29% in the case of Mauritania and 37% in the case of the Lesotho, but a clear majority of African countries reflect levels below 10%.

The study also found that the most prolific institutions on the African continent—nine in Egypt and seven in South Africa—all have higher numbers of inter-institutional collaborative articles than single institution articles. South Africa's high international collaboration rate persists in spite of the fact that the national university funding system acts as a disincentive to inter-institutional collaboration in the sense that collaborating institutions are required to share the government subsidy that rewards staff members who publish. "The high share of inter-institutional collaborative articles from South African universities indicate that the forces promoting inter-institutional collaboration are stronger than the adverse impact of the funding mode," conclude Pouris and Ho.

CHANGING PRIORITIES

They suggest that African collaboration is not driven by local researchers searching for collaborators beyond a relatively small national or regional pool, but by the availability of resources and interests outside the continent—in other words, by international imperatives and often these favour group rather than individual research. "What drives researchers, say in Botswana and Zimbabwe, to produce more than 74% of their collaborative publications outside Africa? South African universities are a few hours away by car. Europe and the US are a number of hours away by plane?" they ask. For Pouris and Ho, the "revealed structure" of co-authorship patterns raises a number of policy concerns. The fact that international co-authorship is higher for scientifically small countries has already been established by earlier studies, but Pouris and Ho suggest that it is precisely because of these scientific limitations that African countries need to be particularly attentive to research priorities in order to optimise developmental goals.

KAREN MACGREGOR

69. EUROPE: PROGRESS, PROBLEMS WITH RESEARCHER MOBILITY IN EUROPE

University World News, 26 September 2014, Issue 336

There has been significant progress in alleviating obstacles to mobility for researchers in Europe—but advances have been uneven and challenges remain in some countries in the areas of recruitment, researcher skills, working conditions and career opportunities—says a Deloitte Consulting report prepared for the European Commission. The third annual report of a three-year study includes for the first time a composite index of European Union research excellence compared with that of other major economies, which it says can be seen as a proxy for the attractiveness of Europe for researchers. "The EU is significantly behind the United States, but well ahead of Japan, South Korea, China, India, and Brazil—in descending order. "Between 2007 and 2012, the level of research excellence in the EU increased by six percentage points to 47.8, and increased in every EU country except Greece. The best-performing EU countries are the Nordic member states, the Netherlands, the United Kingdom, and Belgium, all with scores over 60."

The Researchers' Report 2014 was produced by Deloitte Consulting as a part of a three-year monitoring study for the European Union's directorate general for research and innovation. An up-to-date picture is painted of the research profession in 38 countries. Researchers are defined as "professionals engaged in the conception or creation of new knowledge, products, processes, methods, and systems and also in the management of the projects concerned." All doctoral candidates are considered to be researchers. "An open and attractive labour market for researchers is a key priority of the European Research Area where researchers and knowledge can move freely from one country to another," says the report.

There had been significant progress at the European and national levels in removing or easing some obstacles to mobility, improving PhD training and making research careers more attractive. But progress has been uneven and there are large differences between countries. In a number of states there is "a lack of open, transparent and merit-based recruitment, where some early-stage researchers are ill equipped for the labour market or where working conditions are relatively poor or where career opportunities are rather limited." The report outlines key findings, in categories.

G. Mihut et al. (Eds.), Understanding Higher Education Internationalization, 319–323.
© 2017 Sense Publishers. All rights reserved.

STOCK OF RESEARCHERS

There were 1.63 million full-time equivalent researchers in the EU in 2011 compared to 1.49 million in the United States, 660,000 in Japan and 1.32 million in China. Between 2000 and 2011, the stock of researchers in the EU-28 grew by an annual average greater than 4%. "This was faster than in the US and Japan, but slower than in China," says the report. Researchers, however, account for a significantly lower share of the labour force than in the US and Japan, "even if there are indications that the gap is closing." Also, Europe has "a long way to go before it matches the US, Japan and China in the ratio of business-to-public sector researchers."

Countries reported a range of measures aimed at training enough researchers to meet national research and development targets, including action plans, new or updated legislation, awareness-raising schemes about research careers, and improvements to the quality and relevance of doctoral training or incentives.

WOMEN IN RESEARCH

"Europe is far from having achieved gender equality in research and therefore from optimising its talent pool. Women still face a glass ceiling," says the report. "They outnumber men at the first two levels of tertiary education, but are considerably less likely to occupy a senior academic position, or to sit on decision-making bodies— they are even less likely to head a higher education institution or university." Only 16% of heads were women in 2010. There had been some improvement, "but the rate of progress is highly relative given the gap that needs to be closed in most countries."

OPEN, TRANSPARENT AND MERIT-BASED RECRUITMENT

Openness and innovation go hand in hand, the report points out. "Countries with open and attractive research systems are strong performers in terms of innovation." Recruitment based on merit and academic excellence throughout a career was key for research excellence and optimising research talent. A number of countries reported taking steps to make recruitment more transparent. "Nevertheless, many researchers' perception is that there is still a long way to go. They believe that protectionism and nepotism are still widespread in a number of countries, and that institutions do not have sufficiently open and transparent recruitment practices. The problem appears to be particularly acute in some Mediterranean countries." There had been an increase in importance attached to publishing jobs on portals such as EURAXESS Jobs and obtaining the "HR Excellence in Research" logo. Jobs advertised on EURAXESS increased more than five-fold between 2010 and 2013 to more than 40,000.

Several countries had made it compulsory to publish research job vacancies beyond national boundaries (including Austria) or on EURAXESS (including Croatia, Italy, and Poland), and a number of countries had national online systems for advertising research positions. The European Commission is working to produce a recruitment toolkit, including good-practice examples, templates, and other material useful for employers of researchers.

EDUCATION AND TRAINING

There had been progress in increasing the stock of researchers and in providing quality training in line with the Principles for Innovative Doctoral Training, or IDTP, endorsed by European ministers. There had been significant take-up of the IDTP in several countries and a working group of the European Research Area, or ERA, had developed a roadmap for further action. A range of measures to attract people into science and provide quality training had been taken, including regulatory and policy measures, action plans, tax and financial incentives, mentoring and professional development, improved structuring of doctoral programmes, and placements in the private sector.

Between 2000 and 2013 there had been a more than 60% increase in the share of the 30–34 age group who had completed tertiary education (36.8%) and "the EU-28 is well on its way to meeting its 2020 target of 40%," says the report. The number of graduates in science, technology, engineering, and mathematics—STEM—per thousand population in the 20–29 year age group grew by more than 60% between 2000 and 2011 and by more than three quarters among women. "The increases were more rapid than in the US and Japan." During the same period there was growth of more than 60% in new doctoral graduates in the EU, "slightly more than in the US but significantly more than the one third increase in Japan. The number per thousand is slightly lower than in the US but higher than in Japan."

WORKING CONDITIONS

Research careers presented "a particular challenge" during PhD training and in the early career stages when many researchers are on short, fixed-term contracts or have no contract at all. They are often not covered by social security provisions and benefits. "Thus career paths appear uncertain and years of pension contributions may be lost," says the report. Countries reported a range of actions to improve the status of early career researchers. Career problems could be compounded by poor remuneration and on average, as a percentage of the purchasing power adjusted salary of the best paying countries, "non-European countries pay better than the EU," the study found. Among the best paying countries were the US, Brazil, Switzerland, Cyprus, the Netherlands, Ireland, and Belgium.

European countries continued to support the Charter & Code that aims to improve researchers' working conditions. More than 480 organisations from 35 countries had endorsed the principles underlying the C&C, many of them membership or umbrella organisations. Award of the 'HR Excellence in Research' logo recognised institutional progress in implementing C&C principles, and 180 organisations had received the logo.

COLLABORATION WITH INDUSTRY

Although interaction with the private sector was vital for encouraging exploitation of research results, moving into the private sector for a short period during PhD studies was "still very much the exception, even though it is perceived as potentially beneficial for a researcher's career, access to funding, and the exploitation of research results." "Researchers appear to be held back by lack of preparation in areas such as intellectual property and knowledge transfer. As a result, levels of co-publication between the public and private sector are much lower than in the US or Japan," says the report.

Many countries are promoting partnerships between universities, research institutions, and companies, and measures to improve the skills of doctoral researchers. There are joint projects, exploitation programmes, research traineeships in companies, inter-sectoral mobility programmes, industrial PhDs, and combining teaching and private sector research. "Belgium, Croatia, Denmark, France, Greece, and Norway have all taken steps in the last couple of years to create two-way flows between industry and academia, generally with the aim of bridging the gap between research and market applications," the report says.

MOBILITY AND INTERNATIONAL ATTRACTIVENESS

Mobility is a core concept of the ERA and is often associated with excellence, dynamic networks, improved scientific performance, improved knowledge and technology transfer, improved productivity "and ultimately enhanced economic and social welfare," says the report. "Evidence shows that the researcher population is highly mobile internationally. Around 31% of EU researchers in the post-PhD phase have worked abroad (EU or worldwide) as researchers for more than three months at least once during the last 10 years."

Most researchers perceived the mobility experience as positive: 80% of internationally mobile researchers felt mobility had a positive impact on their research skills; more than 60% believed mobility had strongly increased their research output; and 55% thought career progression had improved as a result of their mobility. But 40% perceived mobility as negatively impacting on two aspects— job options, and progression in remuneration. The reasons behind this are as yet unclear but include issues such as a lack of recognition of mobility and "forced" mobility," says the report.

The share of non-EU doctoral candidates as a percentage of all PhDs indicates the openness and attractiveness of a research system. "The average share for the EU is 24.2%." To overcome remaining barriers to mobility, the European Commission proposed changes to the Scientific Visa Directive and has committed to supporting setting up a Pan-European supplementary pension fund for researchers and an insurance scheme. Measures to remove obstacles to researchers' mobility include national mobility schemes, for instance the APART programme in Austria, tax incentives (Denmark), non-financial incentives (extended-stay research scholar visa in France), or promoting dual careers, such as the Dual Career Network of universities near the Franco-Swiss-German borders.

The main report is complemented by data annexes, 38 detailed country profiles, around 50 examples of good practices and a set of "scorecards" which provide a quick visual presentation of where countries stand in relation to the main themes.

NANETTE SVENSON

70. CENTRAL AMERICA: THE VALUE OF INTERNATIONAL ACADEMIC COOPERATION

International Higher Education, Spring 2013, Number 71

Central America, like many small developing regions, contributes little to worldwide research efforts. It accounts for less than 0.05 percent of global research and development and only 0.07 percent of all Science Citation Index publications. While this would seem to make Central American scientific and technological advances unworthy of study, quite the opposite is true as progress on this front will likely determine the extent of the region's development over the next decades.

Seven countries comprise this subcontinent lying between Mexico and Colombia: Belize, Costa Rica, El Salvador, Guatemala, Honduras, Nicaragua, and Panama. Each is different in many ways, but all fall into the "middle-income" World Bank category of developing countries. So, despite a 40 percent poverty rate, Central America is not poor enough to qualify for most donor aid. Neither is it large or rich enough to generate internally the scientific growth, required for propelling development. Interestingly, more than half of the world's economies fall into the same middling category—almost double the number in either the higher- or lower-income classifications. Thus, the circumstances facing Central America, particularly for participation in global scientific exploration, are not unique. International academic cooperation offers a powerful means of addressing this concern and bridging some of the existing gaps.

OBSTACLES

Central America faces numerous challenges to developing research capacity. Higher education enrollment has increased in recent years—thanks to a proliferation of private universities and various labor-market financial incentives—and now averages around 25 percent of the age cohort; however, completion rates are estimated at well below half of that. With the exception of Costa Rica, quality is also questionable. No Central American university appears in the international rankings; public investment in education is under the Organization for Economic Cooperation and Development's average 5 percent of gross domestic product; few professors hold advanced degrees; quality-assurance mechanisms are emerging but

G. Mihut et al. (Eds.), Understanding Higher Education Internationalization, 325–327.

still underdeveloped; and curricula are generally outdated, overly theoretical, and inapplicable to productive sector work.

Additionally, the region invests little in scientific research. Contrary to its industrialized counterparts, 70 percent of the investment is public, with little to no private support. This represents a considerable limitation, as governments struggle to budget for fundamental health and educational expenses—much less scientific and technological activity. Consequently, research is seen as a luxury, most policymakers are uninformed about its potential returns, and Central America has among the lowest research and development investment rates worldwide. Institutionalization efforts are also lacking, which hinders scientific programming sustainability. Finally, the region operates principally in Spanish. This facilitates cooperation within Latin America, but impedes collaboration with North America, Europe, Oceania, and Asia, where the bulk of scientific exploration and publishing is happening.

Even with these obstacles, Central America does have something to offer the global scientific community. Its natural resources, indigenous tradition, and historical migratory importance—among other characteristics—make it a region to study. Its proximity to North America, relative political-economic stability, and literate human capital base also contribute to providing an operational platform. Leveraging these assets to bring education to the point of developing significant scientific capacity is the next step.

PROMISING INITIATIVES

International academic cooperation can do much to augment scientific research budgets and build capacity. In fact, international funding currently accounts for nearly 20 percent of Central America's scientific spending. One of the most promising areas in this regard is that of cross-border university- and research institute-led programs. A number of these have been established over the past several decades and are beginning to yield important dividends. This is especially true where collective synergies have been developed, around areas of common regional interest—such as, agriculture, environmental management, and health.

The Tropical Agricultural Research and Higher Education Center (CATIE) in Costa Rica is one such example. Established over 60 years ago through the Inter-American Institute of Cooperation on Agriculture and now supported by the World Bank and other international donors, CATIE is a regional research and education center, focused on agriculture and natural-resource management. It has graduated more than 2,000 students, operates over 100 research projects, employs professors and researchers from 25 countries, and publishes widely in Spanish and English.

Other examples, similar to CATIE, include the US Smithsonian Tropical Research Institute in Panama; the United Nations University for Peace in Costa Rica; the Pan-American Health Organization Institute of Nutrition for Central America and Panama in Guatemala; and the Latin American School of Social Sciences, supported by the United Nations Educational, Scientific, and Cultural Organization, with programs throughout the region—including Costa Rica, Guatemala, El Salvador, and Panama. All of these initiatives create regional hubs for specialized knowledge generation, education, research, and innovation in areas critical to Central American development. To the extent they can draw on international scientific research capacity and funding, as well as incorporate regional actors and students, they will continue to advance opportunities for knowledge transfer.

MOVING FORWARD

Central American governments, at both regional and national levels, must contribute to these efforts more consistently and effectively. Fortifying the national entities responsible for scientific innovation is essential, as is improving monitoring and evaluation methods for producing data on ongoing scientific activity. Costa Rica is farthest ahead with this, followed by Panama and Guatemala, but much remains to be done in all countries. More strategic targeting of specific scientific and technological capacities to be developed and the linking of development aims with scientific capacity building are important, too, for better identifying priorities and allocating resources.

Central American universities must also do more to further this process. Even with their limited resources, alignment of graduate studies curricula with research methods that are more reflective of the Frascati principles, used elsewhere as the global benchmark, would represent a solid first step in this direction. Strengthening English-language skills would complement this effort. Both of these initiatives would better prepare faculty and students to seek out and participate in international research partnerships. Instigating more of the types of international academic cooperation programs, described above, would not only stimulate academic learning in the region but also give universities an added leverage with national governments for increasing research budgets.

Developing Central American scientific and technological capacity is a daunting task. Nevertheless, resources and models are available, and progress is being made in isolated areas. These advances should be nurtured and expanded. Better utilizing international scientific and technological capacity, to further regional development objectives, stands to benefit greatly the countries of Central America. It could also inspire middle-income countries facing similar challenges in other developing regions to do the same.

MAREK KWIEK

71. EUROPE: "INTERNATIONALISTS" AND "LOCALS" IN RESEARCH: SIMILAR PRODUCTIVITY PATTERNS ACROSS EUROPE

International Higher Education, Special Issue 2015, Number 83

The relationship between international cooperation and research productivity have been widely discussed in the research literature, and there is a general assumption that international collaborative activities in research lead to an increase in research productivity. International research collaboration is most often found to be a critical factor in predicting high research productivity.

A recent study investigated how strongly international collaboration in research is correlated with higher than average research productivity and whether the relationships found hold across all academic disciplines. Analysis was conducted with reference to two separate groups of academics, termed internationalists and locals. We define "internationalists" as academics indicating their involvement in international research collaboration and "locals" as academics indicating their lack of involvement in it. We used the data created by the global CAP and the European EU-ROAC projects on the academic profession—"The Changing Academic Profession" and "The Academic Profession in Europe: Responses to Societal Challenges," respectively. The primary data come from 11 European countries, with 17,211 usable cases.

INTERNATIONALIZATION PRODUCTIVITY, AND ACADEMIC FIELDS

Our research demonstrates that across all major clusters of academic fields, the difference in productivity rates between European "internationalists" and "locals" is statistically significant. Those European academics who were collaborating with international colleagues in research had published, on average, substantially more articles in academic books or journals, than their colleagues in the same academic field who were *not* recently collaborating internationally.

The percentage of academics collaborating internationally in research across Europe is high and it is an activity reported, on average, by two thirds of academics. There are huge cross-disciplinary and cross-national differences, though. The share of "internationalists" varies significantly across the five major clusters of academic fields that we studied: life sciences and medical sciences, physical sciences and

G. Mihut et al. (Eds.), Understanding Higher Education Internationalization, 329–331.

mathematics, engineering, the humanities and social sciences, and the professions (teacher training and education science, and administration, economics, and law). Academics in the cluster of physical sciences and mathematics are by far the most internationalized (three quarters of them are collaborating internationally) and academics in the cluster of the professions are the least internationalized (only about half are collaborating internationally).

"Internationalists" across eleven European countries across all academic fields had published, on average, about twice as many articles as "locals." In some academic fields, "internationalists" produced, on average, about 140 percent more articles (the engineering cluster) or about 120 percent more (the physical sciences and mathematics cluster), while in others (the humanities and social sciences, and the professions) they produced about 70 percent more articles in a three-year reference period (2005–2007 for CAP and 2008–2010 for EUROAC countries). "Internationalists" in life sciences and medical sciences—the academic fields with the highest productivity rate—produced, on average, 8.80 articles, which was about 80 percent more than "locals," who produced 4.91 articles, on average. The academic field with the highest productivity rate differential between "internationalists" and "locals" in Europe is engineering, with average productivity rates of 6.97 articles for the former group and 2.91 articles for the latter.

In all 11 European countries studied, international collaboration in research is correlated with a substantially higher number of publications. Only for the Netherlands, the most highly internationalized system in Europe, are the results not statistically significant. If we assume that the mean number of publications of "locals" is 100 percent, then the field mean for "internationals" varies from about 240 to more than 400 percent. International collaboration pays off most in terms of knowledge production in engineering (on average, academics collaborating internationally produce four times more publications), and the least for the humanities and social sciences and the professions (producing about two and a half times more publications).

Cross-national differences apply: leaders in internationalization are the relatively small systems of Ireland and the Netherlands (with more than four in every five academics collaborating internationally, on average), followed by Austria, Switzerland, and Finland (with three out of four academics collaborating internationally). The two least internationalized systems are the relatively large systems of Poland and Germany, with slightly less than half of all academics collaborating internationally (about 48 percent). The remaining countries can be termed internationalization moderates.

CAVEATS

There are two reservations: one regarding the direction of causality in the research productivity-international cooperation relation and one regarding publication numbers. The identification of high research productivity correlates (e.g., international collaboration) does not necessarily imply the identification of causal relations. International cooperation in research may be generally undertaken by more productive academics, as such academics are sought by the most productive academics across all systems. Also, more productive academics tend to have better access to funding for international cooperation. There is also an important difference to be made between publication numbers and their scientific significance. Numbers do not necessarily determine scientific value, but it is often assumed in the studies on social stratification in science that a higher number of publications tends to lead to more consequential research than a lower number.

CONCLUSIONS

Research productivity of European academics is highly correlated with international research collaboration: the average research productivity rate of European academics involved in international collaboration ("internationalists") is consistently higher than the rate of European academics not involved in international collaboration ("locals") in all clusters of academic fields and in all 11 countries studied. The distinction between "internationalists" and "locals" permeates European research. Some systems, institutions, and academics are consistently more internationalized in research than others. For "internationalists," the international academic community is a reference group, while "locals" publish predominantly for the national academic community. Internationalization increasingly plays a stratifying role in academia, though—more international collaboration tends to correlate with higher publishing rates, and those who do not collaborate internationally may be losing more than ever before in terms of resources and prestige.

MANAIL ANIS AHMED

72. SAUDI ARABIA: INTERNATIONALIZING RESEARCH IN SAUDI ARABIA: PURCHASING QUESTIONABLE PRIVILEGE

International Higher Education, Special Issue 2014, Number 78

As part of its ambition to create a "knowledge economy" and ultimately diversify revenue sources, Saudi Arabia has been working aggressively to boost research production. The Kingdom is young and its university and higher education system even more so. Focusing initially on building schools and later tertiary teaching facilities, it was not able to establish scholarly research production until very recently. However, research activity has been given a massive push over the past few years. The country has made great strides in this regard with the building of many higher education institutions and research facilities.

THE ROLE OF RANKING

Accompanying the race toward the creation of new universities and other educational institutions has been the pursuit of quality. Whereas robust national systems of quality assurance (such as the National Commission for Academic Accreditation and Assessment) have come into existence, there is also a need to benchmark against more global and publicly visible systems. As global university rankings have gained widespread acceptance and become the dominant form of consumer-oriented information producers, Saudi universities have been preoccupied lately with being featured in these lists.

In the report—"Global University Rankings and Their Impact" by Andrejs Rauhvargers—commissioned by the European University Association in 2011, it says: "One problem or "unwanted consequence," as rankers sometimes call the negative impacts of rankings, is that both society and policy makers are tempted to judge all higher education in the world by the standards that rankings use to detect the top research universities, rather than applying one of the core principles of quality assurance—the "fitness for purpose" principle." And he continues: "Thus, one "unwanted consequence" of global league tables is that higher education institutions with other missions than that of being top research universities may have to re-justify their profile at a time when mission differentiation is at the top of higher education agendas across Europe."

G. Mihut et al. (Eds.), Understanding Higher Education Internationalization, 333–335.

GENEROUS FINANCIAL INCENTIVES AT THE EXPENSE
OF THE LOCAL RESEARCH ENTERPRISE

This problem becomes immediately apparent in the case of Saudi universities. Whereas the first university in the country was established as late as 1957; and whereas there is a huge and pressing need to educate a fast-growing population of youth to effectively enter the workforce and become productive members of society, there is also a pressure on the country's institutions to produce publishable research output in English that can be leveraged for the various different international university ranking systems.

BENEFITS, RISKS, AND CONTROVERSIES

In such a situation, a default internationalization of research has come about, perhaps a faster internationalization than was possible, or even desirable, in the development of the rest of the Saudi academy. This internationalization has reaped huge rewards with regard to boosting the country's research production. In fact, three Saudi public universities have been featured in various international rankings over the past decade—and others, large and small, are making their way there now.

An interesting aspect of this research-based internationalization is that it has so far been focused in the areas of the life, natural, information, and engineering sciences—the humanities are nowhere to be seen, and the social sciences are few and far behind. But the most problematic aspect of this internationalization is that institutions, both large and small, are allocating—and paying out—substantial proportions of their research budget to invite highly cited international researchers to publish with the paying institution listed as the researcher's secondary affiliation. This practice was highlighted in a controversial article in Science Magazine in December 2011 and has since been widely debated in both local and global fora as being problematic. The contracts offered to these "visiting researchers," "research fellows," or "international partners" generally require a minimum number of publications per each contract period, and only a nominal requirement of physical presence at the host institution.

THE PRICE OF "ACADEMIC CAPITALISM"

Whereas some academics deride the practice of paying others to make it seems like one's own institution did the work, others think of it as merely another aspect of capitalism—being able to buy the best global talent by paying top dollar for it and in the process deriving credit for research production. The practice of hiring prolific, highly cited international researchers in order to boost the research reputation of any given institution remains a contested one. However, this debate does bring into focus the problems associated with the urgent internationalization of research in a country like Saudi Arabia.

The more widely accepted desirable outcomes of higher education internationalization—i.e., the exchange of people, knowledge, ideas, and research production systems across boundaries—have in this case been supplemented by a too-easy prepared solution with regard to research production and development. It is one thing to invite foreign scholars and researchers to help build an indigenous, vibrant, and sustainable research culture that can eventually thrive independently of any outside help. It is entirely different to supplant local research production and to coopt foreign resources that have little vested in the research development of the host institution or country beyond co-authorship. Thus, the internationalization of research in Saudi Arabia is not devoid of controversy.

A MIDDLE WAY

Perhaps it would be better to advise a more gradual, comprehensive internationalization of both teaching and research at Saudi universities. This would involve an openness toward traditional models of research production (such as the documentation of oral histories and the acknowledgement of verifiable "chain-based" historic research resources) and the placing of more value on local knowledge and indigenous methods of knowledge production and transmission. The kingdom could also benefit far more from diverting resources to support research produced locally: by providing rigorous training in international research methods, sponsoring the translation of Arabic research output into English, and in the process educating Saudi researchers about the importance of peer review, academic influence through citation, and ultimately the production of high-quality research to an international standard.

By doing the above, Saudi Arabia would be able to build a gradual and robust local research culture, creating a valid space for research production that acknowledges differences in international research methods, while incorporating best practices from academia worldwide. Given strong state support, and keeping in mind the potential inherent in the country's nascent research enterprise, a research culture of its own is surely not too far in the Saudi future.

YOJANA SHARMA

73. CHINA: JOINT RESEARCH: ALTERNATIVE TO BRANCH CAMPUS?

University World News, 3 July 2011, Issue 178

Tie-ups between China and Western universities are announced almost every month. But a new collaborative research centre being set up by England's Birmingham University in Guangzhou in southern China highlights another model of cooperation, with none of the drawbacks of the more popular "branch campus." Western universities, particularly in Britain and the US, are beginning to find that sustaining a branch campus in Asia or the Middle East requires a great deal of time and resources and faculty are becoming more reluctant to spend time at overseas branches, leading to recruitment and quality issues. "I would not go as far as to say the branch campus model is finished," said KK Cheng, a professor of epidemiology at Birmingham University who is spearheading the research centre collaboration with Guangzhou, announced this week. "But very early on, we at Birmingham decided that is not our priority. Instead, for China we have pursued a model of a graduate school and research institute, training PhD students and post-docs in more than just lecture rooms."

The University of Birmingham Guangzhou Centre, which will open in the next few months, "will help identify, design, and coordinate the delivery of joint research projects in Guangzhou, the province of Guangdong and the Pearl River Delta region," the university said in an announcement last week. "We have liaison offices in Shanghai and Beijing. Initially we saw that many Western universities were exploring the Shanghai prospect. They were visited weekly by Western universities seeking partnerships. Shanghai is quite burnt over in terms of partnership," said Edward Harcourt, Director of International Relations at Birmingham.

Branch campuses in China mainly enrol undergraduate students and require a large number of fee-paying students to be financially viable. "A lot of overseas universities go to China and want to set up a campus and they mainly cater to undergraduates. Some have a better time doing it than others. Some are more successful, some are less so, but many of them are top-down initiatives," said Cheng. "This often means the Western institutions make up their minds that they want to go into China first, then look at where they can be useful or complementary." Problems for institutions such as Duke University in America, where staff are opposing an administration-led bid to set up a Duke branch campus on the outskirts of Shanghai

G. Mihut et al. (Eds.), Understanding Higher Education Internationalization, 337–339.

in Kunshan, have highlighted some of the difficulties. "There is a lesson people can learn from Duke," Cheng argued.

While there are different models of branch campuses—including full campuses with a mixture of local and home country faculty teaching a variety of specialist disciplines, and smaller outposts that teach only in-demand subjects such as business—within the university staff and faculty may not be behind an administration that is gung-ho about a branch campus in China. Even when branch campuses are set up, faculty may be reluctant to spend time teaching there, even for short stints. However, the Birmingham Guangzhou Centre will be a graduate research institute, which will conduct high quality collaborative science and social research. "We think it is more sustainable to set up [research] in areas that our own faculty are interested in, as well as helping them produce more high quality research papers for publication. That way our faculty will be more interested in going there," said Cheng.

A major feature of the centre will be a clinical trials unit in Guangzhou. "If we conduct clinical trials, it will also support PhD students," Cheng explained. At first, the research will be funded by Birmingham University and Guangzhou municipality on a shared basis. But Cheng believes major research and clinical trials could attract funding from large agencies in the West, and later from the pharmaceutical industry. One of the attractions of biomedical research, which forms the bulk of science research collaborations between China and other countries, is that China provides access to a population cohort size that would be difficult to find for clinical trials in the West.

It is clear that a major interest on the Chinese side in such university collaborations is to increase the number of research citations and to be published in major Western research journals—an important measure of global scientific prowess. Research collaborations with Western partners has helped Chinese academics gain access. The Guangzhou Biobank Cohort Study, into genetic and environmental influences on the development of chronic diseases, which has been a long-running collaboration between the Guangzhou municipality, Birmingham University and Hong Kong University, resulted in a large number of academic publications in prestigious journals—some 68 since 2006. "That helped put Guangzhou on the scientific map," said Cheng. It also gained Birmingham enough trust to pave the way for the new Guangzhou research centre, which will scale up many other projects including clinical research. Although the number of papers being published by Chinese scientists in top research journals is rising, the country is not well represented in medical journals that publish papers on clinical trials and evidence-based medicine.

China has invested hugely in science laboratories and research and development, but there is still a big gap between discovery and innovation and delivery. Clinical trials research and other research and development could help bridge that gap. "Many pharmaceutical companies are eying China as a major market for drugs," said Cheng, but they need access to relevant local evidence-based research. He also sees "an opportunity here to engage more widely." Cheng pointed to China's announcement in 2009 that it would spend some US$131 billion revamping its dysfunctional health care system. "Every city in China has a five-year plan to develop primary care. They will need some 300,000 GPs [general practitioners] by the end of the decade. There is a real shortage of GPs."

China is looking to more advanced countries to help in health care capacity building. Cheng also sees an opportunity for training primary care general practitioners in Guandong: "We are doing a lot of work with the Guangzhou health bureau. These are much more extensive relationships than simply delivering a few lectures or overseeing research." Meanwhile, he said the best research has to be relevant beyond publications and citations. "Publishing papers is not enough. Research must also help policy-makers, officials, and researchers understand local problems. We hope the research, for example on the link between passive smoking and disease in Guangzhou, will have an impact on policy. The research helps to wake people up." But the main reason why major research collaborations are seen as long term and sustainable is that "Guangzhou, like many Chinese cities, wants to move up the value chain," said Cheng.

China's government understands that its economic growth cannot simply be from export-led manufacturing of cheap consumer goods. It also wants to increase innovation, including in healthcare and pharmaceuticals, as well as in areas such as energy technology and environmental research and technology, which are other areas of research collaboration at the Birmingham Guangzhou Centre. "The case for being in Guangzhou is compelling. No one needs any persuading that China is an economy to be reckoned with. There are lots of opportunities," said Cheng.

PART 12

TEACHING AND INTERNATIONALIZATION

INTRODUCTION

This section discusses the relation between internationalization and teaching, the central mission of universities. Articles focused on questions around the language of instruction, internationalization of the curriculum, and "internationalization at home" (IaH) are included here.

Hans de Wit and Betty Leask offer a comprehensive assessment of the impact that internationalization has had on the curriculum. The incorporation of an intercultural and global dimension in teaching, as well as discussion about the relevance of the concept of global citizenship are included. Next, Michele Rostan addresses the advancement of English as lingua franca within the academic space. She delves into the reality of teaching in a second language in countries where English is not an official language.

Unsurprisingly, recent initiatives have attempted to measure the quality of teaching and learning around the world. Elspeth Jones argues that soft-skills typically acquired through study abroad need to be imbedded into the local curriculum, and promoted through "internationalization at home." This would allow all students—not only the mobile few—to benefit from experiential and intercultural learning. To some extent, internationalization of the curriculum is not optional. In an article focused on Japan, Jeremy Rappleye, and Edward Vickers emphasize the importance of complementing the nationalist curriculum in the country with an internationally-focused curriculum to facilitate multilateral cooperation and economic success. The section concludes with a piece written by Jan Petter Myklebust and Jacquie Withers, whose article offers insights on the internationalization of PhD education in Norway.

Together, the articles in this section discuss the importance of exposing all students to a more internationalized curriculum. While advocacy to increase and improve "internationalization at home" is often justified in light of economic realities, this by no means represents the only—or the most important—rationale to promote teaching with global awareness, among other elements of IaH.

G. Mihut et al. (Eds.), Understanding Higher Education Internationalization, 343.

HANS DE WIT AND BETTY LEASK

74. GLOBAL: INTERNATIONALIZATION, THE CURRICULUM, AND THE DISCIPLINES

International Higher Education, Special Issue 2015, Number 83

In the last decade, institutions of higher education, national governments, and (inter)national organizations have become more proactive, comprehensive, diverse, and innovative in their approaches to internationalization. Critical reflection on their outcomes—in particular their impact on student learning—has resulted in a search for approaches to internationalization that have deeper meaning and greater impact.

The search for new approaches is evident in the increasing use of terms such as "deep internationalization," "transformative internationalization," and "comprehensive internationalization." While such terms are increasing in number and frequently used, the challenge is to align rhetoric with practice. These terms are consistent with using internationalization as a driver of quality and innovation and reflect growing interest in ensuring the majority of students and staff are engaged in and changed by the internationalization agenda. They also have the potential to stimulate the development of approaches that address existing inequalities in educational opportunity and outcomes in the world today. Haphazard approaches to internationalization that focused on a minority of students or on profit rather than education are not consistent with such terms and insufficient in universities operating in a globalized world. In this super-complex world, multiple dimensions of being are required of both individuals and institutions. In this world, coherent and connected approaches to international education, which address epistemological, praxis, and ontological elements of all students' development, are urgently needed. Focusing attention on these goals has the capacity to transform an institution's approach to internationalization and the identity of the institution.

The curriculum is the vehicle by which the development of epistemological, praxis, and ontological elements can be incorporated into the life and learning of today's students, ensuring that they graduate ready and willing to make a positive difference in the world of tomorrow. Recently, questions related to the relationship between the internationalization of higher education, the curriculum, and the disciplines have been raised. Some of these questions are discussed briefly below.

G. Mihut et al. (Eds.), Understanding Higher Education Internationalization, 345–348.

IS GLOBAL CITIZENSHIP A POSSIBLE AND DESIRABLE OUTCOME?

The development of responsible global citizens may be one way in which universities can have an impact on local communities and global society. But how do we define "global citizenship" as an outcome of internationalization? What knowledge, skills, and values will the global citizen display? How would we develop and measure these in the context of the curriculum of a program of study? Is global citizenship indeed possible in a world in which the nation-state dominates politically and the gap between the rich and poor of the world is widening?

Some argue that the pursuit of global citizenship as an outcome of international education is not even desirable, that it will inevitably exclude some. This could lead to the creation of a stronger transnational elite, further increasing the privilege and power of some groups compared with others.

These are important issues that are often overlooked in the pursuit of global citizenship as an outcome of internationalization of the curriculum.

WHAT IS THE ROLE OF MOBILITY?

Mobility is still the main focus of many institutional approaches to internationalization. This is in part because mobility is easy to translate into numbers, percentages, and targets. Measurable targets are required for the rankings of universities nationally, regionally, and globally. However, even if the ambitious goals set by the Ministers of Education of the Bologna signatory countries are met, around 80 percent of students will not be able or willing to study abroad. This highlights the importance of the "at home" component of internationalization, which not only looks at the outcomes, impact, and quality of internationalization, but is focused on internationalized learning outcomes for all students instead of the mobility of the minority. This raises the question: "How can we shift, in many institutions, from an almost exclusive focus on mobility for the elite to a focus on curriculum and learning outcomes for all students, mobile or not?"

HOW DOES CONTEXT INFLUENCE CURRICULUM INTERNATIONALIZATION?

Institutional mission, ethos, policies, and priorities influence approaches taken to internationalization. The local context—the social, cultural, political, and economic conditions—provides opportunities and challenges for internationalization of the curriculum. National accreditation requirements for registration in professions often focus on local legislation and policy. Different national and regional contexts provide different options for internationalization of the curriculum. The global context is also important. Globalization has contributed to increasing the gap between the rich and the poor of the world, and the exploitation of the "South" by the "North." The domination is not only economic, it is also intellectual: the dominance of Western educational models, what research questions are asked, who will investigate them, and if and how the results will be applied. Discipline communities are a strong driver of approaches to content selection, teaching, learning, and curriculum design in the national and global contexts. Critical decisions about whose knowledge will be included in the curriculum and how to teach and assess learning, are determined by the discipline community. Disciplinary, institutional, local, national, regional, and global factors interact in different ways to facilitate and inhibit, drive, and shape approaches to internationalization, including the way in which learning outcomes are defined, taught, and assessed. Hence, we see approaches to internationalization of the curriculum that are both similar and different within and across disciplines.

HOW DO WE DEFINE INTERNATIONALIZATION OF THE CURRICULUM?

Can we come to some international, if not global, agreement on at least the general characteristics of the concept and the process of internationalizing the curriculum? This definition needs to be broad enough to allow context sensitive, discipline-specific interpretations, that are detailed enough to ensure key components of the curriculum are addressed and all students are influenced and included. The definition by Betty Leask (2015) addresses these points: "Internationalization of the curriculum is the process of incorporating international, intercultural, and global dimensions into the content of the curriculum as well as the learning outcomes, assessment tasks, teaching methods and support services of a program of study."

A SHIFTING FOCUS

These unresolved questions highlight a shifting focus in approaches to internationalization—away from ad hoc, marginal, and fragmented activities toward broader, more diverse, and more integrated and transformative processes. Although there is still a strong focus on the abroad side of internationalization, there is an ever stronger call for attention to the internationalization of the curriculum at home. There is increasing recognition of the need for institutions to pay more attention to involve more, and even all, students in internationalization. The focus is, however, shifting slowly and more is imagined than achieved.

Internationalization is not a goal in itself but it is a means to enhance the quality of the education, research, and service functions of higher education. The context influences the why, what, and the how of internationalization; therefore, the way in which internationalization of the curriculum is interpreted and enacted, is both similar and different across disciplines and fields of study. There is no one model of internationalization fit for all higher education systems, institutions, and disciplines.

MICHELE ROSTAN

75. GLOBAL: ENGLISH AS "LINGUA FRANCA" AND THE INTERNATIONALIZATION OF ACADEME

International Higher Education, Spring 2011, Number 63

English is considered as the Latin of the 21st century and a language playing a relevant role in the internationalization of academe. Data collected through the Changing Academic Profession (CAP) survey—referring to 25,000 academics working in 18 countries located in 5 continents—allow to investigate whether and to what extent English is the contemporary academic "lingua franca," and how it contributes to the internationalization of the academic profession in different countries.

ENGLISH AS LINGUA FRANCA

At the global level, 53 percent of the academics involved in the CAP survey primarily employ English for their academic activities: 17 percent of the academics use it as their mother tongue and 36 percent as their second language. English is much more used as lingua franca for research activities than for teaching activities: while 51 percent of academics employ English for research, only 30 percent actually use it for teaching. This gap mainly concerns non-native speakers. Among native speakers, almost all academics use English both for teaching and for research purposes. On the contrary, twice as many academics employ English as their second language in research than those who use it as their second language for teaching.

ENGLISH-SPEAKING COUNTRIES

English can play a different role in the internationalization of both higher education and the academic profession, depending on the official language of a country. Countries participating in the CAP survey can be divided into three groups. First, in three countries English is either the official or the main language: Australia, the United Kingdom, and the United States. In these countries, the overwhelming majority of academics teach in English as it is their mother tongue, but a significant minority uses English for teaching as their second language, while few academics teach using a different language than English. Briefly, in these countries practically all academics teach using the contemporary lingua franca, giving institutions and higher education systems a competitive advantage in the global student market.

G. Mihut et al. (Eds.), Understanding Higher Education Internationalization, 349–352.

Second, in four countries with a special bilingual or multilingual context, English is one of the official languages, together with one or more other languages: Canada, Hong Kong, Malaysia, and South Africa. In these countries English is used for teaching by the majority of academics as it is either their mother tongue (Canada) or their second language (Hong Kong, Malaysia, and South Africa). Moreover, a significant minority of academics mainly use a different language for teaching, but a smaller minority also exists that teaches in English as the second language (Canada) or the main language (Hong Kong and South Africa). All in all, in these countries 65 to 75 percent of academics teach in English. As a consequence, these countries also enjoy quite a strong competitive advantage, globally.

The role played by English as the second language in these two first groups of countries is somehow different. In three multilingual countries—Hong Kong, Malaysia, and South Africa—many academics (57% to 71%) use English for teaching as their second language. In most cases, these people are national academics employing a language that is not their mother tongue. So, it can be argued that in these countries as non-native speakers, academics may have two goals: introducing an international dimension into teaching and providing a common language for education in a multilingual national context.

In Canada, Australia, and the United States, the majority of academics employing English for teaching as their second language—more or less two out of three— are national citizens, likely belonging to linguistic minorities or having acquired the national citizenship during their career. International academics are a minority, around one out of three. This situation probably depends on the long-lasting capacity of international attractiveness of the three countries' higher education systems. In the United Kingdom most academics employing English for teaching as their second language are international academics, mostly European, witnessing the attractiveness of the UK higher education system.

In countries where English is either the official, or one official, or the main language, almost all academics, or a strong majority, employ English in research either as their mother tongue or their second language. In these countries, employing English in research cannot be considered as an indicator of participation in international research. The use of English gives academics working in these countries an ipso facto advantage as it is the dominant means of communication in the international scientific community. Yet, when English is academics' mother tongue, employing it in research does not necessarily imply participating in international research networks. Moreover, using English as second language may simply be necessary to take part in national research activities.

NON-ENGLISH-SPEAKING COUNTRIES

The third group of countries includes those where English is not an official language. According to the CAP data, this group can be split into two subgroups. On one side, in three countries a small but considerable part of academics (10% to 20%) are committed to employing English as the mean of instruction, as an effort to attract international students and/or to provide domestic students with useful language skills: Finland, South Korea, and Norway. In these three countries, almost all or most academics teaching in English are national academics whose mother tongue is the official language of the country or one of the official languages. On the other side, in eight countries with strong linguistic identities, English is not, or seldom, used for teaching: Argentina, Brazil, China, Germany, Italy, Japan, Mexico, and Portugal. In most of these countries (except China, Italy, and Japan) academics belong to non-English-based international language communities.

In four countries (Italy, Finland, Portugal, and Norway), English is used in research by the majority of academics, and in other three countries (Germany, South Korea, and Brazil), it is used by a significant minority. Finally, in four countries (Argentina, Mexico, Japan, and China) English is used in research by a small minority.

In countries where English is not an official language, the use of it by national academics whose mother tongue is not English is a necessary tool for participating in international research. As a consequence, employing English as the second language in research can be viewed as an indicator of integration within international research networks. On this basis, two groups of countries can be identified. The first group includes the six countries where the percentage of academics employing English as their second language in research is above average (Italy, Finland, Portugal, Norway, Germany, and South Korea). Academics working in these countries can be featured as well integrated in the international research networks. The second group includes the five countries where the percentage of academics employing English as their second language in research is below average (Brazil, Argentina, Mexico, Japan, and China). Academics working in these countries are not well integrated within the international research networks.

INTERNATIONALIZATION—CERTAIN CONCLUSIONS

The CAP data support the conclusions that English is the contemporary "lingua franca" within academe and that research is the most internationalized academic activity. Besides, they also provide a map of the internationalization of academe, based on the role of the English language. According to CAP data, it can be argued that academics working in 13 countries, representing 64 percent of the sample (Australia, Canada, Germany, Finland, Hong Kong, Italy, South Korea, Malaysia, Norway, Portugal, United Kingdom, United States, and South Africa) are more internationalized, albeit for different reasons, while those working in five other countries, representing 36 percent of the sample (Argentina, Brazil, China, Japan, and Mexico), are less internationalized.

While in the countries where English is not an official language, the use of it as second language can be considered as a clear indicator of the internationalization of academe, in English-speaking countries the relationship between the use of English and the internationalization of academe is less straightforward. In these countries,

351

higher education institutions and academics enjoy an advantage as almost all or most of the academics use English, but the use of English as such cannot be considered as an indicator of participation in international research networks. Moreover, the use of English as second language for teaching has different meanings, depending on the nation context. It possibly refers either to academics' contribution to the internationalization of their higher education or to their contribution to its national integration or to the international attractiveness of higher education systems.

ELSPETH JONES

76. GLOBAL: GRADUATE EMPLOYABILITY AND INTERNATIONALIZATION OF THE CURRICULUM AT HOME

International Higher Education, Special Issue 2014, Number 78

Over the past two decades and more, frequent surveys of employers have found that, while graduates may have the technical skills required for a given role, they often lack the so-called soft skills that are key to effective working. Sometimes called employability skills, these include team-working, negotiation, and mediation, problem-solving, and interpersonal skills, flexibility, organization, and good communication. These surveys have been conducted in a wide array of countries from Australia to Zambia, and similar sets of requirements have been found repeatedly across the world.

Academics are often oblivious to such calls from employers, perhaps believing that the intellectual rigor of their program may be compromised by a focus on "mere skills." Indeed, it is undeniable that education is about much more than getting a job at the end of the process. Yet, global dimensions in working environments are no longer limited to multinational corporations and are now integrated into professions and roles, which had previously been seen as more locally based. It could be argued, therefore, that we are failing our students unless we prepare them effectively for contemporary employment, and a range of scholars have urged that university curricula should be better aligned to employer needs. The ability to interpret local concerns within a global context and to judge the impact of global issues on one's personal and professional life should surely be an attribute of all graduates in contemporary society.

EDUCATION ABROAD AND THE DEVELOPMENT OF EMPLOYABILITY SKILLS

What is remarkable is that many of the skills required are precisely those which studies have found to be developed through international experience of study, work, volunteering, or service learning. It has been demonstrated that even short periods of such activity, if students are effectively prepared and guided through the experience, can achieve these results, along with the many other benefits offered through international experiences. Studies in several countries have identified profound transformational learning in various geographical locations. The research covers a

G. Mihut et al. (Eds.), Understanding Higher Education Internationalization, 353–355.

range of activity which challenges the student to a greater or lesser extent. Results show clearly that exposing students to alternative perspectives and cultural contexts can result in a questioning of personal identity, values, beliefs, and mindsets, and can offer significant results in terms of personal growth, self-efficacy, and maturity and enhance students' intercultural competence.

Proponents of experiential learning may argue that it is the physicality of the experience which results in such transformation, nevertheless the international/ intercultural element seems to play a role. Furthermore, it could be argued that those students who already possess some of these skills, or who have a propensity to develop them, are particularly attracted to the opportunity of studying, working, or volunteering abroad. These points give pause for thought but still the findings are both significant and repeated in one study after another.

IMPLICATIONS FOR UNIVERSITIES

This has a number of implications for policy and practice within institutions. First, the link between international experience and the development of employability skills is not widely recognized at the institutional level. This means that, secondly, its importance is not transmitted to students either in encouraging more of them to take part in education abroad, or in helping them understand the skills they have developed as a result of doing so. Thirdly, this link is not communicated to employers; note that they call for more soft skills, not for more students with international experience.

Finally, and perhaps most significantly, there is a lack of exploration of what this means for the curriculum of all students, not simply the mobile minority. If education abroad can support employability in this way, can internationalization of the curriculum at home offer similar benefits for the static majority? As yet, there is insufficient evidence of student learning outcomes from internationalized curricula in the domestic setting to indicate the full potential of this approach.

INTERNATIONALIZING THE CURRICULUM AT HOME

It has been argued that the real benefit of international experience for the kind of transformational learning noted above comes through the many "disorienting dilemmas" a student is faced with outside the comfort zone of their home environment. A number of academics are seeking to offer virtual mobility through technological means in order to share differing national and cultural experiences. But other opportunities are closer to home; cultural "otherness" comes in many forms and there are different kinds of comfort zones. Students in a contemporary university are likely to include people from differing religious, national, or ethnic backgrounds, of different sexual orientations, or with differing physical abilities. If "otherness" is understood as anybody whom you perceive as different from yourself, cultural others are not merely those from different countries or language groups.

354

Sharing perspectives across this alternative cultural divide means that, with imagination, creative "intercultural" opportunities can be used within a domestic curriculum. For example, if international community volunteering can result in personal transformation, could the same be true for local "intercultural" volunteering such as with different religious or faith groups, drug addiction centers, shelters for homeless people, women's refuges or homes for mentally or physically challenged individuals?

The answer is that we do not know whether internationalization (or "interculturalization") of the curriculum "at home" can be as successful as education abroad, including in the development of transferable employability skills. What is clear, however, is that we have yet to make the most of the diversity in our universities and local communities to support intercultural learning in domestic settings. However, if we accept that transformational learning, of the kind identified in the literature on international mobility, relates to the intercultural and experiential dimensions of that international experience, it is likely that replication in domestic intercultural contexts may offer some equivalence, at least.

In order to achieve this, international and intercultural must be understood as complementary aspects of the broader notions of equity, diversity, and inclusion within our institutions, something not yet accepted in all universities. Relevant intercultural learning outcomes will need to be incorporated into curricula for all students—not simply opportunities for international mobility—and innovative assessment tasks developed which measure whether the outcomes have been achieved. The assumption that study abroad offers the golden remedy must be challenged. The demands of today's global professional contexts require us to offer an internationalized curriculum for all our students not simply the mobile few. Perhaps more importantly, the enhanced perspectives that result can help the development of more just and tolerant societies.

JEREMY RAPPLEYE AND EDWARD VICKERS

77. JAPAN: NATIONALISM VS INTERNATIONALISM[1]

University World News, 20 November 2015, Issue 391

In October 2014, The New York Times spotlighted an apparent contradiction in what it termed "Japan's divided education strategy." Whilst pushing leading universities to become more globalised, the government was simultaneously making schooling more "nationalistic"—revising curricula for history and moral education. The article underscored the riddle at the heart of Japan's educational response to globalisation: How can any country become both more global and more "nationalistic" at the same time?

In an unprecedented move, the Ministry of Education, Culture, Sports, Science and Technology, or MEXT, promptly issued a response on its website. The then minister of education Shimomura Hakubun argued that "there is no contradiction between Japan placing great value on its traditions, culture, and history on the one hand, while coexisting in the international community on the other." His response was not new: the same logic can be found running through previous education reform plans, from Yasuhiro Nakasone's Rinkyoshin (Ad Hoc Council on Education) in the 1980s to Prime Minister Shinzo Abe's Kyoiku Saisei Kaigi (literally, the Council for Educational Rebirth) today.

The statement first confirmed that the government is indeed now strongly committed to globalising its universities. In order to "develop human resources that can compete on the global stage," more foreign students and scholars will be recruited, and the number of young Japanese abroad doubled to 120,000 by 2020. But Shimomura also stressed that a "weak sense of identity" meant that young Japanese venturing abroad suffered from an inability to "explain aspects of their own country." He argued that education at all levels must strengthen Japanese identity as a necessary precondition for becoming a "truly globalised person." He insisted that this did not involve promoting "nationalism" or "contempt for other countries." In conclusion, he even cited Prince Shotoku Taishi's Seventeen Article Constitution from the seventh century to suggest that current reforms are driven by a "spirit of harmony" inherent to Japanese tradition.

GLOBAL HIGHER EDUCATION FOR SOME

So which is it? Is Japan's current education policy contradictory or harmonious? As it happens, The New York Times article was wrong on several counts. Only 37 of

G. Mihut et al. (Eds.), Understanding Higher Education Internationalization, 357–361.

Japan's almost 800 universities—a mere 5%—are receiving funding under the Super Global Universities programme, the most ambitious attempt to change Japanese universities since World War II. Although these will produce many future elites, the majority of Japanese students will not have a "global" higher education. Moreover, the article was wrong in asserting that government efforts to internationalise are confined to the tertiary sector. English teaching is now being introduced at earlier grades of elementary school. In 2003, the ministry launched the Super English Language High Schools programme, and in June 2012 a vast increase in the number of Japanese high schools offering the International Baccalaureate, or IB, curriculum was announced.

Nonetheless, the broader point concerning the contradictory nature of current educational reforms still stands. Unfortunately, as former minister Shimomura's protestations illustrate, these contradictions appear to be nearly invisible at the national level. It is only when one ventures into actual classrooms or listens closely to globally ambitious Japanese youth that one confronts the conflicts.

INTERNATIONAL EDUCATION FOR AN INTERNATIONALISING JAPAN

There are now nearly 6,000 primary or secondary schools across the country where at least some of the students are not Japanese. This number will increase rapidly in coming years due to the declining birthrate, continuing immigration and international marriages. Is it either possible, or desirable, for Japanese teachers to present a single vision of Japanese "tradition, culture and history" to foreign students or those of mixed parentage in the hope of building a "strong" Japanese identity? Such students must be integrated into Japanese society—but what is the best way of doing it? Or take the challenge of encouraging Japanese youth to "go global" by studying abroad. Leading universities such as Tokyo University are already considering making overseas study a requirement for graduation. But many students we talk to, who have already participated in such exchange programmes, confess that their chief difficulty lies not in understanding themselves, but in an inability to understand the starting point of, say, Chinese or American worldviews. Many therefore tend to spend more time while abroad with other Japanese than with their foreign counterparts

Compelling Japanese students to spend more time at school studying national "traditions, culture, and history" is only likely to increase their alienation from the outside world. This will make them even less capable of participating in serious discussions about Japan's global role. By continuing to emphasise the drawing of simple dividing lines between Japanese and non-Japanese, current government policy threatens to accelerate the uchi-muki (inward-looking) mindset of young Japanese. But what if the real solution lies not in drawing such lines, but in erasing them? What if Japanese leaders and citizens alike began to think about "identity" as relational and ever-changing, not eternal and immutable? We believe that such a fundamental shift is key to the success not just of university internationalisation, but to restoring the health and vigour of Japanese society more broadly.

A DISTINCTIVE VOICE IN THE GLOBAL CONVERSATION

In this article, we have written as two foreign faculty at leading national universities in Japan, graduates from "world-class" Western institutions, with years of experience teaching in Japan at high school and university levels. We are committed to Japan for the long term: this is our home too. We want to see the ambitious current reforms succeed for the sake of Japan's future, for the sake of our students. And as citizens of countries—America and Britain—whose role in constructing the current global order has been deeply problematic, we believe that the wider world is poorer without Japan's presence, voice, and values.

So let us be clear: we are not advocating wholesale replacement of the current system with a foreign import or global "best practice." Instead, we are calling for education at all levels, but especially in leading universities, to offer space for real dialogue between the diverse cultures, languages and experiences of both Japan itself and the wider world. In short, we want to see universities become sites where "Japanese" identity and values are renewed for a global age.

Like many Japanese, we are aware that the competition, consumerism, and self-promotion that dominate contemporary global society clash with an emphasis on cooperation, thrift, and gratitude that is deeply ingrained in Japan. But as foreigners, we know that these values are not "unique" to Japan, but are shared by many elsewhere. This is precisely why there is so much resistance around the world today to ultra-competitive, hyper-consumerist "neoliberal globalization."

Unfortunately, however, rather than demonstrating how qualities thought of as traditionally "Japanese" are shared with many in other societies, education policy-makers remain intent on emphasising Japan's "uniqueness." The effect of this is to foster attitudes that are, at best, dismissive of "outsiders" or, at worst, fearful and hostile. Preserving the aspects of our lifestyle that we value becomes a matter of building barriers against irreconcilably alien foreigners. Moreover, when values are seen simply as products of some unique, ineffably "Japanese" essence, questions about what we can learn from other societies, and what they might learn from us, become very hard to discuss. When Japanese youth overseas are challenged to explain Japanese culture and society, if all they can muster are harmonious smiles and vague quotes from Shotoku Taishi, then the conversation will be brief and disappointing. Rather than acting as persuasive ambassadors for a resurgent Japan, they will only confirm stereotypes of their country as a quaint island kingdom cut off from the rest of the world. They will confirm what many foreigners already believe: there is nothing the world can learn from Japan.

So what is the alternative? It is to give Japanese youth an opportunity to critically explore their values before they encounter the outside world as adults. Education reforms should aim to make classrooms at all levels places where youngsters are encouraged to challenge and critique received notions of "Japaneseness."

CHANGING VALUES

Conservative commentators constantly complain that today's youth are losing the sense of "Japanese" identity. But as foreigners we encounter a set of values that are not so fragile as such commentators allege. These values are strongly rooted in the depths of Japanese society, not in the mercurial political realm or only amongst an older generation.

Values are not learnt simply as abstract concepts in the classroom, but primarily through daily practice and in interactions with family, friends, and neighbours. We know this because we feel that we have in some sense "become Japanese" without ever being students in Japanese classrooms, won over by the values we see as central to everyday life here. So schooling should help Japanese youth to become conscious of their values and thus able to explain them. But how should it do this? As we have learnt after many years living in foreign countries, real consciousness of identity and difference is something that comes through experience, not from textbooks.

Everyone has a "weak sense of identity" until they come up against values or lifestyles different from their own. And such encounters have the potential not just to reinforce our beliefs, but to transform them—quite possibly for the better. Those responsible for education policy, generally lacking significant overseas experience, have failed to understand this. They cling to a vision of homogenous Japan, technologically innovative, but culturally unchanging. But the country they hanker after no longer exists, if it ever did.

Like every society, Japan is constantly changing, forcing each generation to re-examine their values and identity in the face of new challenges. For young Japanese today, these include the need to adapt to a new order in East Asia and to accommodate growing diversity within Japan itself. This will happen not through memorising textbook platitudes about "harmony," but through interaction and dialogue with those who are different. The ability to understand and communicate one's identity comes precisely from working with people who do not share the same set of basic assumptions.

OPPORTUNITIES TO INTERACT

For us then, the problems associated with internationalisation—the supposed "weakness" of Japanese youth identity, Japan's inability to communicate its values, and widespread uncertainty about a global future for Japan—are not the result of a failure to teach "Japaneseness," but symptoms of a lack of opportunities to interact with "outsiders." The ministry's ideas about "identity" reflect the long-standing assumptions of those at the core of the Japanese establishment—that identity is an objective, culturally specific quality that can easily be packaged up and taught.

But the elements of society that are most "globalized," such as students returning from abroad and foreign residents, know that "identity" is relational. We understand that confidence in the global space comes through embracing interaction with the "outside," not reinforcing rigid divisions between "inside" and "outside."

From this vantage point, Japan's inability to produce "truly globalised" people looks completely different. Uchi-muki attitudes are the inevitable result of an overemphasis on teaching the values of the core establishment since the early 1950s. So long as the most global elements of Japanese society remain marginalised, education will fail to produce the change policy-makers say they want. More tragically, if Japan chooses to portray itself as exotic and "unique," the universal appeal of its values, with all they have to offer the rest of the world, will be quickly dismissed.

Alternatively, education could challenge and transcend arbitrary distinctions between "inside" and "outside," "core" and "periphery," "Japanese" and "non-Japanese." A new generation of Japanese youth might then emerge—more confident, more articulate, more comfortable with difference, and less confused by the contradictions between what they learn at school and what they experience internationally. Policy-makers and citizens alike need to strive to make educational institutions places where peripheral "outsiders" and an out-of-touch core interact and transform one another. Then Japan's educational "rebirth" can really begin.

NOTE

[1]   This is the third article in a three-part series written by Jeremy Rappleye and Edward Vickers and published by University World News.

JAN PETTER MYKLEBUST AND JACQUIE WITHERS

78. NORWAY: INCREASING INTERNATIONALISATION IN PHD EDUCATION

University World News, 2 September 2012, Issue 237

A recent survey suggests that Norway boost its efforts to internationalise PhD education and includes the recommendation that for PhD dissertation evaluation, at least one member of the three-member committee should be drawn from outside Norway. A June report, *PhD Education in a Knowledge Society: An evaluation of PhD education in Norway* (NIFU, 2012), maintains that Norway's PhD education system is of a high quality, being well funded and well organised and offering "very good working and learning conditions for PhD candidates, as well as good career prospects." The report was published by the Nordic Institute for Studies in Innovation, Research and Education (NIFU) and commissioned by the Research Council of Norway on behalf of the Ministry of Education and Research. It argues that since the previous similar evaluation in 2002, "Norway has taken a definitive step towards becoming a standardised PhD education system with a strong focus on monitoring quality and efficiency."

Among the report's key recommendations is "improving practices in international recruitment at the PhD level, and finding ways of reducing the administrative burden of international recruitment of PhD candidates." The report continues: "Norway needs to be thinking more broadly about how the internationalisation of PhD education is occurring and how it should be promoted—with a focus that goes beyond concerns for outward mobility and longer stays abroad."

MORE FOREIGN INPUT INTO PHD EVALUATION

At the same time, the country is pushing to include more foreign academics on its PhD evaluation committees. The NIFU report details how the researchers sent out a survey questionnaire to the members of PhD evaluation committees who are from outside Norway. The objective was to map how highly these "external members" judge the quality of the country's PhDs. In the survey, which had a response rate of 79%, members were asked their opinion of the quality of PhD dissertations recently assessed. Those surveyed were asked to rate quality in terms of a number of different factors: originality; depth and coverage; theoretical level; methodological level and skills in written presentation; contribution to the advancement of the field;

G. Mihut et al. (Eds.), Understanding Higher Education Internationalization, 363–365.

and external (applied, societal, cultural, or industrial) relevance. There were five response options, ranging from "excellent" to "poor."

Overall, 20% of the respondents rated the survey elements "excellent," with a further 40% rating them "very good" and 25% to 60% evaluating them as "good." The quality aspect that was ranked highest was skills in written presentation, as either "excellent" or "very good" by two-third of the evaluators, followed by depth and coverage listed by 65% and originality by 60% in the excellent-very good category. When broken down according to PhD dissertation evaluators from different regions, interesting patterns emerged from the survey responses: North American evaluators gave the Norwegian PhD theses better ratings than their European colleagues, who in turn were more positive in their responses than members from the other Nordic countries.

On how the thesis evaluated contributed to the advancement of the field, 48% of the Nordic evaluators said "excellent" or "very good," compared to 64% of those coming from the rest of Europe and 68% of those from North America. When broken down according to academic field, PhD dissertations in the natural sciences and the humanities got the strongest ratings, while those in the social sciences and agriculture or veterinary medicine, were ranked beyond average. Theses in engineering or technology and medicine or health received very high scores among the North American examiners.

The majority of the survey respondents said the assessment procedures were rigorous and fair to the candidate, but also more time-consuming than in other countries. In Norway a joint examiners' evaluation report is required before the doctoral defence, which is not the case in most other countries.

NEED FOR INTERNATIONALISATION IN PHD EDUCATION

In arguing the need for internationalisation in PhD education to be reconsidered, the NIFU report points out that "the world of science and academic labour markets are increasingly global." The report states that in Norway currently about 33% of PhD graduates are not Norwegian citizens, and in the areas of natural sciences and technology 73% of PhD programme units report having a majority of international PhD applicants, reflecting "increased opportunities for internationalisation in PhD education." The report concurs that the increasing international recruitment that is being seen in Norway at the PhD level is positive "but poses short and long term challenges for the higher education institutions." The report specifies: "Recruitment procedures and quality control of PhD applicants is important, as is the integration of international PhD candidates and finding efficient ways to promote international experiences for all Norwegian PhD candidates."

One of the concerns raised by the NIFU report is the issue of "critical time" for the research training part of the PhD, and "the risk that too many and too diverse a set of demands are being placed on the PhD period, in a way that has negative long-term consequences for the development of science." The report concludes in this regard that: "Better integration between the master and PhD levels and further training in the post-doc period are international trends which might help to address such challenges in Norwegian PhD training."

REFERENCE

Nordic Institute for Studies in Innovation, Research and Education (NIFU). (2012). *PhD education in a knowledge society: An evaluation of PhD education in Norway.* Retrieved from https://brage.bibsys.no/xmlui/bitstream/handle/11250/280895/NIFUrapport2012-25.pdf?sequence=1&isAllowed=y

PART 13

PEACE, DIPLOMACY, AND SOCIAL SERVICE

INTRODUCTION

This last section, number thirteen, focuses on instances when internationalization can become part of the social mission of universities. As it is widely acknowledged that global cooperation and understanding are key to ensuring lasting world peace, the role of higher education as a space for skill building in these areas is seen as critically important.

The first article in this section, written by Jenny Lee, highlights the challenge faced by international students in light of the rise in neo-nationalist sentiments. The article introduces the examples of the negative lived experiences of Chinese students in South Korea and of Zimbabweans in South Africa. The next article offers a compelling analysis of the obligations held by universities when branch campuses are founded in areas with known human rights violations. Gearóid Cuinn argues that the responsibility of universities extends to protecting those that have been affected by conflicts, general unrest, human rights violations, and natural disasters. Hans de Wit discusses the responsibility of universities and international organizations to increase their capacity and welcome more refugee students from Syria and elsewhere. Indeed, the role of higher education in achieving global cooperation is ongoing and crucial. Jane Knight highlights the importance of knowledge diplomacy as a means of operation for universities. Under a paradigm of diplomacy, universities can mediate, negotiate, and facilitate collaboration between and within nation states that may result in addressing world challenges. The last article in this section, authored by Daniel Obst, summarizes the power of cooperation between institutions—at the core of the internationalization imperative—by describing attempts to restore the relationship between Iran and the United States.

Internationalization can and should contribute towards building a peaceful world. Important challenges rarely affect a single nation. Universities facilitate the process of learning from the experiences of others, offer space for research and reflection, and mediate the encounter with the Other. Indeed, internationalization may be seen as a form of diplomacy, and the skills developed on internationalized campuses as critical building blocks in establishing and maintaining peace.

JENNY J. LEE

79. GLOBAL: NEO-NATIONALISM: CHALLENGES FOR INTERNATIONAL STUDENTS

International Higher Education, Winter 2016, Number 84

There are more students studying outside their borders than ever before, with numbers doubling over the past decade, and forecasts that these numbers will rise even more rapidly in the years to come. Yet, with the rise of international demand, come added challenges for universities seeking to become more globally adaptive to their internationally diverse students. While some cultural adjustment is to be anticipated, what international students might be less prepared for are difficulties that are attributable less to any shortcomings of the student, but to the shortcomings of the home environment. Despite institutional leaders' best efforts, members of the university and local community might not be prepared or willing to welcome those perceived as outsiders. Resistance against international students has been well documented in various media outlets, in the form of discriminatory acts, from subtle stereotyping to physical attacks.

Although most international students have a very positive experience studying abroad, there are others who suffer silently. Based on some recent survey research of international students across seven universities in South Africa, when asked to whom they would report if they encountered unfair treatment, 32 percent indicated that they would not report to anyone.

RISE IN REGIONAL MOBILITY

With the rise in global mobility, there has been a rise in regional mobility as well. International study within one's region is occurring most notably within the European Union, but regional study is also taking place in East Asia, Latin America, Southern Africa, and other parts of the world. Due to regional cooperation agreements, improved university quality, and increased cross-border travel, there has been an emergence of regional hubs that are attracting increasing numbers of students seeking an international degree, but desiring to stay closer to home. With this phenomenon, one might suppose there would be fewer discriminatory concerns for those maybe appearing less like "foreigners" abroad. Challenges such as language barriers, homesickness, and cultural adaptation might be assumed to be less troubling for those from neighboring countries than those from more distant regions. However, this is not the case.

G. Mihut et al. (Eds.), Understanding Higher Education Internationalization, 371–373.

NEO-NATIONALISM

In the United States, international students from non-Western and developing countries tended to report more unfair treatment and hostility than students from Europe, Canada, and Australia, which I describe as forms of neo-racism. Neo-racism is discrimination not solely based on biological differences, but also includes differences in culture in this postcolonial era. Neo-racism would help to explain why students from China, for example, might encounter a very different set of troubles in the United States, in comparison to Chinese American students. Neo-racism, however, would not aptly apply to international students being discriminated against within their region. As such, my latest research has uncovered a new form of discrimination that has less to do with one's race and more to do with one's nationality. Whereas nationalism refers to identification with one's nation, neo-nationalism, like neo-racism, extends this concept to the new global economy. Simply put, neo-nationalism is defined as discrimination based on national identity. With increasing internationalization, national identity is being reintroduced and reconceptualized as forms of global competition. That is, neo-nationalism has the potential to negatively impact an international student's experience, particularly in studying in one's region. Negative treatment might occur even despite sharing the same race as the majority culture, and may even result in worse treatment compared to a student from a different race and geographical region.

CASES OF SOUTH KOREA AND SOUTH AFRICA

South Korea and South Africa are two emerging market countries that have both experienced major increases in immigration, including from international students. These countries play significant roles as regional hubs, providing international higher education to nearby countries. Among both overall migrants and cross-border students, the major source of these populations comes from shared borders. Meanwhile, both South Korea and South Africa, much like the major global destinations of the West, have also been subject to negative reports of hostile treatment targeted against unwanted "foreigners."

South Korea hosts approximately 86,000 international students and attracts most of this population from China (69%). In a comparison between students from different regions, East Asian students reported greater difficulties and unfair treatment compared to students from Europe, North America, and even other parts of Asia. Chinese students in particular reported feeling less welcomed compared to those from other countries, including other East Asian countries. A Chinese student explained, "Korean students tend to socialize well with students from Western countries and also not bad with Japanese students. But they don't do so with, particularly, Chinese students." Such experiences were explained as based on negative stereotypes about China, and were manifest in a range of discriminatory acts. Common examples included the following: "I made my best effort to search jobs but I was rejected since I was foreigner. Actually, managers didn't recognize it while we were speaking, but I told them honestly since I thought I should not be embarrassed of being Chinese. Then, soon they rejected me." Another student said, "The dorm mother said she never accepted Chinese to live here, since they were dirty and noisy." Such accounts cannot be explained as discrimination by race, but based on national origins.

Such discrimination based on nationality, despite sharing the same race, is not isolated to East Asia. In the case of South Africa, the majority of its approximately 73,000 international students are from Southern Africa (74%), with the largest group from its border country, Zimbabwe (27%). As in South Korea, international students in South Africa reported mistreatment on the basis of nationality. A student explained, "Zimbabweans are treated badly because of our political and economic challenges." Another African student shared, "People seem to be uncomfortable with my being Nigerian." Accommodation is a common problem for international students; as one Zambian student reported, "We as foreigners are usually treated with contempt by South Africans. When it comes to accommodation, we are treated unfairly. We would be charged twice the amount that South African citizens pay." In comparison to other international students, a student from Malawi explained, "Home students are more welcoming to students outside Africa than to those from within Africa (...) home students do not associate with African international students. However, they are always friendly to those coming from overseas."

COMPLEX CHALLENGES AHEAD

Although the dominant hosts in the West continue to grapple with successfully integrating international with local students, similar challenges exist for regional hosts, despite educating a majority of culturally similar international students. While neo-racism might be observed in major Western destinations, such as the United States, United Kingdom, and Australia, neo-nationalism might also be at play, particularly in emerging economies that serve as educational destinations within the region, such as South Korea and South Africa. As some recent research has revealed, the difficulties that international students encounter are global. Even so, neo-racism and neo-nationalism are two different but powerful challenges in this increasingly complex global society.

GEARÓID Ó. CUINN

80. GLOBAL: TRANSNATIONAL EDUCATION AND HUMAN RIGHTS OBLIGATIONS

University World News, 1 April 2016, Issue 407

In recent years, Western universities have demonstrated an appetite for international expansion and the establishment of overseas branch campuses. Today there are an estimated 230 satellite campuses operating globally, a figure that excludes franchises, partnerships, "twinning" agreements, and many failed attempts (Cross-Border Education Research Team, n.d.). Approximately 60 Western education institutions or programmes currently operate in the Persian Gulf region alone. While the aim is to diversify revenue streams and build an international reputation, these efforts also invite significant risk. A steady stream of headlines show how universities have had to contend with (or ignore) human rights challenges in their host nation, issues ranging from restrictions on freedom of expression (Washington Square News, 2014) to the use of forced labour (Shaw, 2014).

Professor Sigrun Skogly and I attempted to map the implication of such frictions from a domestic perspective and asked whether the export of education programmes overseas imports human rights risks. To do this we focused on the multiple forms of oversight and accreditation which are intrinsic to the education programmes being exported overseas (Ó Cuinn & Skogly, 2016). The UK's Quality Assurance Agency for Higher Education, for example, is an independent body involved with extensive international higher education activity, working with countries such as Albania, Sri Lanka, Pakistan, and Uzbekistan (Havergal, 2016).

When fulfilling a public function, such bodies are often bound by human rights law obligations and, in the European context, this includes obligations found in the European Convention on Human Rights. If that public function is exercised overseas, it does not mean human rights obligations no longer apply. However, due to limited debate on these issues the significance of human rights obligations to such activity remains practically unexplored. Often there appears to be a misplaced faith that the campus gate insulates a branch campus from the ills of a local setting.

EUROPEAN COURT OF HUMAN RIGHTS

We examined the case law of the European Court of Human Rights to see how oversight functions extending to a branch campus engage human rights obligations.

G. Mihut et al. (Eds.), Understanding Higher Education Internationalization, 375–377.

What quickly became clear is that transnational oversight allows for the "extra-territorial" application of human rights standards thanks to the cooperative nature of the interaction. Ultimately, any state that consents to hosting a degree programme from another country also consents to the standards that underpin it. Thanks to this consent, the transnational oversight of a branch campus, whether as quality assurance or an accreditation scheme, remains governed by the standards of the sending country. We then set out to explore what this would mean in practice when human rights violations are at stake. What would this legal framework mean in practical terms for universities and their oversight authorities?

We chose to conduct our analysis using the controversial accreditation of an Irish education institute in Bahrain operated by the Royal College of Surgeons in Ireland or RCSI (Hillard, 2014), which has received significant international attention following the Arab Spring protests (Fisk, 2013). Its clinical training facilities were the scene of a broad spectrum of human rights abuses: hospitals were allegedly used for torture, sectarian discrimination was rife and has affected student placements and an overtly militarised hospital administration continues to target injured protesters. The broader context of Bahrain also appeared to affect academic freedom on the Irish campus (Gantly, 2013) and RCSI-Bahrain has admitted to questioning students on behalf of the regime during the initial response to the protests (Gantly, 2011).

Medics who gave interviews during this time were imprisoned and one Irish trained doctor remains in detention. Meanwhile the main hospital used by RCSI, Salmaniya Medical Complex lost its approval from a Canadian accreditation authority (Devi, 2013). One month prior to an accreditation visit by Ireland's Medical Council to Bahrain a women's rights activist was arrested and imprisoned for tweeting criticism about a hospital used in the Irish education programme (Amnesty International, 2014).

RELEVANT HUMAN RIGHTS ISSUES

In this context we determined that obligations contained under the European Convention on Human Rights were materially relevant to accreditation standards. This means that, where human rights abuses are found to occur, an obligation may arise to address these issues through the accreditation process. For example, the case of Ireland's Medical Council accreditation in Bahrain requires making a determination on the appropriateness of supervision and the suitability of facilities to provide training in medical ethics.

As the Medical Council performs a public function, relevant human rights issues must be taken into account and steps taken to deter the well-documented allegations of torture, mistreatment, restrictions and violations of medical ethics in the facilities it monitors. Likewise, from the methodological perspective, fear and self-censorship ought to be contended with in advance as they can completely undermine procedures originally designed to assess standards in an open and free environment. If, over time, there is no sign of change, an obligation to withdraw involvement could arise.

In sum, the transnational oversight of education programmes is not detached from human rights obligations and a legal responsibility exists for proactive due diligence and meaningful monitoring. Rather than inhibiting transnational education, these findings ought to be seen as a means to properly uphold standards for the benefit of communities on both ends of the transnational connection.

REFERENCES

Amnesty International. (2014, November 7). *Bahrain: Activist faces jail for 'defamation on twitter':* *Ghada Jamsheer.* Retrieved from https://www.amnesty.org/en/documents/ mde11/044/2014/en/

Cross-Border Education Research Team. (n.d.). *Quick facts.* Retrieved from http://cbert.org/

Devi, S. (2013, May 30). Rights abuses linked to Irish surgical college in Bahrain. *The Lancet.* Retrieved from http://www.thelancet.com/journals/lancet/article/PIIS0140-6736 (13)61138-1/fulltext

Fisk, R. (2013, March 24). Bahrain hit by doctors' desertion. *Independent.* Retrieved from http://www.independent.co.uk/voices/comment/bahrain-hit-by-doctors-desertion-8547097.html

Gantly, D. (2011, October 12). Exclusive breaking news: RCSI says treatment of students in Bahrain "unacceptable." *Irish Medical Times.* Retrieved from http://www.imt.ie/news/exclusive-breaking-news-rcsi-says-treatment-of-students-in-bahrain-unacceptable-12-10-2011/

Gantly, D. (2013, June 10). Freedom was a resigning matter—Prof Tom Collins. *Irish Medical Times.* Retrieved from http://www.imt.ie/features-opinion/freedom-was-a-resigning-matter-10-06-2013/

Havergal, C. (2016, February 29). QAA to support Albanian university reviews. *Times Higher Education.* Retrieved from https://www.timeshighereducation.com/news/qaa-support-albanian-university-reviews

Hillard, M. (2014, May 9). Critics claim Irish visit to Bahrain medical university will be stage-managed. *The Irish Times.* Retrieved from http://www.irishtimes.com/news/ health/critics-claim-irish-visit-to-bahrain-medical-university-will-be-stage-managed-1.1788985

Ó Cuinn, G., & Skogly, S. (2016). Understanding human rights obligations of states engaged in public activity overseas: the case of transnational education. *The International Journal of Human Rights, 20*(6), 761–784.

Shaw, C. (2014, August 29). MP urges UCL to "stamp out" forced labour on Qatar campus. *The Guardian.* Retrieved from https://www.theguardian.com/higher-education-network/2014/aug/29/university-college-london-forced-labour-qatar-campus

Washington Square News. (2014, August 24). *New Abu Dhabi campus to open amid controversy.* Retrieved from http://www.nyunews.com/2014/08/24/abu-dhabi/

HANS DE WIT

81. GLOBAL: BEYOND THE SYRIAN REFUGEE CRISIS

University World News, 11 March 2016, Issue 404

The Syrian refugee crisis has already been going on for a year and its end is not yet in sight: the war goes on and the economic, social, and political situation in the country itself and in neighbouring countries is worsening. The numbers of refugees arriving in Europe daily is still high and resistance is increasing. After a slow initial reaction from the higher education community, the number of initiatives launched by individual institutions, donor organisations, and NGOs has been remarkable, even though these actions are only solving a minor part of an immense problem.

In its recent newsletter, Al-Fanar Media showed clearly how access to higher education in neighbouring countries like Iraq, Egypt, Lebanon, Jordan, and Turkey is limited to a very small proportion of Syrian students, and this week University World News republishes an impressive appeal by a Syrian academic refugee to universities in neighbouring countries to use him and his colleagues to help educate young Syrian refugees. There is still a long way to go to increase access for Syrian youth to higher education. A whole generation seems doomed to be lost.

INCREASED MOBILITY

The response to the Syrian refugee crisis provides lessons about the important role education in general, and higher education in particular, can play in addressing the increasing mobility of (illegal) immigrants and refugees around the world. Where politicians see building gates and camps (as in Europe) and walls (as in the United States) as their only solutions and do their best to contain the problem in the bordering countries which are already struggling with considerable numbers of refugees, there is no long-term vision of how to avoid an increase in illegal immigration or how to solve the problems at their root, in the regions themselves. Most developed countries have reduced their development aid budgets over the past years and/or have aligned them more with their commercial interests. Education, and in particular higher education capacity building in developing countries, is under financial constraints.

At the same time, one can see an increasing focus on competition for international talent needed to fill the gaps in the knowledge economies. How is it possible that Europe, the United States and Australia invest in recruiting international students and scholars while at the same time ignoring the presence of potential talent among refugees and immigrants already in their countries and in camps? Increasing higher

G. Mihut et al. (Eds.), Understanding Higher Education Internationalization, 379–380.

education capacity in neighbouring countries to address the needs of refugees there would be a tremendously useful investment. Canada is a positive exception with its acceptance of 25,000 refugees, including students from Syria. It might already be too late for the current Syrian youth still living in the country or resettled in camps elsewhere, but to avoid future massive migration flows, increased investments in higher education in the region and in scholarship schemes to study abroad are a necessary and effective measure.

National governments and international entities like the World Bank, the European Commission, and UNESCO should plan long-term strategies to increase higher education capacity and quality in the developing world, beginning with countries like Iraq, Turkey, Lebanon, and Jordan, but also those in Central America and Africa.

JANE KNIGHT

82. GLOBAL: MOVING FROM SOFT POWER TO KNOWLEDGE DIPLOMACY

International Higher Education, Spring 2015, Number 80

International higher education, in its role as a political actor, is strongly attracted to the concept of soft power. Developed by Joseph Nye about a decade ago, soft power is popularly understood as the ability to influence others and achieve national self-interest(s) through attraction and persuasion rather than through coercion, military force, or economic sanctions—commonly known as hard power.

Many academics hail soft power as a fundamental premise of today's international education engagement. Common examples of soft power in higher education include the Fulbright Program, British Council activities, German Academic Exchange initiatives, Erasmus Mundus projects, and others. Clearly, these are respected and long-standing programs that make enormous contributions. But why do we call them instruments of "soft power," when at their heart they promote exchange of students, faculty, culture, science, knowledge, and expertise. Yes, there are self-interests at play, but there is a mutuality of interests and benefits involved for all partners. International higher education is not traditionally seen as a game of winners and losers—it focuses on exchange and builds on the respective strengths of institutions and countries. Importantly, it recognizes that benefits will differ among partners and countries. In our highly interdependent world, higher education facilitates the cross-border flow and the exchange of people, knowledge, values, innovation, economy, technology, and culture. But why is it framed in a "power paradigm" like soft power? Are the values of self-interest, competition, or dominance going to effectively address issues of world-wide epidemics, terrorism, failed states, the bottom billion in poverty, and climate change? The answer is no. This is based on the reality that solutions to worldwide challenges cannot be achieved by one country alone.

An alternative to the power paradigm is the framework of diplomacy. Diplomacy, interpreted as the management of international relations, focuses on negotiation, mediation, collaboration, compromise, and facilitation. These are different tactics and concepts than those attached to power dominance, authority, command, and control. Is knowledge diplomacy more appropriate to frame the role of higher education in international relations, than the soft power paradigm?

Knowledge is a cornerstone of today's interconnected world. The evolution from the new information and communication technologies of cyberspace, to the big data

G. Mihut et al. (Eds.), Understanding Higher Education Internationalization, 381–382.

of infospace, to the knowledge processing of knowspace brings new opportunities and complexities to international higher education. However, there is no denying that knowledge can also lead to power imbalances within and among countries. This reality is exacerbated when higher education and knowledge are seen as tools of soft power. The alternative of using collaboration and mediation strategies of diplomacy requires serious consideration.

International higher education has the opportunity of moving beyond its preoccupation, with the knowledge economy, and takes a proactive role to ensure that knowledge is effectively used to address worldwide challenges and inequalities, by recognizing the mutuality of interests and benefits. Is higher education ready to take a lead in promoting the notion of knowledge diplomacy and not remain stuck, in the soft power frame of self-interest and dominance?

DANIEL OBST

83. US-IRAN: RESTORING RELATIONSHIPS IN HIGHER EDUCATION

University World News, 3 July 2015, Issue 374

Last month the Institute of International Education, or IIE, led a delegation of US higher education leaders to Iran, meeting with counterparts from Iranian universities and research institutes in Tehran, Shiraz, and Isfahan, to explore how to reopen and expand educational and scientific dialogue. After almost a year of planning and preparation, our delegation opened a historic new chapter in educational relations and people-to-people exchanges between the United States and Iran. While there is still much to learn about Iran today, one thing is clear from our visit: there are tremendous opportunities and a strong desire in both the United States and Iran to expand academic collaboration between our two countries.

A MULTI-GENERATIONAL FOUNDATION

The IIE delegation included five public and private institutions: Ball State University; Pitzer College; Rutgers, the State University of New Jersey; the University of Southern California; and Wayne State University, as well as representatives from IIE's Center for International Partnerships in Higher Education.

Our group was warmly received by high-level officials from many of Iran's top universities and research institutes, including the University of Tehran, Shahid Beheshti University, Sharif University of Technology, and the Iranian Research Organisation for Science and Technology, or IROST, most of whom were quite well-versed in the many facets of the US higher education system. The majority of academics and university administrators we met in Iran had been educated in the United States, and many had children that are studying in the United States today.

According to the 2014 Open Doors Report on International Educational Exchange, published by the IIE with support from the US Department of State's Bureau of Educational and Cultural Affairs, there were nearly 10,200 Iranian students and close to 1,400 Iranian scholars at US colleges and universities in 2013–14. The connection between Iranian faculty and American universities is not new. It is notable that Iran was the leading sender of international students to the United States in the 1970s, with more than 51,000 students enrolled in US universities in 1979. At Allameh Tabataba'i University in Tehran, for example, the rector brought together a number

G. Mihut et al. (Eds.), Understanding Higher Education Internationalization, 383–385.

of faculty members who had earned multiple degrees at institutions such as the University of Texas at Austin, Florida State University, University of Tennessee-Knoxville, University of Wisconsin-Madison, Wichita State University, Florida International University, University of Missouri, and the University of Illinois.

Their degrees ranged from statistics, theoretical economics, financial management, industrial management, and accounting to counselling and educational planning. Many Iranians who had received PhDs in the United States subsequently returned to Iranian universities to start new doctoral level programmes in their respective disciplines. This rich history of educational exchange between the two countries provides a particularly strong foundation for new and sustained educational cooperation.

AREAS FOR POTENTIAL ACADEMIC PARTNERSHIPS

Most institutions we visited have developed links with higher education institutions abroad, especially with European universities. However, almost none had formal relationships with US institutions. Going forward, universities in both countries are looking to form partnerships to enable the exchange of students and faculty and advance joint research. The first step will be to look at past memoranda of understanding, or MoUs, that have been lying dormant, some for 40 plus years, and determine which ones can or ought to be revived, and to look at current faculty interest for new areas of engagement.

The Iranian institutions we met with and our US delegates expressed particular interest in collaborating around research areas of mutual interest, including nanotechnology, stem cell research, medical and health sciences, and other fields. Despite the international sanctions, the facilities and the knowledge base at the institutions we visited seemed particularly well developed. Another surprise to the US delegation was how many women there were among the science faculty and in the student body.

Especially noteworthy is that almost every Iranian institution expressed interest in conducting joint research in the areas of water conservation and environmental management. With years of declining precipitation and increases in waste and contamination, water shortage is a paramount issue in Iran. The United States is facing similar challenges, especially related to the long-term water shortages affecting the Colorado River basin and thus most states west of the Rocky Mountains. At a minimum, more collaboration and research on these issues and others related to environmental sciences and climate change will be very valuable for both countries.

Another potential area of collaboration was related to a scholarship opportunity that is offered by the Iranian government to support Iranian PhD students to spend six to nine months in another country while working on their dissertation research. Approximately one third of the 1,500 scholarship students are currently doing their research in the United States, but there is potential to use this scholarship as a means to build closer relationships by centralising the coordination of the scholarships and focusing on key areas of mutual interest.

While a few US faculty members and students have reportedly visited Iran to participate in conferences or workshops, the 2014 Open Doors statistics show that no US higher education institution reported sending students to Iran for academic credit. Despite this, our delegates agreed that there are significant opportunities for American students and faculty, and they would be warmly welcomed if they were to come to Iran. We were especially pleased to learn about the widespread interest among Iranian universities in hosting American students and the interest of the US delegates in providing opportunities for their students to study in Iran. The semester-based credit system makes Iranian universities especially promising for US study abroad students. Several institutions, including the University of Tehran and Shiraz University, expressed interest in developing short-term study abroad opportunities for US students that would include cultural and language immersion in addition to the academic programme.

In the meantime, the delegates noted that there is a great need for more Iranian studies programmes in the United States, and part of this gap could be met in the short term by drawing on the expertise of visiting Iranian faculty and advanced doctoral students. US and Iranian higher education officials agree that the study of Iran has not been well defined; it is not effectively addressed in Arab studies or Middle Eastern studies programmes since Iran is neither an Arab country nor geographically part of the Middle East. Developing Iranian studies programmes, in collaboration with partners in Iran, would contribute to Americans' knowledge of the area while also helping build the pipeline for US study abroad to Iran.

Academic freedom is of particular concern to higher education institutions in the US and around the world. President Hassan Rouhani and others have called for more academic freedom in Iran's universities in order to encourage innovation and tolerance. More engagement with international academic institutions would certainly help universities to show their progress and shed light on any remaining restrictions or concerns. While there is much work to be done in the coming months and years, we hope our efforts will serve as a catalyst for sustained higher education partnerships that will encourage cooperation and understanding between the United States and Iran.

ABOUT THE CONTRIBUTORS

Georgiana Mihut is a Research Assistant at the Center for International Higher Education and a doctoral candidate in Higher Education at Boston College. In addition to international higher education, her primary research interests include the impact of university reputation on graduate employability and quality assurance in higher education. She recently published the article *What Germany and Romania have in common: The impact of university prestige on graduate employability*, coauthored the ACE and CIHE report *Internationalizing higher education worldwide: National policies and programs,* and published the article *International advisory councils and internationalization of governance. A qualitative analysis.* Georgiana holds an Erasmus Mundus Joint Master's degree in Research and Innovation in Higher Education, a Master of Arts degree in Education and Globalization from University of Oulu, Finland, and a Bachelor of Arts in Political Science degree from Babeş-Bolyai University, Romania.

Philip G. Altbach is research professor and the founding director of the Center for International Higher Education at Boston College. He was the Monan University Professor at Boston College for two decades. He has held appointments at Harvard University, the University of Wisconsin at Madison, and the State University of New York at Buffalo and has been a visiting scholar at Stanford University and the University of California at Berkeley. He was Distinguished Scholar Leader of the Fulbright New Century Scholars Program and was Fulbright Research Professor at the University of Mumbai, India. He is a Fellow of the American Education Research Association and was given the Houlihan Award by NAFSA: Association of International Educators and the Howard Bowen Research Award by the Association for the Study of Higher Education. He has been appointed to honorary professorships by the National Research University–Higher School of Economics in Moscow, Russia, and Peking University and Xiamen Universities in China, and has been Onwell Fellow at the University of Hong Kong. Philip Altbach has written or edited more than 50 books. He has served as editor of the *Review of Higher Education* and the *Comparative Education Review.*

Hans de Wit is professor of the practice and director of the Center for International Higher Education in the Lynch School of Education at Boston College. A native of the Netherlands, where his career as an administrator, researcher, and teacher has spanned three decades, de Wit joined the Lynch School in 2015 from the Universita Cattolica Sacro Cuore in Milan, Italy, where he served as the founding director of the Center for Higher Education Internationalization, and from the Amsterdam

University of Applied Sciences where he was professor of Internationalization of Higher Education. He is the Founding Editor of the *Journal of Studies in International Education* (Association for Studies in International Education/SAGE publishers), as well as a founding member and past president of the European Association for International Education (EAIE). He has published many books, articles, and reports on international higher education, and contributes a regular blog to *University World News*. He has received several awards for his contribution to the field of international education.

CONTRIBUTORS

Manail Anis Ahmed is a recognized authority on higher education and human capital development in Saudi Arabia. She is a Middle East/South Asia expert with over 16 years of global experience in institutional establishment, management, and administration, as well as strategy and policy for institutions interested in establishing greenfield projects and/or partnerships in the region. She holds a Bachelor in Political Science from Swarthmore College, and a Master's in the Languages and Cultures of Asia from University of Wisconsin-Madison, US.

Ryan M. Allen is a doctoral fellow and PhD candidate in the Department of International and Transcultural Studies at Teachers College, Columbia University, majoring in International and Comparative Education and specializing in Political Science. He recently co-edited a book entitled *Kuo Ping Wen: Scholar, Statesman, and Reformer*. He has also published research on soft power, university rankings, and Chinese educational development. Ryan was awarded the Confucius China Studies Program Fellowship in 2017 and recently completed his field research at Beijing Normal University, researching the impact of university rankings on the higher education sector in China. He also teaches Political Science and History at Berkeley College in New York City.

Veena Bhalla retired from the position of Secretary of the Association of Indian Universities in 2017. Currently she is working as a consultant (International and Student Information Services Divisions). She has written academic papers on examination reforms, distance education, and international education. Dr. Bhalla has published 35 papers, co-authored 5 books and has assisted in editing 8 books. *Foreign Providers of Higher Education: Realities, Implications and Future Options* (2006), *Inflow of International Students into India: Trends, Inferences and Suggestions* (2012*), International Students in Indian Universities: Source Countries, Gender Ratio, Levels of Education and Choice of Discipline* (2014) and *Internationalization on Higher Education: in India: Annual Survey of International Students 2013–2014* (2016) are some of her publications on internationalization of higher education. Dr. Bhalla is a member of *International Advisory Group of Project Atlas* of International Institute of Education, US.

Lukas Bischof is a visiting research fellow and advisor at the Higher School of Economics (Moscow), a consultant associated with CHE Consult (Berlin), and independent consultant and trainer (www.lukasbischof.eu). A trained organizational psychologist, between 2011 and 2016 he served as a full-time consultant for CHE Consult, working with universities, foundations, ministries of education, and the European Commission. He has published on the regulation and quality assurance of national and international higher education systems, institutional quality management, project management, and change management in higher education. He is currently finalizing his PhD on the governance of higher education systems in post-soviet countries.

Peter Bodycott is Professor of Teacher and International Education in the Faculty of Education, Science, Technology and Mathematics at the University of Canberra, Australia. Peter worked for 11 years as an elementary schoolteacher and professional development consultant in Australia, before shifting his career focus to higher education. This career has resulted in various leadership roles as Department, Faculty, and Senior Management in universities in Australia, Singapore, and Hong Kong. His teaching specializations include intercultural adaptation, internationalizing higher education, literacy teaching in early and middle years, and English as a second or foreign language. Peter's research covers a broad number of areas. His most recent published work explores internationalization of the curriculum, second language identity in study abroad, international education policy and practice, and intercultural education.

Patrick Boehler has published on China and Southeast Asia in four languages for publications in the US, Europe, and Asia. After stints with Austria's ministries of defense and foreign affairs in Vienna and Beijing, he began his reporting career in Kuala Lumpur with the Malaysian online news portal *Malaysiakini* and, later, *The Irrawaddy Magazine*, a Myanmar exile publication in Thailand. He holds a doctorate in political science and has taught journalism at the University of Hong Kong.

Uwe Brandenburg is Managing Partner of CHE Consult, a consulting company in the field of strategic higher education management based in Berlin and Prague, and was a valued member of the EAIE General Council. He has worked in higher education research and consulting since 2006 and specializes in impact analysis, effect measurement, employability, outsourcing of internationalization services and consulting on management, strategy development and organizational change. Prior to his current position, Uwe was director of international affairs for more than 11 years, eight of which were at Humboldt Universität zu Berlin. He has a PhD from the University of Bristol, England, a Master's in economics from the University of Wales at Swansea, and a Master's from Westfälische Wilhelms – Universität Münster, Germany.

Roger Y. Chao Jr. has a PhD in Asian and International Studies from the City University of Hong Kong. He also has a Master's of Education in Mathematics from the University of the Philippines and a European Master's in Lifelong Learning: Policy and Management from the Danish School of Education, Aarhus University, and the University of Deusto. He is currently the Senior Consultant for the International Centre for Higher Education Innovation, a UNESCO Category 2 Centre. He was formerly the higher education specialist for UNESCO Myanmar, and has continued to be engaged in various consultancies with UNESCO. He has published on regionalization and internationalization of higher education, higher education policies, comparative and international education, and sociology of education in various platforms including international peer-reviewed journals, edited volumes, international media, and government and international organizations' reports.

Rahul Choudaha is principal researcher and CEO of DrEducation, LLC, a US-based global higher education research and consulting firm. As a social entrepreneur, he co-founded interEDGE.org, a training solutions provider specializing in inclusion and success of international students. Previously, Choudaha worked for over seven years at World Education Services (WES) in New York City. As Chief Knowledge Officer and Senior Director of Strategic Development, he raised the organization's profile, built research capabilities, deepened institutional relationships, and launched innovative services. Choudaha is known for his expertise in connecting data and global trends to inform growth and innovation strategies. He regularly researches, speaks, blogs, and consults on international student mobility, enrollment strategies, and student success. He is a contributor to *Asia Times, Forbes, Huffington Post* and *University World News*. Choudaha frequently delivers invited keynote talks and session. He has chaired or presented over 100 sessions at professional conferences and has been quoted in global media including the *BBC, Time, NPR*, and *The Wall Street Journal*. Choudaha ideated, convened and moderated a global webinar series with *University World News* which received over 4,000 registrations across four webinars.

Gearóid Ó. Cuinn is an Academic Fellow at Lancaster University Law School. His research focuses on public health governance, business and human rights, and he has a strong interest in the sociology of human rights law and practice. Gearóid is also director of the Global Legal Action Network (GLAN), a non-profit organization that develops innovative legal actions to protect and promote human rights in the Global South.

Sharon Dell is a South Africa-based freelance writer, editor, and journalist specializing in higher education. She has written for *University World News* for a number of years and was appointed the Africa Edition editor in January 2017. She has an Master's in postcolonial literature from the former University of Natal.

John Aubrey Douglass is Senior Research Fellow—Public Policy and Higher Education at Berkeley's Center for Studies in Higher Education. He is the co-editor of *Globalization's Muse: Universities and Higher Education Systems in a Changing World* (Public Policy Press, 2009), and the author of *The Conditions for Admissions* (Stanford Press 2007) and *The California Idea and American Higher Education* (Stanford University Press, 2000 and 2007; published in Chinese in 2008 and in Japanese 2012). He is also editor of the Center's Research and Occasional Paper Series.

Richard J. Edelstein is a Research Associate at Berkeley's Center for Studies in Higher Education where he collaborates with John Douglass, Senior Research Fellow, on studies of the impact of globalization on higher education institutions. He is also Principal and Managing Director at Global University Concepts, a higher education consultancy that advises universities on international strategies. In France he directed an international MBA program for seven years, a joint project of ESSEC Business School in Paris and Cornell University.

John Fielden has practiced as a management consultant in higher education policy and management since 1969. Between 1993 and 2000 he directed the Commonwealth Higher Education Management Service (CHEMS), the research and consultancy service of the Association of Commonwealth Universities. He now runs CHEMS Consulting as an independent consultancy and has carried out over 270 higher education projects in over 42 countries. His main areas of specialty are the management and financial aspects of internationalization, higher education policy studies and regulation of the higher education private sector. In the UK he has worked for all the higher education sector agencies and many universities and colleges. International clients have included the World Bank (working on projects in 10 countries), UNESCO, British Council, and many education ministries and universities throughout the world. Recent publications have covered mapping private HE providers in the UK, and policy papers on their regulation for the UK and for Ireland.

Ariane de Gayardon is currently a researcher at the UCL Institute of Education Centre for Global Higher Education. She received her PhD in Higher Education from Boston College where she was a Research Assistant at the Center for International Higher Education. Her research interests include tuition free public higher education systems in various national contexts and the financing of higher education. Before moving to Boston, Ariane was a teaching fellow at King's College London, where she taught students at the bachelor level. Ariane earned a Master's degree in English and Education from the Université Paris Ouest-Nanterre, as well as a Master's in Engineering from the École Nationale Supérieure des Mines de Saint-Etienne, one of the grandes écoles in France.

391

Anita Gopal (PhD) is a postdoctoral research associate and adjunct lecturer at the University of Maryland, College Park. Prior to this appointment, she was a visiting scholar at the University of Toronto with the Department of Leadership, Higher and Adult Education and the Comparative International Development Center at the Ontario Institute for Studies in Education. Her research focuses on the retention and socialization of domestic and international graduate students studying in science, technology, engineering, and mathematics disciplines; visa and immigration regulations for international students from a comparative perspective; and the experiences of international students' within higher education institutions. She serves as the program chair for the Association for the Study of Higher Education—Council for International Higher Education Pre-Conference.

Cornelius Hagenmeier is an international education administrator and legal academic who is rooted in the German and South African jurisdictions. He obtained his qualification to be appointable as a judge in Germany (assessor juris) before he decided to settle in South Africa in 2002. He holds a South African LL.B. degree (UNISA) and a South African LL.M degree (UCT) and is a non-practicing attorney of the High Court of South Africa. He accepted an appointment at the University of Venda in 2007 in the Department of Public Law and has served since 2011 as the institution's Director of International Relations. In a voluntary capacity, he has been a member of IEASA's Management Council since 2011, for which he has served as treasurer since 2015.

Savo Heleta is the manager of Internationalization at Home and Research at Nelson Mandela Metropolitan University's Office for International Education (OIE) and researcher in OIE's Research Unit for Higher Education Internationalization in the Developing World. He is the author of *Not My Turn to Die: Memoirs of a Broken Childhood in Bosnia* (AMACOM Books, New York, April 2008). Savo's research interests range from higher education internationalization to higher education in post-war settings, and from conflict analysis to post-war reconstruction and development.

Robin Matross Helms is director of ACE's Center for Internationalization and Global Engagement. Robin's previous experience includes international program management for the Institute of International Education, EF Education and CET Academic Programs, and faculty development program management at the University of Minnesota. She has also worked as a consultant to a number of organizations in the international and higher education fields, including the World Bank, the Institute for Higher Education Policy, the Observatory on Borderless Higher Education, and the Collaborative on Academic Careers in Higher Education at the Harvard Graduate School of Education. Her publications include *Internationalizing the Tenure Code: Policies to Promote a Globally Focused Faculty*, *Mapping International Joint and Dual Degrees: U.S. Program Profiles and Perspectives*, and *International Higher*

Education Partnerships: A Global Review of Standards and Practices. Robin holds an AB degree in East Asian Studies from Princeton University, and an MBA and PhD in Higher Education from Boston College.

John K. Hudzik is Michigan State University (MSU) Professor and NAFSA Senior Scholar for Internationalization, President of MUCIA, past president of AIEA (the Association of International Education Administrators) and past President, Board Chair of NAFSA—Association of International Educators. From 1995 to 2010 he was MSU Dean and Vice President of International Programs and Global Engagement, and Acting University Provost in 2005. He serves on numerous policy and advisory boards and publishes frequently on internationalization and its future, including, *Comprehensive Internationalization: Institutional Pathways to Success* (Routledge, 2015). He is a frequent speaker at global conferences and a leading consultant on strategic planning for internationalization. He has received the AIEA Klasek Award for leadership in international education and the EAIE (European Association for International Education) 2014 Trans-Atlantic Leadership Award. He chairs the Scientific Committee of the Centre for Higher Education Internationalization, UCSC Milan, and is a member of the advisory board for the Nelson Mandela University Internationalization Centre, South Africa.

Fiona Hunter works globally as a consultant, trainer and researcher in higher education with private, public, and faith-based institutions. She is also Associate Director at the Centre for Higher Education Internationalization (CHEI) at the Università Cattolica del Sacro Cuore in Milan, Italy, and Co-Editor of the *Journal of Studies for International Education* (JSIE). Fiona's background in languages—she is able to work in English, Italian, French, and Spanish—with a specialization in interpreting and translating is what first brought her to the field of internationalization. Her work focuses mainly on strategic change and internationalization, and recent projects have included work with university leadership in Italy, Romania, Albania, Russia, Israel, Colombia, and Cuba. In 2015 she helped lead an international team of over 30 researchers to produce a study for the European Parliament on the internationalization of higher education. She earned her Doctor of Business Administration (DBA) in Higher Education Management from the University of Bath, UK. She is a former president of the EAIE and has offered training programs on a broad range of issues in internationalization over the years. Fiona is also a member of the EAIE Knowledge Development Taskforce.

Elspeth Jones is an Emerita Professor of the Internationalization of Higher Education at Leeds Beckett University, England whose specializations are in personal, professional, and employability outcomes from international mobility, strategic leadership, internationalization of the curriculum at home and abroad, global citizenship, and intercultural competence development. She has published widely and is Series Editor for the Routledge book series *Internationalization in Higher Education*. She is a member of the Scientific Committee of the Centre for Higher Education Internationalization and the Editorial Board of the *Journal of Studies in International Education*.

Ard Jongsma is a Dutch freelance education journalist. Based in Denmark, he has written about international affairs in education since 1989. Between 1997 and 2007 he was the director of International Correspondents in Education, a global network of education writers, editors, and translators.

Nico Jooste is the Senior Director of International Education at the Nelson Mandela University, where he has served since July 2000. He is involved in the re-thinking of internationalization of higher education globally and arranged the global dialogue on the future of higher education internationalization in January 2014 in Port Elizabeth, South Africa. He is also the director of the research unit focusing on the research of higher education internationalization in the developing world. He is the immediate past president of the International Education Association of South Africa. He publishes widely on higher education internationalization and has presented numerous papers on this topic at international conferences. He is the series editor of the *Colloquium Series on Higher Education Internationalization,* published since 2004. He has also acted as the editor of *Study South Africa* since 2009. Nico holds a PhD in History.

Zakir Jumakulov is a junior researcher at the Research Institute in Nazarbayev University's Graduate School of Education. He obtained his bachelor's degree from L.N. Gumilyov Eurasian National University, followed by a Master's program in public policy at the Michigan State University with the Bolashak Scholarship of Kazakhstan. He conducts research on internationalization of higher education and higher education funding. Zakir's research outputs were recognized with the 2016 Leader of Science Independent Award by National Center for Science and Technology Information of Kazakhstan and Thomson Reuters for publication in highest impact factor journal in social sciences among Kazakhstani authors. In addition, he is a coordinator of the Eurasian Higher Education Leaders' Forum, which is annually held at Nazarbayev University.

Suvendrini Kakuchi is a Sri Lankan journalist based in Japan. She has a long career working in media in Japan and Asia. Her focus is on development issues including education and the environment and Japan and Asia relations.

Alex Katsomitros is a London-based journalist and researcher specializing in education, technology, and innovation. In the past he has worked for the Observatory on Borderless Higher Education and the Association of Business Schools.

Maxim Khomyakov is a director of the center of BRICS studies and a vice-president (international affairs) at Ural Federal University, Ekaterinburg, Russia. Prof. Khomyakov was a visiting scholar at a number of universities, including Texas A&M University and the European University Institute. In 2002–2013 he organized a number of transnational research and teaching projects in political philosophy and religious studies. Since 2015, Prof. Khomyakov has been actively involved in establishing university collaboration in BRICS countries, and especially in establishing the BRICS Network University (nu-brics.ru). Prof. Khomyakov is the head of the Russian National Coordinating Committee and a member of International Governing Board of the BRICS Network University. His research interests include theory of modernity, theory of toleration, Russian philosophy of nineteenth century, and higher education theory. His works include several books and more than 60 scholarly articles.

Bob Kinnaird is a Sydney-based research associate with the Australian Population Research Institute (TAPRI). He was previously National Research Director for the Construction, Forestry, Mining, and Energy Union (CFMEU) National Office (2009–2014). From 2009–2011 he was also on the Australian Immigration Minister's advisory group, the tripartite Skilled Migration Consultative Panel. He previously ran his own independent consulting and research company for over 20 years specializing in migration, labor market, and education issues for private and public sector clients. He was also State Manager New South Wales, for the National Centre for Vocational Education Research Ltd (NCVER). Before that, he was a Senior Executive with the Australian Federal Department of Education, the first Executive Director of the Asian Studies Council (1986–1987), and the first Australian Exchange Officer (Employment) to the Canada Employment and Immigration Commission, 1980–1983. He has a Bachelor of Arts degree from Monash University.

Kevin Kinser is Professor and Department Head of Education Policy Studies and Senior Scientist at the Center for the Study of Higher Education at Pennsylvania State University. He is also a Senior Fellow for Internationalization at NAFSA: Association of International Educators and co-director of the Cross-Border Education Research Team. His research focuses on non-traditional and alternative higher education, particularly the public policies and organizational structures related to private for-profit institutions and international cross-border higher education. Kinser is the author or editor of four books and more than 70 articles, chapters, and scholarly reports, and he is regularly invited to present his research at conferences in the United States and abroad. Because of his research, Kinser is regularly sought out by national and international media outlets for commentary on for-profit and international higher education. He is currently co-editing a book on US quality assurance (forthcoming, Johns Hopkins Press).

Jane Knight of the Ontario Institute for Studies in Education, University of Toronto, focuses her research on the international dimension of higher education at the institutional, national, regional, and international levels. Her work in over 70 countries with universities, governments, and UN Agencies helps to bring a comparative, development and international perspective to her research, teaching, and policy work. She has been a visiting scholar at numerous universities including in the US, India, Japan, Malaysia, United Arab Emirates, Germany, Spain, and South Africa. She is the author of numerous publications on internationalization, is the co-founder of the African Network for the Internationalization of Education and sits on the advisory boards of various organizations, universities, and journals. The awards she has received include an honorary doctorate from the University of Exeter in the UK and Symbiosis International University in India, the Outstanding Researcher Award from the European Association for Institutional Research and the Gilbert Medal from Universitas 21 for her contribution to higher education internationalization.

Marcelo Knobel is a Professor of the Gleb Wataghin Physics Institute of the Universidade Estadual de Campinas (University of Campinas—UNICAMP), Campinas, SP, Brazil. At UNICAMP he coordinated the Creativity Development Center, NUDECRI, from 2002 to 2006, was the executive director of the Science Museum from 2006 to 2008, and was the vice-provost for undergraduate programs from 2009 to 2013. From 2015 to 2016 he served as the Director of the Brazilian Nanotechnology National Laboratory (LNNano). He was member of the board of the Brazilian Higher Education Assessment Commission (CONAES) from 2010 to 2016.

Piyushi Kotecha is CEO of the Southern African Regional Universities Association (SARUA). SARUA seeks, over time, to be recognized for the provision of an effective platform, which enables key regional Higher Education leadership players to engage and contribute meaningfully to regional development. The article included in this volume by Piyushi is part of a series on a regional higher educational response to climate change.

Marek Kwiek holds a UNESCO Chair in Institutional Research and Higher Education Policy and is a director of the Center for Public Policy Studies at the University of Poznan, Poland. Marek serves as an international higher education policy expert for the European Commission, OECD, World Bank, UNESCO, OSCE, Council of Europe, and USAID. His research interests include university governance, academic entrepreneurialism, and the academic profession. He has published 180 papers, mostly internationally (*Science and Public Policy, Higher Education, Studies in Higher Education, Comparative Education Review, Journal of Studies in International Education* etc.). A Principal Investigator or country Team Leader in about 50 international higher education research and policy projects, Marek has spent three years at North American universities and has also been a Fulbright New Century Scholar (2007–2008). He has served as an editorial board member of *Higher Education Quarterly, European Educational Research Journal, British Educational Research Journal* and *European Journal of Higher Education*.

Ada Lai did her Bachelor and MPhil degrees at the University of Hong Kong and obtained her PhD in Sociology from the University of Essex in England. Over the years, she has been involved in various research projects in Hong Kong, China, Australia, and England in the fields of migration, education, refugee studies, labour studies, and gender studies and is currently working as a research fellow at the Vocational Training Council in Hong Kong. Her current research interest revolves around how minority or disadvantaged groups such as migrants, refugees, ethnic minorities, or students of low socioeconomic backgrounds are able to use schools to satisfy the academic demands prevailing in different education systems. In other words, how the institutionalisation of the curriculum at the system and school levels could affect the employment outcomes of different student groups.

Jason E. Lane is deputy director for research at the Rockefeller Institute of Government. He has written broadly on higher education public policy, administration, and globalization. His current work focuses on educational accountability at the state and international levels. Lane has authored or edited seven books and more than 40 articles and book chapters. In addition to his position at the Institute, he is the SUNY Provost Fellow as well as Associate Professor of Educational Administration and Policy Studies at the University at Albany, where he is also co-leader of the Cross-Border Education Research Team (C-BERT).

William Lawton has worked in higher education for 25 years, as a university lecturer and more recently as a researcher and writer. His main areas of expertise are higher education internationalization—especially transnational education, the interplay of TNE and mobility, and the digital HE revolution. William has a longstanding interest in government policy and higher education, especially in regard to the UK, US, Canada, southeast Asia and India. He served as Director of the Observatory on Borderless Higher Education from 2011–2014.

Betty Leask is the Pro Vice-Chancellor (Teaching and Learning) at La Trobe University, Melbourne. She has researched and published extensively on teaching, learning and internationalization in higher education. She has led and participated in six nationally funded Australian research projects on teaching and learning and in 2010 was awarded an Australian government teaching fellowship *Internationalization of the Curriculum in Action*. Betty is Editor-in Chief of the *Journal of Studies in International Education*, the leading international journal in her field, and is an Honorary Visiting Researcher at the Centre for Higher

Education Internationalization at the Universita Cattolica del Sacre Cuore in Milan. Betty was founding Chair of the International Education Association of Australia's Internationalization of the Curriculum Special Interest Group and was Chair of its Research Committee from 2010–2012. Her current role at La Trobe University includes responsibility for leading curriculum innovation and change across the institution. Betty's most recent publication, *Internationalizing the Curriculum*, was published by Routledge in 2015.

Jenny J. Lee is a Professor at the Center for the Study of Higher Education at the University of Arizona and former researcher at the Higher Education Research Institute at UCLA, where she obtained her PhD. She is currently a NAFSA Senior Fellow for internationalization, the Associate Editor for the *Review of Higher Education*, and Co-editor of the book series, *Studies in Global Higher Education*, with Palgrave/Macmillan. She is also on the editorial boards for *Higher Education* and *Religion and Education*. She formerly served as the Director of the Center of the Study of Higher Education, Director of Project SOAR (Student Outreach, Access, and Resiliency), co-Director of Native SOAR, and Chair for the Council of International Higher Education and Board of Directors for the Association for the Study of Higher Education.

Peta Lee is an award-winning South African journalist with several decades of professional writing experience. She has edited and written for numerous newspapers and magazines (both in South Africa and Namibia) and contributed chapters to several books. She was a freelance contributor to *University World News* from 2014 until 2016, and had previously worked on *Higher Education Review*, a specialist supplement appearing in several mainstream newspapers of the Independent Newspapers group. She currently writes business profiles for *The Mercury* newspaper in Durban and edits a community newspaper in the KwaZulu-Natal Midlands.

Modi Li was born in China and grew up in the US. She received a Master's in Higher Education from the Graduate School of Education at Peking University in 2016.

Chrissie Long is a freelance reporter living in Boston, Massachusetts. She moved to New England from Central America where she covered stories of international significance such as the Honduras crisis, the election of the Costa Rica's first female president, and issues of development and foreign market integration. She worked as a political reporter for The Tico Times, specializing in health, education, politics and foreign relations, and occasionally contributes to tourism/features publications. Most recently she served as Costa Rican travel correspondent for About.com.

Karen MacGregor is one of the founding editors of *University World News*, and is currently its Global Editor and director of the Africa Edition. She is a former foreign editor of *Times Higher Education,* and for 10 years wrote about Southern African news and current affairs for a range of publications including *Newsweek* (New York), *The Sunday Times* (London), *The Independent* (London), and *The Globe and Mail* (Toronto). MacGregor, a South African, holds a Master's in International Relations from the University of Kent, UK.

Mary Beth Marklein covered higher education for *USA TODAY* for more than 17 years, and has written stories from Eastern Europe, Southeast Asia and Central America. She also taught journalism to university students in Romania in 2004–2005 and in Vietnam in 2014, both through the US State Department's Fulbright programs. She is pursuing a PhD in higher education studies with an emphasis on international issues.

Don Martin is an expert in the fields of enrollment management, student affairs and higher education administration. From 1980 to 2008 he managed divisions including admissions, financial aid, student development, registration/advising, and career, disabled and international services. He has been employed by some of the best colleges and universities in the United States: Wheaton College (IL), Northwestern University (Medill School of Journalism), The University of Chicago (Booth School of Business), and Columbia University (Teachers College). Along with a team of dedicated professionals, Dr. Martin grew both the applicant pool and the enrollment yield at each institution he served. In addition, students' ratings of their experience at those institutions improved dramatically during his tenure.

John McNamara is director of research for McNamara Economic Research and exercises overall editorial control on research output. John has a broad range of applied economics and research experience having worked as an economist in Enterprise Ireland in Dublin and the Office of Gas and Electricity Markets in London. Before establishing McNamara Economic Research in 2011, John worked for the Economist Intelligence Unit in London as a senior economist in the custom research team where he managed the education portfolio. This involved designing, managing, and delivering education research projects for corporate and government agency clients. John has a Bachelor in Economics from University College Dublin and an Master's in Economics from National University of Ireland, Galway.

Robin Middlehurst is an international adviser on higher education policy and governance and Professor of Higher Education. She is a trustee of the British Accreditation Council and Advisory Board member of the Observatory on Borderless Higher Education. Robin's research and consultancy includes borderless and private higher education, internationalisation, governance and leadership, quality assurance, and quality enhancement. Previously, she was the Director of the Quality Enhancement Group of the Higher Education Quality Council. Robin has held posts at three UK universities over 30 years. Professor Middlehurst has published extensively on higher education policy and management and undertakes consultancy for governments and higher education agencies in the UK and internationally.

Nic Mitchell is a freelance journalist and communications adviser who writes on European higher education and research for *University World News*, *The PIE News* and *BBC news* online. He blogs regularly for the European Universities Public Relations and Information Officers' association, EUPRIO, and on the website of his consultancy, DelaCourCommunications.com. In 2015, he won the Outstanding Higher Education Journalism Award from the UK's Chartered Institute of Public Relations (CIPR) for a BBC online feature about Europe's East to West brain drain since the fall of Communism. Recently, Nic has been working with the Norwegian School of Economics (NHH) in Bergen and Oslo and Akershurst University College of Applied Sciences (HiOA) and Charles University in Prague to raise their profiles with English-speaking students and researchers. His services range from English-language copy-editing of university online and offline publications and websites to journalism and public relations consultancy to support student mobility.

Claire Morel is the Head of Unit for international cooperation at DG Education and Culture of the European Commission, with particular focus on the international dimension of the Erasmus+ program and international policy dialogues in higher education, as well as youth issues. She has worked several years with countries neighboring the EU. Before that, she worked for the Tempus program (for higher education modernization), cooperating with Central Asian countries, and for the European Training Foundation, an agency of the EU based in Turin, on the reform of vocational education and training systems in the Eastern neighboring countries and Central Asia.

Jan Petter Myklebust is a Professor in Comparative Politics at University of Bergen. He is a coeditor of the book *Who were the fascists? Social Roots of European Fascism* (1980). Until 2006, Myklebust served as the director of the Office of International Relations at the University of Bergen. He has been a contributor with University World News since 2009.

Gilbert Nganga is a Kenyan based freelance journalist and a communications consultant.

Brendan O'Malley is an Assistant Professor in the School of Arts and Design at Newbury College. He has previously been a teaching fellow and lecturer at Brooklyn College and The New School. He received his doctorate in History from the City University of New York.

Milton O. Obamba is a research associate with the African Network for the Internationalization of Education, Eldoret, Kenya.

Daniel Obst is President and CEO of AFS Intercultural Programs, a global network of 60 member organizations with nearly 50,000 volunteers and programs in 99 countries. Before joining AFS in 2016, Daniel served as Deputy Vice President for International Partnerships at the Institute of International Education (IIE) where he provided strategic leadership for many groundbreaking IIE initiatives. Daniel led the launch of Generation Study Abroad, which mobilized 700 international partner organizations to help double the number of US students who study abroad. Under his leadership, partners pledged more than $185 million to support study abroad. He was also responsible for all the activities of IIE's network of 1,500 member institutions, publications and higher education services, IIE's Center for International Partnerships in Higher Education, and strategic communications team, including alumni affairs. Daniel currently serves on the US National Commission for UNESCO. Prior to joining IIE, Daniel worked as Producer and Director of Product Development at the tech start-up iAgora.com, an online community for young internationals who live, work, and study abroad. Daniel received his Bachelor in International Relations from the George Washington University (US) and holds a Master's degree in European Studies from the London School of Economics (UK).

Hiep Pham is a PhD candidate at Department of International Business Administration, Chinese Culture University, Taiwan R.O.C. His academic specialties include marketization and globalization of higher education, financing in higher education, and consumer behavior. Pham is also a reporter, working as correspondent in Vietnam for *University World News*.

Gerard A. Postiglione is Chair and Professor of Higher Education, Faculty of Education, the University of Hong Kong. He is former Associate Dean for Research and Head of the Division of Policy, Administration, and Social Science Education. He has published 16 books and over 150 articles and chapters. His books include: *Mass Higher Education in East Asia, Crossing Borders in East Asian Higher Education, Asian Higher Education, Education and Social Change in China*, and *Balancing Higher Education in China* (forthcoming with Johns Hopkins University Press). He is editor of the journal *Chinese Education and Society* and four book series about education in China.

Krishnapratap B. Powar (PhD) was Chancellor of the Dr. D. Y. Patil Vidyapeeth University in Pune, India. In a professional carrier of over 45 years, he worked in various academic and administrative positions. Prof. Power had an outstanding academic career and has important contributions to research and policy planning related to higher education. Books authored by him on higher education include *Accreditation in Higher Education: The Indian Perspective* (1996), *International*

Students in Indian Universities (1997), *Performance Indicators in Distance Higher Education* (2000), *Indian Higher Education: Conglomerate of Concepts, Facts and Practices* (2002), *Internationalization of Higher Education: Focus on India* (2003), *Quality of Higher Education* (2005), *Indian Higher Education Revisited* (2011), and *Expanding Domains in Indian Higher Education* (2012), *Understanding Internationalization in Higher Education* (2013), and *Changing Landscape of International Higher Education: An Indian Perspective* (2015). He has been member of many national and international committees.

Douglas Proctor is Director of International Affairs at University College Dublin (Ireland), where he has management responsibility for the international office and provides leadership to the broader university community on internationalization, international engagement, and international partnerships. Having completed a PhD in International Higher Education at the University of Melbourne (Australia) in late 2016, Douglas serves as a member of the AIEA Editorial Committee (US) and is a Member of the Register of Experts for the Tertiary Education Quality and Standards Agency (TEQSA) in Australia. Douglas has authored papers and reports in relation to his doctoral research, as well as on the global landscape of international education research. With Laura Rumbley from Boston College's Center for International Higher Education, he is currently editing a book in the Routledge Internationalization in Higher Education Series, which will offer new perspectives on the future of internationalization in higher education.

Zha Qiang is an Associate Professor in the Faculty of Education, York University, Canada. He holds a PhD (Higher Education) from the Ontario Institute for Studies in Education of the University of Toronto. His research interests include Chinese and East Asian higher education, international academic relations, global brain circulation, and internationalization of higher education. He has written and published widely on these topics in scholarly journals such as *Compare, Higher Education, Higher Education Policy, Higher Education in Europe*, and *Harvard China Review*. His recent books include a co-authored book (with Ruth Hayhoe et al.) *Portraits of 21st Century Chinese Universities: In the Move to Mass Higher Education* (Comparative Education Research Centre, University of Hong Kong and Springer, 2011), and three edited volumes *Education and Global Cultural Dialogue* (co-edited with Karen Mundy, Palgrave Macmillan, 2012), *Education in China. Educational History, Models, and Initiatives* (Berkshire Publishing, 2013), and *Canadian Universities in China's Transformation: An Untold Story* (co-edited with Ruth Hayhoe et al., McGill-Queen's University Press, 2016).

Jeremy Rappleye is Associate Professor at Kyoto University Graduate School of Education. His earlier work focused on the dynamics of policy formation in Japan, particularly the international dimensions of reforms since the 1980s. More recent work, including *A New Global Policy Regime Founded on Invalid Statistics?*

(Comparative Education, 2017) and *A PISA Paradox?* (Comparative Education Review, 2017), has problematized international learning assessments such as PISA.

Liz Reisberg is an independent consultant in higher education, formerly associated with the Center for International Higher Education at Boston College. In the past she has worked in university administration at several universities and taught in the graduate program in higher education administration at Boston College. She works with ministries of education, universities, and international donor organizations throughout the world. Themes of her research and other activities include quality assurance in higher education, the challenges of access and equity, and new approaches to university curriculum and pedagogy. Much of her work has focused on Latin America.

Michele Rostan is Professor of Economic Sociology and Director of the Centre for Study and Research on Higher Education Systems at the University of Pavia, Italy, where he is also Rector's Delegate for Student Affairs. He is member of the Consortium of Higher Education Researchers, the Academia Europaea, the Italian Centre for Research on Universities and Higher Education Systems, the editorial boards of *Higher Education, The International Journal of Higher Education Research*, and *Studies in Higher Education*. His main research interests concern the relationship between economy, society and higher education, the academic profession, graduate work and employment, and university/industry links. Recently, he edited with Futao Huang and Martin Finkelstein the book *The Internationalization of the Academy: Changes, Realities and Prospects*, Springer (2014).

Laura E. Rumbley is Associate Director of the Center for International Higher Education, and is also Assistant Professor of practice within the Department of Educational Leadership and Higher Education at Boston College. Laura was previously deputy director of the Academic Cooperation Association, a Brussels-based think tank focused on issues of internationalization and innovation in European higher education. She has authored and co-authored a number of publications, including the foundation document for the 2009 UNESCO World Conference on Higher Education, *Trends in Global Higher Education: Tracking an Academic Revolution* (with Philip G. Altbach and Liz Reisberg). Laura currently serves as a co-editor of the *Journal of Studies in International Education*. She is active in the European Association for International Education (EAIE), where she is chair of the publications committee. Laura received her PhD from Boston College following completion of a dissertation focused on internationalization in the universities of Spain.

Aida Sagintayeva is the Dean of Nazarbayev University Graduate School of Education, Kazakhstan. Prior to joining to the Graduate School of Education, Aida served as Vice-Rector for International Cooperation at Gumilyov Eurasian National University, Astana. She has administered the Center for International Programs

(International Presidential Scholarship 'Bolashak'). Dr. Sagintayeva has been involved in educational research projects of the Ministry of Education and Science on shifting Kazakhstan's higher education system towards the European three-tiered degree system. She has coordinated a ministerial initiative focused on Western-styled PhD programs in Kazakhstan, and is the founding President of the Kazakhstan Educational Research Association. Aida's research interests include internationalization of higher education, comparative education and higher education governance. She has authored and co-authored scholarly publications in the fields of higher education governance, internationalization of higher education, and education policy.

Jamil Salmi is a global tertiary education expert. Until January 2012, he was the World Bank's tertiary education coordinator. He is the principal author of the Bank's Tertiary Education Strategy entitled *Constructing Knowledge Societies: New Challenges for Tertiary Education* (2002). In the past 23 years, Mr. Salmi has provided policy and technical advice on tertiary education reform to the governments of about 95 countries on all continents. His latest book (2011), co-edited with Professor Philip Altbach, is entitled *The Road to Academic Excellence: The Making of World-Class Research Universities*. His previous book, published in 2009, addresses the *Challenge of Establishing World-Class Universities*. His forthcoming book is called *The Tertiary Education Imperative: Knowledge and Skills for Development.*

Peter Scott is Emeritus Professor of Higher Education Studies at the University College London Institute of Education, and also Commissioner for Fair Access in Scotland. Previously he was Vice-Chancellor of Kingston University in London and a Professor at the University of Leeds. His most recent book (with Jim Gallacher and Gareth Parry) is *New Languages and Landscapes of Higher Education* (Oxford University Press 2016).

Yojana Sharma is the Asia Director at *University World News* and a multilingual foreign correspondent who has covered major events, UN conferences, and international summits for many years. She has a particular interest in education, international trade, and developing countries, as well as an extensive experience in Asia, Africa, Central America, and Europe. She is now based in London, but has previously worked in Geneva, Brussels, Costa Rica, Nicaragua, Hong Kong and China, Berlin, and New Delhi for major newspapers. She has served as a correspondent for *The Daily Telegraph, The Sydney Morning Herald, Times Educational Supplement* and a regular contributor to *The Scotsman, Far Eastern Economic Review, South China Morning Post, the New Scientist,* and *The Guardian.* Yojana is a regular contributor to the BBC's Knowledge Economy series.

Yunyu Shi was the Chinese visiting scholar at the University at Albany from the year 2013 to 2014. She holds a Bachelor's Degree in Arts (Nanjing University of Science and Technology, China) and a Master's Degree in English Linguistics (Nanjing Normal University, China). After she finished her graduate work, she entered the Jiangsu Provincial Department of Education and has been engaged in educational cooperation and exchange for 10 years.

Yukiko Shimmi is an Assistant Professor and international education advisor at the Graduate School of Law, Hitotsubashi University in Tokyo, Japan. Yukiko received her PhD degree in Higher Education at Boston College where she worked as a research assistant at the Center for International Higher Education. She earned her Master's degree in Educational Psychology at the University of Minnesota as a Fulbright scholar. She also holds a Bachelor in Human Relations from Keio University in Japan. Previously she worked for two Japanese universities in student services and academic affairs with both domestic and international students. Yukiko's research focuses on the impact of study abroad experiences on students from the perspectives of personal and career development. She also studies international visiting scholars and their experiences. Additionally, Yukiko conducts research on policy issues related to the internationalization of higher education in Japan.

Karen Smith was originally trained in linguistics, but has been working within the field of educational research and development since 2003. She is currently Principal Lecturer in Collaborative Research and Development at University of Hertfordshire. Her role focusses on supporting collaborative research with external partners (schools, local authorities, public services, and other organizations). Karen was previously a Senior Lecturer in Educational Development at University of Greenwich.

Joseph Stetar is a Professor of Education at Seton Hall University in New Jersey. Between 2012–2013 he was a Visiting Professor at both the Peking University Graduate School of Education and the Institute of Higher Education Research at Harbin Institute of Technology.

Nanette Svenson. With over 20 years of global development experience, Nanette is an adjunct Professor at Tulane University and consultant for the UN and other international organizations. For the past six years, she has directed Panama programming for the Tulane Global Development Master's program. Prior to this, she helped establish the UNDP Regional Centre for Latin America and the Caribbean and headed its research and knowledge management efforts. She holds a PhD in International Development from Tulane, an MBA from IESE in Barcelona and a Bachelor from Stanford University. Nanette is based in Panama and her research and consulting focus on capacity development, particularly for higher education, and developing regions' education policy. Her article *The Role of Higher Education in Equitable Human Development* was a Springer most accessed/read article of the year in 2016, and her recent book, *The United Nations as a Knowledge System* (2015), has just been released in digital format.

Wesley Teller supports regional networks, cross-sector collaboration, and building capabilities of government in the field of education. Based in Berlin, Budapest, New Delhi, and Bangkok (2005–present), he currently serves as a Senior Project Officer for Higher Education at UNESCO's Asia-Pacific Regional Bureau for Education. He is a Visiting Scholar at Mahidol University, Thailand in the Master of Public Administration Program in Public Policy and Public Administration, Faculty of Social Sciences and Humanities (2017), and a former regional coordinator for Education USA, a global network supported by the US Bureau of Educational and Cultural Affairs, US Department of State (2005–2012). As a PhD Candidate in the Faculty of Education, University of Hong Kong (2014–present), his research interests include how to build state capabilities, improve network governance and integrate effective feedback loops in complex accountability systems.

Guillaume Tronchet is Professeur grégé d'histoire and research associate at the Institut d'histoire moderne et contemporaine (PSL-ENS, University of Paris 1 Panthéon-Sorbonne, CNRS). Former education adviser to the president of PSL Research University and deputy director of the PSL Bachelor of Interdisciplinary Studies, he is now special adviser to the director of the Ecole Normale Supérieure, Paris. He holds a PhD from the University of Paris 1 Pantheon-Sorbonne and specializes in the international history of higher education. He was previously a visiting scholar at Columbia University. He has coedited a book on the history of the Cité internationale universitaire de Paris with Dzovinar Kévonian: *La Babel* étudiante. *La Cité internationale universitaire de Paris* (Presses universitaires de Rennes, 2013). Guillaume is preparing a single-authored monograph on the internationalization of French Higher Education in the nineteenth and twentieth centuries, and also serves as an editorial board member of the *Journal of International Mobility*.

Agnete Vabø is based at the Nordic Institute for Studies in Innovation, Research and Education (NIFU) in Norway. She has expertise in comparative studies of knowledge organizations, change processes in higher education, analysis of recruitment patterns, and the evaluation of research.

Edward Vickers is Professor at Kyushu University, Department of Education. His research has focused on the history of education in East Asian societies, particular on issues of political socialization and identity contestation. He recently co-edited a major volume entitled *Imagining Japan in Post-War East Asia: Identity Politics, Schooling, and Popular Culture* (Routledge, 2013), extending early work on *Education as a Political Tool in Asia* (2010). His most recent work is *Education and Society in Post-Mao China* (Routledge, 2017). He also currently serves as the Secretary-General of the Comparative Education Society of Asia.

Bernd Wächter is the Director of the Academic Cooperation Association (ACA). He studied at the universities of Hull (UK), Giessen and Marburg (Germany).

He worked for the British Council, the University of Kassel, and the University of Applied Sciences Darmstadt, before joining the German Academic Exchange Service (DAAD) as the head of their EU division and German National Agency for the Erasmus Program. He subsequently became the Director for Higher Education (Erasmus) in the Brussels Socrates Office. In 1998, he took up his present post as ACA Director. Bernd has published and lectured widely on international higher education. His focal areas of research comprise the internationalization of higher education, with a particular emphasis on international student and staff mobility, language policy, excellence, and rankings. Importantly, he has co-authored three studies on English-medium instruction across Europe (2001, 2008 and 2014) and been involved in large-scale projects on student mobility. He is also the editor of the ACA Papers on International Cooperation in Education. In 2012, he was awarded the Constance Meldrum Award for Vision and Leadership of the EAIE. Bernd has two great children. He is married to Thora Magnusdottir, a delightful lady from Iceland.

Tomoaki Wada is in charge of internationalization and academia-industry collaboration at the Tokyo University of Science (TUS). He is also an affiliated senior fellow at the National Institute of Science and Technology Policy, or NISTEP. Prior to his appointment at the TUS in 2010, he worked in the Ministry of Education, Culture, Sports, Science and Technology for 30 years. Between 2002 and 2004, he served in the cabinet office as chief secretariat for science and technology policy, where he prepared the draft of the Third Science and Technology (S&T) Basic Plan. In July 2008, he was appointed director general of NISTEP, where he summarized key reports of follow-up studies on the Third S&T Basic Plan.

Esther Wilkinson is a specialist in higher education strategy and planning and the Head of International at Jisc. Her role includes developing Jisc's international strategy and leading business development for Jisc's transnational education support programme, and enabling delivery of UK education overseas. A key part of Esther's role is supporting the Global Research and Education Network CEO Forum. Esther has worked in various roles in higher education, previously as Assistant Director in the Universities UK International Unit delivering UK government and overseas programmes, e.g. HEGlobal and the Dikti Scholarship Scheme, in addition to managing operations for the Unit. Prior to this, Esther delivered a number of projects in the UK Research Councils for over 13 years; these included multi-million Government longitudinal studies in the medical and social sciences, and the setting up of the RCUK Strategy Unit. Other roles included a brief spell as a police officer, and as Planetary Protection Officer on the Beagle2 programme at the Open University. Esther has a BSc Hons, DIC and PhD in Chemistry from Imperial College. Esther also is Director of Red Coaching and Development, a skills training consultancy to facilitate development of leadership, communication and teamwork for researchers in higher education.

Jacquie Withers is a professional English-language editor with a solid, 25-year track record of collaborating with academic, corporate and civil society organization authors to help them prepare their materials for publication. She holds a Bachelor (Honors) cum laude in English Literature and History (1999) and an Advanced Postgraduate Diploma in Organizational and Management Systems (2007), both from the University of KwaZulu-Natal, South Africa. She has extensive, up-to-date experience of editing higher education content, as well as educational and learning materials in general. In recent years she has also specialized in the areas of recognition of prior learning (RPL/APL/APEL), and financial inclusion in poor and marginalized societies. She is fully conversant and comfortable working with the entire publication process.

Li Zhang currently serves as the project manager for US-Taiwan Partnership for International Research and Education (PIRE) at Atmospheric Sciences Research Center (ASRC), State University of New York (SUNY) University at Albany. Before she transferred to SUNY Albany, she worked for SUNY System Administration as an Associate for Academic Programs and Planning. Dr. Li Zhang received her PhD in International Higher Education from the Department of Education Policy and Leadership (formerly named Educational Administration and Policy Studies—EAPS) at SUNY Albany in 2016. Since 2013, Dr. Zhang has been working in the field of international higher education, helping Chinese higher education institutions build partnerships with colleges and universities in the United States. She has helped a dozen Chinese institutions build different types of partnerships with SUNY at different levels. She is also working pro bono as Chinese Group Leader at the Cross-border Education Research Team at SUNY Albany.

Chun-Mei Zhao is Director of Custom Programs at the Stanford Center for Professional Development. Previously, she was Director of SERU International Consortium at the Center for Studies in Higher Education. Chun-Mei received her PhD in Higher Education Research and Policy Studies from Virginia Tech.

GLOBAL PERSPECTIVES ON HIGHER EDUCATION

Volume 1
WOMEN'S UNIVERSITIES AND COLLEGES
An International Handbook
Francesca B. Purcell, Robin Matross Helms, and Laura Rumbley (Eds.)
ISBN 978-90-77874-58-5 hardback
ISBN 978-90-77874-02-8 paperback

Volume 2
PRIVATE HIGHER EDUCATION
A Global Revolution
Philip G. Altbach and D. C. Levy (Eds.)
ISBN 978-90-77874-59-2 hardback
ISBN 978-90-77874-08-0 paperback

Volume 3
FINANCING HIGHER EDUCATION
Cost-Sharing in International perspective
D. Bruce Johnstone
ISBN 978-90-8790-016-8 hardback
ISBN 978-90-8790-015-1 paperback

Volume 4
UNIVERSITY COLLABORATION FOR INNOVATION
Lessons from the Cambridge-MIT Institute
David Good, Suzanne Greenwald, Roy Cox, and Megan Goldman (Eds.)
ISBN 978-90-8790-040-3 hardback
ISBN 978-90-8790-039-7 paperback

Volume 5
HIGHER EDUCATION
A Worldwide Inventory of Centers and Programs
Philip G. Altbach, Leslie A. Bozeman, Natia Janashia, and Laura E. Rumbley
ISBN 978-90-8790-052-6 hardback
ISBN 978-90-8790-049-6 paperback

Volume 6
FUTURE OF THE AMERICAN PUBLIC RESEARCH UNIVERSITY
R. L. Geiger, C. L. Colbeck, R. L. Williams, and C. K. Anderson (Eds.)
ISBN 978-90-8790-048-9 hardback
ISBN 978-90-8790-047-2 paperback

Volume 7
TRADITION AND TRANSITION
The International Imperative in Higher Education
Philip G. Altbach
ISBN 978-90-8790-054-4 hardback
ISBN 978-90-8790-053-3 paperback

Volume 8
THE PROFESSORIATE IN THE AGE OF GLOBALIZATION
Nelly P. Stromquist
ISBN 978-90-8790-084-7 hardback
ISBN 978-90-8790-083-0 paperback

Volume 9
HIGHER EDUCATION SYSTEMS
Conceptual Frameworks, Comparative Perspectives, Empirical Findings
Ulrich Teichler
ISBN 978-90-8790-138-7 hardback
ISBN 978-90-8790-137-0 paperback

Volume 10
HIGHER EDUCATION IN THE NEW CENTURY: GLOBAL CHALLENGES
AND INNOVATIVE IDEAS
Philip G. Altbach and Patti McGill Peterson (Eds.)
ISBN 978-90-8790-199-8 hardback
ISBN 978-90-8790-198-1 paperback

Volume 11
THE DYNAMICS OF INTERNATIONAL STUDENT CIRCULATION IN A
GLOBAL CONTEXT
Hans de Wit, Pawan Agarwal, Mohsen Elmahdy Said, Molatlhegi T. Sehoole, and
Muhammad Sirozi (Eds.)
ISBN 978-90-8790-259-9 hardback
ISBN 978-90-8790-258-2 paperback

Volume 12
UNIVERSITIES AS CENTRES OF RESEARCH AND KNOWLEDGE
CREATION: AN ENDANGERED SPECIES?
Hebe Vessuri and Ulrich Teichler (Eds.)
ISBN 978-90-8790-479-1 hardback
ISBN 978-90-8790-478-4 paperback

Volume 31
GLOBAL OPPORTUNITIES AND CHALLENGES FOR HIGHER EDUCATION
LEADERS: BRIEFS ON KEY THEMES
Laura E. Rumbley, Robin Matross Helms, Patti McGill Peterson, and
Philip G. Altbach (Eds.)
ISBN 978-94-6209-862-6 hardback
ISBN 978-94-6209-861-9 paperback

Volume 32
CRITICAL PERSPECTIVES ON INTERNATIONALISING THE
CURRICULUM IN DISCIPLINES: REFLECTIVE NARRATIVE ACCOUNTS
FROM BUSINESS, EDUCATION AND HEALTH
Wendy Green and Craig Whitsed (Eds.)
ISBN 978-94-6300-084-0 hardback
ISBN 978-94-6300-083-3 paperback

Volume 33
THE IMPACT OF INTERNATIONALIZATION ON JAPANESE HIGHER
EDUCATION: IS JAPANESE EDUCATION REALLY CHANGING?
John Mock, Hiroaki Kawamura, and Naeko Naganuma (Eds.)
ISBN 978-94-6300-168-7 hardback
ISBN 978-94-6300-167-0 paperback

Volume 34
GLOBAL AND LOCAL INTERNATIONALIZATION
Elspeth Jones, Robert Coelen, Jos Beelen, and Hans de Wit (Eds.)
ISBN 978-94-6300-300-1 hardback
ISBN 978-94-6300-299-8 paperback

Volume 35
MATCHING VISIBILITY AND PERFORMANCE: A STANDING CHALLENGE
FOR WORLD-CLASS UNIVERSITIES
Nian Cai Liu, Ying Chen, and Qi Wang (Eds.)
ISBN 978-94-6300-772-6 hardback
ISBN 978-94-6300-771-9 paperback

Volume 36
UNDERSTANDING GLOBAL HIGHER EDUCATION: INSIGHTS FROM KEY
GLOBAL PUBLICATIONS
Georgiana Mihut, Philip G. Altbach, and Hans de Wit (Eds.)
ISBN 978-94-6351-043-1 hardback
ISBN 978-94-6351-042-4 paperback

Volume 37
RESPONDING TO MASSIFICATION: DIFFERENTIATION IN
POSTSECONDARY EDUCATION WORLDWIDE
Philip G. Altbach, Liz Reisberg, and Hans de Wit (Eds.)
ISBN 978-94-6351-082-0 hardback
ISBN 978-94-6351-081-3 paperback

Volume 38
THE TERTIARY EDUCATION IMPERATIVE: KNOWLEDGE, SKILLS AND
VALUES FOR DEVELOPMENT
Jamil Salmi
ISBN 978-94-6351-127-8 hardback
ISBN 978-94-6351-126-1 paperback

Volume 39
UNDERSTANDING HIGHER EDUCATION INTERNATIONALIZATION:
INSIGHTS FROM KEY GLOBAL PUBLICATIONS
Georgiana Mihut, Philip G. Altbach, and Hans de Wit (Eds.)
ISBN 978-94-6351-160-5 hardback
ISBN 978-94-6351-159-9 paperback

CPSIA information can be obtained
at www.ICGtesting.com
Printed in the USA
BVOW06s1103210917
495255BV00003B/10/P